Pendulum: the Psi Connection

John Francis Hitching is a member of the Royal Archaeological Institute, the Prehistoric Society, the Society for Psychical Research, the British Society of Dowsers and the American Society of Dowsers.

Born in 1933, he grew up in Stratford-upon-Avon where his grandfather, Randle Ayrton, had been the leading pre-war Shakespearian actor. He left Warwick School in 1950 and was a newspaper reporter and magazine journalist before being appointed producer of the television programme *Ready, Steady, Go!* As an independent producer, he made many other musical programmes and documentaries both in Britain and in Europe.

While filming at Carnac in Brittany, his boyhood interest in megaliths was reawakened and he spent the next four years researching for *Earth Magic*, his book on that subject. He was impressed with the dowsers he met who seemed instinctively to know why the stones had been erected. Some of their information about psychic matters was so extraordinary that he decided they warranted a full investigation and explanation; hence *Pendulum: the Psi Connection*.

Francis Hitching has appeared many times on television, both in Britain and in the United States, talking on alternative theories of archaeology and on the psychic make-up of people. He and his wife, whom he has known since childhood, live with their three daughters near London.

D1513181

Pendulum:
the Psi Connection

Francis Hitching

Fontana/Collins

First published in Fontana 1977

Copyright © Francis Hitching 1977

Made and printed in Great Britain by
William Collins Sons & Co. Ltd, Glasgow

For my family

Acknowledgements

This book could not have been completed without the help and encouragement of the many people who offered me information and introductions, and to all of them I offer my thanks. I am particularly grateful to Professor John Taylor, Dr Zaboj Harvalik and Dr Eduardo Balanovski for guiding me through the mysteries of electromagnetism; if, in spite of their patience, there are any errors, these are entirely mine. My friendship with Bill Lewis taught me a great deal about dowsing, but others in this field have also given invaluable advice; especially, Dr Arthur Bailey, Bernard and Enid Smithett, Raymond C. Willey, Major-General James Scott Elliot and Robert Leftwich. In the United States, I was looked after and guided by Christopher Bird, Stephen and Chris Bosbach, Jack Livingston, Norman and Marje Runnion, and David and Cynnie Birenbaum.

I acknowledge my debt to all those quoted in the book; in particular Alan Angoff of the Parapsychology Foundation Inc.; Professor Madeleine and Dr Jena Barnothy; Dr Ruth Borchard; Robert Ater; Dr Adrian Boshier; Norma Lee Browning, whose book *The World of Peter Hurkos* provided me with the opening quotation to Part One of this book; Professor Hans Eysenck; Dr Gordon Flint; Tom Graves; Peter Hammond; Dr Harold Puthoff; and Dr Russell Targ. Lastly, the *Journals* of the British and American Societies of Dowsers proved to be essential source material.

Contents

CONTENTS

Introduction

Deep within our minds, something uncontrollably mysterious seems to be going on. We call it the paranormal, or psi, and it has tantalized, challenged, and ultimately baffled the finest scholars in the world. Most of us suspect instinctively that it exists; yet in spite of countless successful laboratory experiments, and fleeting individual demonstrations of the supernatural in almost every person's life, we still need convincing. Why doesn't it happen more often? Why does it seem to disappear under conditions of strict proof? Why is it so frequently surrounded by fraud? Are we meant to toy with such matters?

Yet even to ask these questions implies that there is something unknown to be searched for; and perhaps the most curious thing is not so much whether the paranormal exists, but why, for most of us, it happens so unpredictably and so seldom.

This book is about the few people who in every generation through history have said the opposite – that for them, the psychic happens whenever they want it to. Traditionally, their gift was known as divination; nowadays, it is usually called clairvoyance or dowsing. Most good dowsers today say they ought to be able to find anything, anywhere – not just water, but minerals, missing people, information about the past – and that they have all learned to use their talent more or less at will.

Now these are big claims, but they are exciting ones too. We live in a time when there is a revival of interest in the ancient 'mysteries'; and also when there is a great deal of scepticism, inherited from several hundred years of rationalism and Newtonian science. Throughout all this time dowsing has quietly persisted, apparently fulfilling a widespread need. In today's more hospitable climate for the psychic, it has two great advantages as a subject for study. Firstly, it ought to be possible to find out just how efficient and accurate it is. Secondly, dowsers say we can nearly all acquire the same talent.

However, as it turned out, this book isn't just about dowsing. An American physicist, Dr Arthur S. Wilson, recently told a Colorado symposium on the effects of electromagnetism on life that his students, instead of settling down to orthodoxy, were seeking answers to such questions as 'is there such a thing as ESP? why are we anxious? what causes hypnosis? do biological clocks affect humans? and the like'. It may be more than a co-incidence that my research had already taken me to precisely those four questions (as well as many others), all of which can be seen to have a common thread that draws them towards an explanation of how the unlikely feats of dowsing may come about.

Basically, we need to know how on earth people can perceive things hidden from the five classical senses. This involves not only physics, chemistry, biology and so on, but also the people who say they can do this – and here, as any investigator quickly finds, there is a well-trodden and slippery area of self-deception and trickery that surrounds all such matters. I have looked for this danger, and tried to avoid it. Along with most people, I am probably predisposed to accept, in a general way, that the inexplicable happens. However, now in my forties, and having had a career in journalism and then film-making, I have travelled a good deal, and the number of interviews I have conducted must run into thousands.

You cannot talk to as many people as that, checking up afterwards on what they have said, and remain credulous. These years of finding out facts from people have proved to me many times that it is a common human frailty to embroider a truth, and that most people have an unconscious desire to please – and thus to tell a listener what he thinks the listener wants to hear. I also know, because it is one of the arts of story-telling itself, how people will ignore an awkward fact, or alter it, if this makes the tale more rounded and complete; how people's memories are unreliable; and how two people's descriptions of the same set of events are frequently so different as to make one wonder if they have seen the same thing.

So in reporting for this book what I have seen, or recounting the stories that have been told me, I have been careful to take these things into account – indeed, to be especially cautious, because of the nature of the subject. Even so, not all the instances of dowsing that are included would pass muster at the Society for Psychical Research, of which I am a member. The standard of proof in that body requires independent witnesses, signed documentary evidence, and the elimination of the possibility of collusion or accidental success. It is surprisingly rare to find an instance of dowsing in which all these requirements have been met, the main reason being that when it works, it is basically a practical and useful talent serving a human need (unlike the more abstract exercises in ESP such as experiments in telepathy, metal-bending, or card-guessing), and dowsers as a whole see no need to justify themselves by anything except their results.

So, when deciding whether or not to include the story of a dowsing achievement, my standards of proof have usually been those of a juror in a court of law, who looks at all the evidence and then believes that something is true or untrue, rather than the absolute standards of modern ESP investigation.

My research took me to many places in Britain, and on a long round-trip of North America for a map-dowsing experiment organized in collaboration with the SPR. I believe this is the most extended and thorough test yet undertaken of the extraordinary claim by dowsers that they can accurately divine information using nothing but a map and a pendulum, and it yielded remarkable results (see chapter 7). Throughout the book, wherever the research did not involve personal interview or observation, I have identified the principal sources.

Part One looks at some of the ways that dowsers work, now and in the past. It is a formidable record, and one which at the start I had no idea existed in such depth. The how-to-dowse section is built up from the simplest and most straightforward contemporary advice. For me personally, it has worked. I make no claim to be a successful or reliable dowser, but I have taught myself to recognize a dowsing impulse, and have no difficulty in accepting that unconscious muscular reactions trigger off exaggerated movements of the rod or pendulum.

Part Two deals with the many people who have tried to find an explanation for dowsing through some kind of radiation, and the almost insoluble difficulties of doing so. I say 'almost', because research here led to a handful of people working on the

11

outermost fringes of science, where physics, chemistry and biology combine, who are demonstrating that we all have an astonishing, and hitherto unsuspected sensitivity to minute signals coming from our environment. Something beyond the bounds of present scientific knowledge is operating within us, and I have tried to give a readable summary of this demanding, potentially revolutionary area of discovery.

Finally, *Part Three* makes the connection between dowsing and the remainder of the parapsychological spectrum. I found, in California, a supposedly infallible and repeatable way in which clairvoyance – or 'remote viewing' – can be made to happen within any group of people, and have given the formula. By this stage in the research, the paranormal was becoming almost familiar, and to a certain extent the structure of the book reflects this view. Like dowsing itself, it was a personal search – a search to find out if dowsing works, and if so, how it works, and how well. What emerged may not be quite the final destination, but I feel myself to have gone a long way down the road.

My thanks are due to all those quoted in the book, many of whom have given me their time and hospitality, and have been kind enough to advise me on the detail of what I have written; my thanks especially to John Taylor and Eduardo Balanovski for checking my science, and Bill Lewis and Arthur Bailey my dowsing.

London, February 1977

Part One: the Phenomenon

The senses are more powerful than we normally find them to be. Man has developed and evolved as he is today because he is subject to certain desires. His psychological and physiological apparatus is conditioned for the satisfaction of his desires; thus he makes a very limited and selected use of the power of his senses. There are things he does not wish to hear, things he does not wish to see. He uses his sensory organs only to the extent that they satisfy his desires. Nature is a great economist. She does not give what does not have to be used. Through great practice, and sometimes painfully, he may, little by little, gain use of these sensory powers that have lain dormant from disuse.
– Dr K. Sampurnanda, Governor of Rajasthan, scholar of Sanskrit and Yoga.

1 The World of Dowsing

An observer venturing freshly into the private world of those who work with forked rods and pendulums soon finds a disconcerting theatricality. Unbidden, a rod will twist violently up or down, sometimes contorting so strongly and uncontrollably that blood may be drawn from the palms of the person who persists in holding it. Or a pendulum, suspended motionless from an apparently stationary hand, will gradually start to move, its momentum gaining steadily until it is circling rapidly round and round – and then, as unpredictably as it began, slow down and return to neutral. Or a man, walking to a spot where there is believed to be an underground stream, will pause there, begin to tremble, and soon shake in a paroxysm of involuntary jerks that will cease only when he moves onwards.

An outsider tends to shy away from such events. They are an embarrassment, like coming upon someone who has fainted, or who tells you with perfect certainty that the end of the world will occur next Sunday week.

It is similarly discomforting, for those of a rational and fastidious nature, to eavesdrop on a meeting of dowsers. The word dowser itself has a strangeness: nobody knows its origin, although it has been in use at least since the sixteenth century; it describes a person who, by use of some instrument such as a forked twig or pendulum, attempts to gain knowledge about matters hidden from the normal senses. Dowsers have been known as water-diviners in Britain and water-witchers in North America (the United States, incidentally, would not have been settled in the way it has without their ability to tell farmers where to sink a well). But nowadays, when several dowsers meet together, you would hear talk not only about how professionals among them can find almost anything, but even stranger claims: how they can divine the precise age of an object they may be shown; how they can be given a map – a sketch-map even – and they will mark the exact position of what is being sought.

These extraordinary claims seem quite matter-of-fact to dowsers themselves. They insist that their only talent is to have rediscovered a lost sensitivity which was once common to all mankind; and depending on which book you read or which authority you listen to, you will be told that between ten and ninety per cent of all of us can learn to do the same. In other words, that no matter how mystifying the process by which it happens, nor how apparently magical the results, we are all far more receptive to unseen information than we usually let ourselves believe – perhaps, more sensitive than the most delicate electronic receivers yet made.

Half a dozen of the world's most advanced medical laboratories have a piece of equipment known as the superconductive quantum interferometric device – in short, a squid.[1] This invention is based on the discovery that some metals become electrically superconductive below a certain critical temperature and can therefore be used to measure minute amounts of current. Among other things, it is used to map the magnetic field created by brain activity: brainwaves. It can barely manage this. A few inches from the head, the strength of magnetic field registering as a brainwave is around one *million millionth* the strength of a small horseshoe magnet, and this is the limit of a squid's sensitivity. It now seems proved that an exceptional dowser can detect changes in a magnetic field even smaller than that.

A brainwave experiment

The man who set up the experiments demonstrating this is Dr Zaboj V. Harvalik, the latest of a small band of scientists who have been prepared to take the subject seriously. He lives in a large, peaceful, elegant house on the wooded banks of the Potomac river just outside Washington, DC. Inside this, one might easily cast him as the inventor of many a children's TV serial, with still a strong mid-European accent in spite of many years in the United States, his office desk crowded with neatly-stacked papers and files. He willingly demonstrates to visitors a profusion of home-made electrical gadgets that have winking lights, buzzers, skeins of incomprehensible wiring, and invisible electromagnetic beams. Above him is his favourite device, a purpose-built ionizer. It teeters from the ceiling, hanging there like the ribs of a badly-broken umbrella or a tangle of giant hairpins, directly above where he sits. When switched on, it discharges negative ion particles into the air; Zaboj Harvalik generally uses it for about an hour a day, to increase his sense of well-being and the size of the unseen aura which surrounds him (and all of us). 'It gives the electrically beneficial and stimulating effects of standing under a shower or a waterfall, without getting wet,' he says.

He has powerful academic credentials, having latterly been Professor of Physics in the University of Arkansas, and then adviser to the US Army's Advanced Concepts Materials Agency in Alexandria, Virginia. Now retired, he devotes most of his time to recording scientific aspects of dowsing in the field, and unless you invent equipment with which to do this, as he has, the equipment would not exist. However, in the summer and autumn of 1969 he needed no complicated apparatus for the experiment which he was carrying out, which was to discover whether dowsers could identify, from a distance, a change in another person's mood.

The experiment consisted of two people standing back to back so that they could not see each other, one a dowser, the other the subject. The distance between them varied methodically during the test from two to twenty feet. The dowser held a pair of L-shaped angle rods made from coathanger wire, one in each hand; their function was to indicate a 'dowsing reaction' – when the dowser recognized something unconsciously, his muscles would give a minute twitch, his wrists would tilt imperceptibly, and the angle rods would swivel towards each other, thus magnifying the effect. They are commonly used dowsing tools, often given to beginners.

While Zaboj Harvalik kept out of sight, so as to give no clue to either of the participants (but in a position where he himself could see and record what was happening), the dowser waited, rods at the ready, for a dowsing reaction to occur. The other person had instructions to remain calm for a while, and then, at a time of his or her own choosing, to think suddenly of something violent or exciting, and concentrate hard on the images connected with this. The aim was to see whether this brought about a simultaneous dowsing reaction, and if so at what distance. The dowser announced aloud as soon as the reaction occurred, so that the other person could determine immediately if it coincided with the change of mood.

'The results were absolutely conclusive,' says Harvalik. 'All 28 subjects – 19 males and 9 females – managed to produce a dowsing reaction of varying strength, occasionally as far away as 20 feet. The strongest reactions were produced by sex-related "exciting" thoughts, and thoughts of fear. To me, it was completely convincing evidence that a good dowser can pick up what is coming out of another person's mind.'[2]

Now if dowsers can truly detect a signal as minute as a brainwave, it perhaps begins to make more credible the many stories of supernatural achievements – or super-sensitivity – which you will hear recounted at meetings of dowsers, or read in their literature. Historically, dowsers have often been treated with suspicion by ordinary people and derided by most scientists, and this tended to encourage an inward-looking defensive and secretive attitude, even among themselves. One of today's experienced water-finders from the west of England, George Applegate, has spoken of how at one time he 'had the cold shoulder from many practising water-diviners who were somewhat jealous of their professional art'. To modern eyes, the journals which they circulated read claustrophobically: a mishmash of unsubstantiated claims, pseudo-scientific explanations and semi-religious treatises written for internal consumption by people who believed themselves – maybe justifiably – to be maligned and misunderstood.

Much of that is changing. There are now societies of dowsers in many countries in the world who see it as their function not just to preach to the initiated, but to welcome outsiders and gather good evidence to present to the world.[3] The American Society of Dowsers, formed in 1961 with just eleven members, had grown by 1976 to more than 1600. It is incorporated as a non-profit, educational and scientific body, one of whose purposes is 'to assemble all manner of dowsing theories, ideas, techniques, applications, instrumentation, experiences, etc., for study and evaluation'. About a quarter of the members meet each

September at a convention which has traditionally come to be held among the red-leaved maples and sycamores of Danville, Vermont, where lectures, seminars and demonstrations are conducted on various aspects of the art. The longer-standing British Society of Dowsers, with a membership of 600–700, holds biannual congresses, and here, too, there is a ready acceptance for any sympathetic outsider.

But even though the attitude is changing, much of what is said and written by dowsers is still very hard for a newcomer to take. Within half an hour at such a convention or congress, you will hear tales not just of successful well-boring, but also how a good dowser can tell you the depth to drill, and the amount and quantity of water which will emerge; you will find dowsing and psychic healing discussed in the same breath; there will be mention of unseen magical properties to be found at prehistoric sacred sites, and stories of how journeys on the other side of the world can be traced instantaneously on a map in your own home. The mood at such meetings is a disturbing one of perfect assuredness that the extraordinary things being talked about are, however remarkable, commonplace; and so before we go into the eerie details of just what dowsing may or may not achieve, how valid it is, how successful, how consistent, and how it possibly happens, I think it is vital to start with the few generally agreed premises on which it rests. For alongside the unprovable and the unbelievable, there is an emerging consensus about basic principles.

The physiological basis

One thing that quickly becomes evident is that on the physiological level, at least, dowsing is a demonstrable fact.[4] Watch a dozen dowsers moving over the same patch of ground, and you will see their instruments – rods, wands, twigs, pendulums – move vigorously about. They do not always function in the same way (one man's rod may flick up, another's down) and this confusion of techniques is perhaps one reason why it is initially a baffling subject for study; but there is no doubt of the physical reality – the rods indeed move, even when there is no visible reason why they should. From time to time, scientists have measured various changes in the body that accompany this; they include alterations

19

in the electrical resistivity of the skin, in pulse rate, temperature, and so on.

So undoubtedly something odd is going on, whatever the cause. The effects of a dowsing reaction range from being negligible, or perhaps cumulatively somewhat tiring, to the violently unpleasant. The nineteenth-century geologist H. W. Whitaker, not himself a great believer in the effectiveness of dowsing, was nevertheless able to give a graphic description of what happened to the rod in the hands of William Lawrence, one of the two greatest water-finders of his day:

> Lawrence, an old white-haired benevolent-faced man, walked about the place for some time, it appeared fruitlessly, holding between each finger and thumb a piece of flat steel wire bent round into a sort of horseshoe shape. This, he told us, would detect minerals as well as water, so that when it presently began to agitate as it did, scriggling, and wriggling, and twisting, and turning in his fingers, he could not say definitely that it was water he had come upon, until he took in his hand a strong forked hazel twig, holding an end of each fork in each hand, and keeping his elbows tightly down to his side.
>
> I can only describe the antics of that twig as a pitched battle between itself and him! It twisted, it knocked about, it contracted and contorted the muscles of his hands and arms, it wriggled, and fought, and kicked, until it snapped in two; and then – what made it painful to watch until you got used to it – the old man reeled, and clutched hold of anyone nearest to him for a few moments. It evidently exhausts him very much, though afterwards I asked him what effect it had on him, and he said it only made his heart beat *most* violently for a short time.[5]

Evelyn M. Penrose, employed by the Government of British Columbia in 1931 as an official water- and mineral-diviner, found the rod turned so violently it tore her hands into blisters; but more than that, the discovery of large quantities of underground water could make her physically sick. 'The first indication I get of oil is a violent stab through the soles of my feet like a red-hot knife,' she wrote. 'When over the oil itself, I am turned and twisted about like a doll on the end of a string, and can hardly keep my feet.'[6]

Such reactions are, of course, exceptional, and few dowsers complain of anything more than a generalized feeling of lassitude, or a mild tingling shock as from an electric current; most feel nothing at all – and that is the reason for the variety of dowsing instruments. For the next generally agreed principle is that these are simply there as indicators of the fact that an otherwise un-noticeable reaction has taken place. Since this reaction seems to take a different form with different people, there is inevitably a profusion of tools. The way they move is important for each individual, but the fact of them moving is even more important – for at that particular moment a personal dowsing reaction has occurred.

Finally, the third agreed principle is that all dowsing is based on a search. The dowser is looking for an answer to a question, and he gets it through a reaction. Thus, walking over a piece of ground, he is unconsciously asking: 'Is there water here?' When he reaches a certain place, the reaction occurs, the rod flips, and the answer is: 'Yes.' If he now wants to find the depth, he simply asks a series of counting questions: 'Is it more than 20 feet?' – the rod flips, and he gets another yes; 'More than 30 feet . . .? more than 40 feet . . .?' and so on until the rod stops flipping.

Dowsers believe that by the same basic simple method they ought to be able to find anything. In theory, all they have to do is concentrate on what they want to find, and ask their questions accordingly; that is how they look for minerals, or treasure, or missing people. Cyril Wilson, an abstract painter who divides his time between Scotland and the island of Ibiza in the Mediterranean, where he has an unparalleled record of finding water beneath arid and stony hills, puts the technique at its most succinct: 'What you think is what you'll find.'

So that is the three-pronged basis on which dowsing rests: you ask a question, you get a reaction, and the dowsing tool indicates the answer. It is, of course, more subtle and elusive than that when the moment comes to make it all work; but there seems little doubt now that for the best dowsers this basic technique is practical and infinitely adaptable.

One other thing may be noteworthy at this stage. Most good

dowsers have long ago given up trying to analyse and rationalize *how* dowsing works, except to say with a vague shrug that it is outside existing scientific knowledge. Instead, they have learned to accept that, however baffling, for them personally it's a fact. They think the best introduction to the subject is to find a dowser, watch him work, and talk to him. I did so, many times, and what follows now is a sample of what I found. Many of the characters reappear from time to time elsewhere in the book, and so for convenience I am introducing them here in alphabetical order.

Master dowsers

Bob Ater, a friendly, comfortable-looking man in his late forties who runs a dowsing consultancy in Maine, has a technique with maps that does not involve any of the traditional dowsing tools; for him, a pencil suffices. He demonstrated it to two brisk young reporters, Emily and Per Ola d'Aulaire, who attended the 1975 Danville convention to research a story for the *Saturday Evening Post* (subsequently abridged by *Reader's Digest*).[7]

They handed him a sketch-map, drawn in pencil on the back of an envelope, of their property 300 miles away in Connecticut, and challenged him to tell them where their water well was.

'I'll see what I can do,' he told them. 'I don't know if I'll be successful or not – but anyway, I'll have a go.' So, as he tells the story, he held the pencil over the drawing and thought about their well – where might it be?

As I looked down at this drawing I pictured myself as a bird or something, hovering over their property. My mind was in a meditative state, picturing this well, and my pencil slipped down to a certain spot on the map right behind the house, and I marked it.

I was spot on, apparently. Then I looked at the map some more, and out in the field between the house and the back of the property I saw an oblong shape – that is to say, I saw it in my mind, because there was nothing on the map except white paper – and I said to them that I thought there was something there, perhaps a foundation of some kind.

At first they thought I was wrong. They couldn't remember

anything like that. Then one of them suddenly thought of an old garage foundation right where I had marked it, only nowadays it was all covered with raspberry bushes and weeds.

Then I ran my pencil along the outline of the house, asking in my mind for the pencil to be pulled off in the direction of any pipes that might be there. There was one place where my pencil felt as if it wanted to go off to the right, and it made a sort of snaky line which I drew in as I felt it. I said, gee, I don't know what this is, but there certainly seems to be something here.

You could see from their faces that this time I'd got through. They looked startled – sort of shocked and surprised. One of them told me why: where I put the line was exactly the place they had left their hosepipe for watering the garden.

I know the feeling they had, because I get it myself. I've had some pretty good successes with map-dowsing, and some monumental failures as well, and I can never tell which it is going to be. When it works, it makes me very happy – but it always comes as a shock and a surprise.

The D'Aulaires duly reported Bob Ater's three instant successes in their article, but when they came to sum up their findings at the end, there was still a note of scepticism – 'we're not sure if we believe . . .' they concluded. To which the *American Dowser* commented tartly that it was yet another example of the difficulty of getting outsiders to accept dowsing, no matter how positive the demonstration. There is a well-known and probably apocryphal story in dowsing circles about a farmer who, after much unsuccessful geological advice, had been found a good water source by a dowser, just where he wanted it, and with enough for all his future needs.

Afterwards, the farmer was asked if he now believed in dowsing, to which he replied: 'Well, yes and no. Yes, I believe it because it works – I've got some water and I didn't have any before. But on the other hand no, I don't believe it – because it's impossible!'

Dr Arthur R. Bailey, Ph.D., M.Sc., F.I.E.R.E., M.I.E.E., is a droll, level-headed Yorkshireman in his early forties who became President of the British Society of Dowsers in 1976 after a number of years as its scientific adviser. A University lecturer in his chosen subject of electronics, he is nowadays more amused than amazed at the reluctance of other scientists to take dowsing seriously, although there was an earlier time when he made a persistent effort to convince them.

In connection with this, he took himself to an archaeological site in the East Riding area of his county, in order to match his dowsing techniques against analysis of the site by normal modern archaeological methods. The site had already been laid out in a grid, and Arthur Bailey walked over the ground with a pair of angle irons keeping in his mind the question: 'Is there something of archaeological interest right here?'

For him, the amount that the angle rods move is an indication of the strength of the dowsing reaction; all through a long day he paced methodically up and down the site, calling out 'weak', 'medium' or 'strong' to an archaeological research student alongside him. By evening, they had accumulated enough data to produce a complete plan of the site, with the shapes of buried chambers and long-demolished walls emerging plainly.

Now this is exactly the same technique used by archaeologists with portable proton magnetometers, which measure magnetic anomalies, and soil resistivity meters, which measure variations in the electrical resistance in the soil; with both instruments, a diagram of artificial ground disturbance can be built up as a guide to where it will be subsequently most fruitful to excavate.[8]

It turned out that Arthur Bailey's plan and the scientifically measured contour maps corresponded remarkably. Transparencies were made of each, so that they could be superimposed, and Arthur Bailey prepared a lecture, entitled 'The Use of Dowsing as a Technique in Archaeo-Prospection', to be given to a 1969 symposium at Oxford University, organized by the august British Academy, and to be attended by most of Britain's leading archaeologists.

Of course, I was aware that there would be a certain amount of hostility, and right at the beginning of the lecture I warned them that although dowsing was an emotive subject for some people, I felt sure that as good scientists they would be able to take an objective view and would not be stirred emotionally.

I couldn't have been more wrong. The outburst that greeted my lecture was quite incredible. One person stated to me categorically that he had proved that dowsing did not work. How you can ever prove that something does not work I am not at all sure. All you can actually show is that under certain circumstances it doesn't work – not that it never works. It is very difficult to prove an absolute negative.

More or less every person present detested what I told them. If they had said that I must be a fraud I could have understood it. But what they were basically saying was that my results must be wrong, because they didn't fit in with their ideas.

I think this is the problem that dowsing has to face: because it doesn't fit in with most people's ideas of the universe, they tend to reject it.

Stephen Bosbach is a slim, vegetarian teacher of handicapped children in Tucson, Arizona, who in his late twenties regards himself as a novice dowser in spite of considerable success locally finding wells in the geologically difficult volcanic area that exists nearby. He and his wife Cris practise meditation regularly, and they are much taken by the metaphysical aspects of dowsing – 'the way it can unlock a part of your mind that maybe you didn't realize you could use'.

He believes that in principle, there is no question that cannot be answered by dowsing methods. However, he has found that accurate answers come more often in areas where the dowser already has some background knowledge; perhaps, he says, because the questions can be framed more precisely.

He gave me an example of this when the three of us went together, in the spring of 1976, to the Hopi Indian reservation some fifty miles north of his home (then in Flagstaff, Arizona). In connection with some studies of early man, we had been talking to local traditional Hopi leaders to try to understand something of the legends telling how their sacred sites were originally chosen. Early one evening, in a bedroom of the reservation's single sparsely-furnished motel, I asked Steve Bosbach if he could find anywhere nearby, by dowsing, evidence of an unknown site dating to a period BC.

Using a small plastic forked rod that flicked upwards in his fingers every time there was a 'yes' in answer to his questions, he began to look for one. 'Is there such a place within twenty miles of here?' An upward flick – yes. 'Within ten miles?' Again an upward flick. 'Within five miles?' – this time, the rod twisted down: no. So he thought it was between five and ten miles; now he established a direction, by turning his body round the points of the compass until the rod flicked into action to show which way we should go and search. Then further questions to establish if it was near a road (about 400 yards, according to the rod's indications); accessible (yes); higher or lower than the road (higher); which road (first track to the right off the main highway).

So we set off in a travel-worn Ford pick-up to the road junction. He stopped to check with a question: 'Is this the correct turning?' An upward flick of the rod, and we moved on. Every so often he pulled up to check distance and direction. 'Are we within four miles of the site . . . ? Three miles . . . ? Is it to the left of the road . . . ?' As we approached, the track grew dustier and bumpier. Around us, great flat-topped mesas of eroded rock reared like a lunar landscape hundreds of feet above the desert floor. On top of one of these, the rod indicated, would be the site we were seeking.

When we finally halted and switched off the engine, it was as quiet and lonely as any place on earth. There was no sign of human habitation, nor even of animal life. The track meandered to the horizon. Above us, nearly sheer, was the mesa which had somehow attracted Steve Bosbach half an hour or so previously in the motel. In his 'teens, his hobby had been mountaineering; now, he was off and up the rocks like a goat. He reached the top four or five minutes before Cris and me, and before we had finished the climb we heard him call: 'I hope you've brought your camera.'

I had done; and when I reached his side I saw what he meant. Planted in the baked crust of the earth was the remains of an irregular circle of stones, about thirty feet in diameter, the stones evidently chosen for their natural geometric shapes: triangular, or cubical, or wedge-shaped. They were small – none with more than two feet showing above ground – but absolutely distinctive: they had once been carefully collected and deliberately placed. Roughly in the centre was a single stunted tree and a flat slab of rock, its surface polished clean by burning winds. As I took photographs, the sun began to set.

I do not know when the site was last used, nor whether it truly dated back more than 2000 years before that evening when we stood there; little enough is understood about the lives of archaic Indians in those early times, and it was like no site I have ever seen.

But I had no personal doubt that having asked Steve Bosbach to find me an ancient sacred place, he had done so.

Robert Leftwich is, by any standards, one of the most remarkable and extraordinary men you would be likely to meet in a lifetime.[9] Now just turned fifty (the age at which from childhood he decided he was going to retire, and typically did so), he is a contentedly married, bright-eyed man whose whole manner is one of barely suppressed energy vibrating somewhere within him and seeking release through his day of crowded activity. In machine-gun dialogue, he will tell you within half an hour of your first meeting of his asceticism; of how he needs no more than a few hours' sleep, and consciously divides his day into times when there must be physical work, and other times for reading, meditation or psychic activities; how his life is devoted to ever-greater measures of self-control and development of the power of the 'mind'; how he can 'will' things to happen, and for that reason is never short of money; how at certain times he can voluntarily achieve astral projection (a relatively common phenomenon classified in ESP case-history as 'out-of-body' experiences, when you seem able to float away as in a dream and view your own body from a distance).

He lives in a substantial detached house just outside Crowborough in Sussex, and is touchingly proud of the fact that it is on the highest inhabited ground in all the county. His large, carefully-catalogued library on an eclectic variety of subjects – comparative religion, philosophy, dowsing, the occult, antiques, to name but a few – overflows into all rooms. In his garden – some of which he sold as building land in order to secure his promised early retirement – are signs of the energies and enthusiasms that have gripped him from time to time: a small swimming pool with a pumping system partly operated by hydraulic equipment invented by himself as a schoolboy; and underneath the grass, some twenty feet down, a network of subterranean tunnels and caves that he excavates daily with pick and trowel as part of his belief that his body must be kept physically in order. 'Sussex has a history of mysterious tunnels. I have found some of them by dowsing, and it suddenly occurred to me that if I was going to build a folly during my retirement, something to be remembered for, it would be more fun to have one underground than on top.' So the network grows continuously, and should they ever become so extensive that they are likely to undermine the whole area, you are left in no doubt that Robert Leftwich will find another way to divert his surplus energy.

Some of his stories, unless you have come to know him very well over a long period, or unless you are familiar with occult literature, are frankly unbelievable; he tells them nevertheless, completely unabashed, with an air of schoolboy honesty. My favourite came when he was complaining, in a puzzled fashion, about how he was able to find no practical moral use for his occasional ability to leave his body and view distant places. After giving me chapter and verse of some relatively trivial occasions on which this had happened, he said: 'To prove it one day, at a time when I was living in London, I thought I'd get up to a bit of harmless mischief. I went on one of these trips and floated away to my local bank. It was after closing time, and the bank manager was in the vaults unlocking the main safe. I watched him do it, took a careful note of how he went about it and what the combination was, and then came back into my body and pulled myself up out of my chair. The next day, I went and told the manager the combination, but not how I'd got it. It created a considerable commotion. I believe they had to change the combination, and this caused a major enquiry.

'That's the trouble with astral projection. It's easier to think of dishonest than honest ways of using it. Or maybe I could find out secrets from an unfriendly Government . . .'

As well as being a good anecdotalist, there is absolutely no doubt that he is at the same time a remarkable dowser, and although in his own mind this is closely connected with all the other psychic aspects of his life – psychokinesis, telepathy, and so on – it tends to be his dowsing successes which are best documented. He keeps a thick file of press cuttings, and correspondence from satisfied customers. They include the Caltex oil company, which called him over to Spain to help them overcome difficulties which they were having with a new refinery in the early stages of construction. The building involved the erection of several 300-feet-high towers, which needed substantial, solid foundations. But the site was in a former mining area, and was riddled beneath ground with a network of irrigation and drainage tunnels, for which the plans were lost, and which were too deep to be located by conventional detecting devices. It was essential to site the towers in areas clear of these tunnels, and the company had already made several false starts on the foundations before they flew Robert Leftwich over from London on the advice of one of their managers, a friend of his.

'The job only took a couple of days,' recalls Leftwich. 'I walked up and down with a rod, and told them where to stick in posts marking the outlines of the tunnels. After a bit, the site foreman asked if he could have a go, and it turned out that he was just as accurate as I was, so we finished the last part of the work together. Since then, I have had confirmation that when they carried on putting up the towers, they didn't hit a single tunnel – very satisfying.'

William A. Lewis, a retired electrical engineer who lives just outside the market town of Abergavenny in South Wales, is universally regarded by his fellows as among the half-dozen best dowsers in the United Kingdom. A tall, thin, diffident man, his experience stretches back some thirty years; I have found him especially interesting not just because of his evident successes in water-finding, but because of the wide range of his interests and his applications of dowsing – aspects of prehistory, tracing missing objects, diagnosis and healing. Also, like Robert Leftwich, he is careful to keep a record of the jobs he has done, and is happier than some dowsers to admit occasional error or defeat. 'You can't improve unless you are prepared to look at your mistakes and try to find out why they happened.'

Because of the long experiment (described in chapter 7) which we jointly undertook, I have spent more time with him than any other dowser. Like Arthur Bailey's archaeologists, I started with an attitude of considerable incredulity, so unlikely were some of the exploits he patiently described and explained; nowadays, after many hours of conversation, and a careful examination of his papers, I find it easier to accept the matter-of-fact way in which he talks about the times he has achieved the apparently impossible.

There probably comes a moment in researching any subject as difficult and intangible as dowsing that marks a turning-point in attitude. For me it came in February, 1976, sitting with Bill Lewis in his sitting-room and talking idly after lunch about different dowsing techniques. He was showing me a loose-leaf book of articles taken from newspapers and journals which he sometimes uses to check various facts. It includes some anatomical drawings that he uses as an aid in diagnosis – he places his left forefinger on each area of the body in turn and says, after a dowsing reaction, if it is a place that needs attention.

He was demonstrating this, explaining as he went along, by running his finger down the spinal column drawn skeletally on the page, when he abruptly asked: 'Hey, what's the matter with your wife?'

It was a totally unexpected question, the more startling because Judith was indeed temporarily not well. However, I didn't let on; I just said: 'Go on – tell me.'

The tape recording of what he continued saying goes like this: 'Ooh, it's painful. It must be a break . . . no not a fracture, more like a compression, something like that . . . an accident . . .'

At that point, I told him to stop. He was getting too accurate for comfort, and I had a quite irrational fear that if he went on the diagnosis would in some way become uncontrollable. For Judith had just come back from a skiing trip, where in a collision on the last day she had badly bruised her coccyx (the small bone at the base of the spine). The way Bill Lewis described it and pinpointed it was so vividly accurate that for the first time in my life I felt personally and immediately touched by the supernatural. I could think of no conceivable way (and cannot now) in which he could have picked up the knowledge by means other than paranormal: she was 150 miles away in London, he hadn't at that stage ever met her, and I hadn't talked about the accident nor (as far as I know) consciously thought about it or worried about it while I was with him that day.

There seemed to be one small discrepancy in what he described. The movement of the pendulum clearly indicated that the trouble was in the third bone up the spine, whereas the hospital staff, when she was being X-rayed, had diagnosed that it was the lowest bone that was damaged.

A few days later, we had the results of the X-rays. Much the worst-affected bone was, as Bill Lewis had insisted, the one that his pendulum had divined.

Jack W. Livingston, a robust, tough, cigar-chomping 65-year-old, formerly a supervisor in charge of organizing heavy earth-moving equipment on construction sites and dam-building in the Sierra foothills of California where he lives, is one of dowsing's archetypes: the man you would cast as the down-to-earth rural water-finder, the fellow who tells you where to site your well and, whoosh, a few hours later up comes the water. He's like that, and that's the way it happens. He started practising the art at the age of seven in Canada, and the last time he wrote, he added the footnote: 'Well locations now number 743, still going strong.'

Latterly, he has been charging thirty dollars a day plus expenses, but he emphasizes that this is the least part of the cost. In the area where he has lived for more than twenty-five years, the so-called 'mother lode' country of California, the hard rock costs upwards of ten dollars a foot to drill. 'Tell someone there's water two or three hundred feet down, and there's a lot of money riding on whether you're right. Fortunately, pretty well always, I am.'

Every location he has dowsed is recorded in a notebook, including details of the predicted depth and flow. In the past quarter-century, only about a dozen have failed to come up to expectations, or been substantially at variance with his forecasts. The occasion he found most deeply satisfying, since he is a cheerfully pugnacious character keen to do battle with orthodox experts, was in the neighbouring town of Pine Grove, which in 1965 was suffering from an acute water shortage, and paying large sums to have it trucked in. The town's Water Advisory Committee brought in two scientists, an engineer and a geologist, who said there would be a stratum of water-bearing rock at around 150 feet below a nearby hill. So a bore-hole was sunk through to 157 feet, at which point it struck bed-rock and was still dry.

Jack Livingston read of this and drove over to offer his services. Within a couple of hours, he had found them a spot more or less central in the public park; he predicted 150 gallons a minute at 130–40 feet, and even more lower down. 'I knew it was a good one. When you're on to a lot of water, your rod feels like a big fish is striking; if there isn't much the rod will twitch like it was a little minnow. Anyway, they started drilling, with a crowd of local people round, all watching the drill and getting the drillers to shout out the depth. At one-thirty feet there was still nothing. Then at one-thirty-six feet, we hit. It blew clear over the drill rig, and half the folk got soaking wet and stood there laughing and cheering. They've never gone short of water to this day. Last I heard, they drilled to 200 feet and were getting nearly 300 gallons a minute. It was a spectacular well, that one.'

Besides water-finding, Jack Livingston's main interest is in an associated field that is probably the most controversial area in modern dowsing: he senses that some underground 'streams' (which may occasionally be some kind of mysterious force rather than water-bearing fissures) are dangerous, and that prolonged exposure to them is enough to trigger off serious illnesses, especially cancer and arthritis. He also believes that such streams can be temporarily neutralized by driving metal stakes above their course. So far, there is no remotely acceptable scientific proof to show that this is so, although it is discussed so frequently by dowsers that no investigation of the subject can ignore it.

Jack Livingston believes everybody should keep an open mind about the unlikely, and has a good phrase to encourage this: 'Never say something can't be done, because you may be interrupted by someone doing it.'

Major-General James Scott Elliot, Companion of the Bath, Commander of the Order of the British Empire, Distinguished Service Order (1943) and Bar (1944), born 1902, educated Wellington College and Sandhurst, Regular Army officer

1923–56, took up archaeology and dowsing more or less simultaneously on his retirement into civilian life.[10] Since then, he has held eminent positions in both occupations: President of the Society of Antiquaries of Scotland 1962–5, and President of the British Society of Dowsers 1966–75. As befits a senior military gentleman, he is a methodical and logical person with whose soft-spoken arguments most people find it hard to disagree. Without doubt, his two biggest contributions to dowsing have been to make it seem, when he talks of it to outsiders, respectable rather than arcane; and to simplify (some say to over-simplify) the way it is practised.

He is a straightforward question-and-answer man who insists on himself and his pupils working only on searches that can provide demonstrable results. He is prone to somewhat magisterial statements, and reserves a certain amount of scorn for 'stick wavers and pendulum swingers', as he terms them, 'who must be persuaded either to train seriously and become reliable dowsers, or to put away their tools and remain interested spectators. It is from the ranks of these untrained semi-sensitives that, I am sorry to say, much of the harm to the reputation of dowsing comes; for, although untrained and unpractised, they take on jobs and fail and so bring dowsing into disrepute.

'I am not saying that we shall not make mistakes, because we all will from time to time. But they must be guarded against, so that they are rare. Unless we are professional about our work officialdom will not accept us, and of course the best way to gain acceptance is by a record of *no* failures.'

He has overcome his own initial difficulty in believing in dowsing by the simple trick of accepting it as an irrational and incomprehensible gift that nevertheless, somehow, works. His definition of dowsing, told to an American Society of Dowsers convention, is: 'The ability to use a natural sensitivity which enables us to know (by some means we don't understand) things that we cannot know by the use of the day-to-day brain, by learning, by experience, or by the five senses.

'It is, I believe, a matter of the mind; and there is very little that cannot be found (or found out) by dowsing means.'

He has many proven and recorded achievements of his own, particularly in archaeological finds. There was also one odd-ball success which, although trivial, is deeply fascinating in the way it touches on what dowsers call 'remanence' – their ability to pick up information from the past, as if wherever something or somebody has been, they leave behind a trace for ever. This is, of course, scientifically even more dubious than unseen noxious rays from underground streams (about which Jim Scott Elliot urges caution), but on the other hand it is a phenomenon that is now well attested.

On this occasion, he was telephoned by a friend of his, a girl who worked in one of London's many small art galleries, and which had been partially closed for three weeks while she went on holiday. Now, having returned, she wanted to reopen it; but before going away she had hidden the keys either in her flat or in the gallery, and had totally forgotten whereabouts. Foolish though she felt, she rang Jim Scott Elliot to see if he could help.

He knew the gallery well, and vaguely remembered the flat, having visited it once. He asked her to describe it in more detail, making a sketch-plan of it as she did so. Then he put the telephone down, redrew the map a little more carefully, and made a similar plan of the gallery and the furniture in it. It was the gallery he dowsed first, and after half an hour rang the girl to suggest she looked in the top left-hand drawer of the desk there. She looked, and found keys. 'Sorry, wrong ones,' she said. 'They're the spare keys to the flat.'

So next he dowsed over the map of the flat, and rang her later to suggest three places where he was getting a reaction:

1. Behind books on a book shelf some three feet to the left of the fireplace in the living-room of the flat;

2. In the right-hand drawer of the work top in the kitchen;

3. In the long hanging cupboard in the bedroom, five feet from the end furthest from the doorway.

By any standards, Jim Scott Elliot was remarkably successful. The first place was where she usually hid keys, although there were none there this time (remanence); the second contained two long-forgotten spare keys to the front door; and in the third, just where he said, a basket hung behind the clothes – and in the basket were the missing keys.

Clive Thompson, by profession an architect in the north of

England, and recently appointed a vice-president of the British Society of Dowsers, has a story of how he showed himself to be more efficient than a scientific device. Near a friend's home, a main electric cable needed to be traced before the track above it was dug up with a pneumatic drill. The Midlands Electricity Board sent along a man with an electric induction detector to mark its path. Rather like a metal detector, this is a portable but relatively cumbersome electronic transmitter/receiver with a probe that picks up electromagnetic disturbance set up around the cable and amplifies it into a buzz that can be heard through headphones. A good deal of checking from side to side is necessary, in order to pin-point the position where the signal is strongest.

Clive Thompson, whose sense of fun is well developed, walked ahead of the MEB official, using a dowsing rod of his own design shaped like a double V, picking up a reaction from the cable and jabbing his heel into the damp ground to mark where it lay beneath the surface. Within minutes, he was thirty yards ahead of the official, who was able to do no more than confirm that Thompson's marks were dead on line (which was subsequently confirmed when the cable was dug up).

After half an hour or so, the official packed up for the day, saying that it was a waste of his time being there when the dowser could detect and locate the main more quickly.

Raymond Willey is secretary of the American Society of Dowsers, one of the eleven founder members in 1961 who decided to gather together people of similar interests, and who has seen the membership rise in fifteen years to more than 1600. A gentle, silver-haired man now in retirement, he talks with sweet reasonableness and utter conviction about the improbable successes that he has managed to achieve. He recently wrote a book, *Modern Dowsing*, which as well as being a comprehensive how-to-dowse manual contains examples of the way he has integrated the art with his day-to-day life on levels that are sometimes important, sometimes trivial: he has used dowsing methods to pin-point hidden leaks in his roof, and an unsuspected fracture in his car battery; in his career, when he worked for a multi-national corporation on organization and method studies, he frequently short-cut his way through a complex series of choices and statistics by dowsing for the answers – and to the bafflement of his colleagues, from whom he concealed his dowsing techniques, the answers generally worked.

Like most people in the Society, he is inclined towards a metaphysical explanation of why he is able to obtain information in this way. 'Dowsing is the exercise of a human faculty which allows one to obtain information in some manner beyond the power and scope of the standard human senses,' is his definition of the art. 'It is a legitimate part of human functioning. You learn to enjoy a legacy, a gift from nature. You can feel that you are employing your total abilities, expanding your full personality. You are bringing back into contemporary culture human skills that have been neglected and even disparaged by many intellectual leaders during recent centuries.'

Once, he wanted to check the whereabouts of a well in a suburb of Albany, NY, which had been sunk on the advice of another dowser some years before. By question-and-answer, Ray Willey established to his own satisfaction that additional water could be found if the well were sunk deeper, and he wanted to check this finding by dowsing privately on the site itself before giving his considered advice. 'Early one evening, after work, I drove as close as I could to the fields where I understood the well to be. First I dowsed a direction to the well; then I got a distance reading of just under a quarter of a mile. There was a farm road most of the way, which ended at the edge of a hayfield. The hay was high and uncut, and I dowsed a fresh direction line through it. Then I walked ahead, the grass about waist high round me. I'd only gone a few yards when I hit my shin hard and painfully on something hidden there. It was the top of the casing of the well, just six inches in diameter. Nobody could tell me afterwards that dowsing didn't work – I'd got a bruised leg to prove it.'

Where Ray Willey parts company with most of his colleagues is that he firmly believes in a dowsing force that acts directly on the pendulum. He has gone to great lengths to demonstrate that this is indeed so, with apparatus such as two heavy rubber balls suspended from four-feet-long cords on a bar which he holds in his hand; he then summons up the dowsing force and 'wills' the balls to start revolving in opposite directions. 'If it were me doing it, it would show up in a very positive hand movement,' he says. 'But it doesn't. I've demonstrated this on television, and nobody could see my hand working. Another time, I suspended a bowling ball from a twenty-inch cord attached to a masonry socket. When I held the socket, I could get the ball in motion without moving my hand.'

He agrees that whatever may cause the pendulum movement, a person has to hold it. There has been no occasion in the history of dowsing experiments when a pendulum or a rod has been induced to move when left on its own in a fixed position.

Footprints on time

In every generation, there are two or three people in the world whose ability to track down events is uncanny even by the standards of other good dowsers of their day – the men and women who, often in the macabre circumstances of suicides or violent deaths, are regularly and especially able to trace the movements of missing people. To me, the feats of such dowsers, however well-attested, simply transcend the imagination. With nothing to help them except a photograph, a letter, a piece of clothing, or a few strands of hair, they are able on occasion not just to pin-point where somebody (alive or dead) happens to be at that moment, but also – guided by some force that they all say comes from elsewhere – indicate the paths and the stopping places that the person in question recently travelled. It is the psychic equivalent of a bloodhound picking up the scent of a month-old trail.

All dowsers agree that it is the most difficult and elusive of jobs, and none claim to be right all the time. But when they succeed, it is dowsing's intellectually most exciting proof to sceptics, because there is usually no way of explaining such a success as having happened by chance, no way of denying its independent confirmation – and no way of explaining it within the parameters of existing scientific knowledge.

Just how many people through the ages have consistently been able to manage these feats it is hard to judge. Historically, it seems to have been very small, with no more than a handful of names of eighteenth- and nineteenth-century dowsers whose exploits in this field have been recorded. Nowadays, it may be rather more common than comes to light, for much of it involves work with police or Government departments which traditionally are not keen to publicize their connection with the occult.

Most of the dowsers so far introduced would say that they are successful occasionally. Bob Ater, hearing on a radio news bulletin that two college students were lost in a thunderstorm on Mount Washington in New Hampshire, took out a map of the area and allowed his pencil to be guided up one trail, down again, and back up a second track. He telephoned the rescue operation at Mount Washington Observatory with the information. A few days later, they called him back to say that the missing hikers were exactly where he had indicated, and had taken the paths he had marked. The same sort of trace even seems to be left behind by objects. At the request of the owner, Bill Lewis outlined the movements of some stolen saddlery near the market town of Chester, more than 100 miles away from his house; he somehow managed to pick up the point where the stolen property had been divided and taken in different directions, as recovery of the property subsequently showed.

Literally hundreds of such cases, more or less well documented, have been published in dowsing journals. But what is so deeply mystifying, even eerie, is the way that long after people are dead, a dowser of exceptional sensitivity finds he can pick up their presence just as if they were alive – 'we can distinguish something that the people have left behind,' I have heard it explained.

In the 1930s, the most renowned of such dowsers was John Clarke, of Kettleby in Yorkshire; in the 1940s and 1950s, the Devon countryman William Burgoyne; and contemporarily, perhaps, the Irishman Thomas Trench, Captain Vo-Sum, formerly of the South Vietnamese Navy, and the Dutch clairvoyant Gerard Croiset. Each of these men has been successful on numerous occasions in pin-pointing not only the place where someone has died, but the route taken in the few hours or days before death; and they all speak in a remarkably similar way about how it feels to be able to 'pick up' this invisible – well, this invisible what? No scientific device can measure what they try to describe, so in scientific terms it doesn't exist. It is as if they sense a series of ghostly footprints on time, an etheric disturbance that hangs in the air like a thin, unseen mist. Yet however intangible, for them it is demonstrably real.

The language they use to describe it is that of radio transmission, since this is presumably the closest analogy that they can manage: words such as 'radiation', 'wavelength' and 'tuning' are common. John Clarke, who in just three months from March to May, 1933, traced the bodies of six drowned people in the Nottinghamshire area, described the way he began a search: 'I first pick up, on the pendulum, the person's radiation, using some article of clothing or a spot where I know he has been.' Or Thomas Trench, describing how, in one of the best-documented cases in the British Society of Dowsers' files, he located on a map from 500 miles away, the body of a murdered Belgian policeman six months after the February 1966 riots in which he had been killed: 'The photograph and description were placed on the top edge of the map, which was oriented N–S, and the pendulum was tuned in over them before beginning the search.'[11]

For all of these dowsers, once the tuning process (whatever that may be) is complete, it then becomes a question of staying on beam, of letting themselves be guided or drawn in the direction the missing person took. I have a tape-recording of William Burgoyne[12] describing the first time he went on such a search, in 1944, for two boys from the nearby village of Slapton, who had gone missing the previous day. The police were already searching the marshes nearby when, having read of John Clarke's methods, he decided to see if he could help. Shortly before going out, the boys had changed their clothes, and he borrowed a pair of braces which one of the boys had been wearing. He describes the way in which, intuitively, he feels he picked up the trail:

'All of us, as we walk through the air, leave vibrations behind us. If I take an article of the person I'm looking for in my hand with the rod, with the vibrations of that sample I can step into the vibrations of where the person has walked, and I get a reaction. Once the rod stops turning, I know I'm off the line, and I have to walk backwards and forwards until I pick it up again.'

Somewhat to his surprise, since this was the first time he tried it, he quickly picked up the trail just outside the village. It led directly to a bridge over a river. The police inspector in charge of the case, deeply sceptical at first, was convinced when William Burgoyne let him hold one branch of the forked rod, and felt it twist. Together, they followed the river bank, and some way along it there was a violent pull on the rod. A boatman took them out to midstream, and after a few zig-zag manœuvres, Burgoyne was in no doubt that the bodies were beneath the boat. The spot was marked, the police search in the marshes a mile away was called off, and later that afternoon the bodies were dragged to the surface.

For the next quarter of a century until he died, William Burgoyne volunteered help to the police, and was asked for it, several times a year. His daughter recalls: 'He was a deeply religious man, who believed that he received divine guidance in this part of his work. He never charged a fee, because he regarded it as a spiritual gift, and if he tried to make money he would lose the power. He developed his faculty so that all he needed was a photograph in the newspaper and a map of the area; then he would ring up someone he knew at Scotland Yard and tell them his results.'

On the tape recording the simplicity and honesty of the man sound unmistakable. In 1953, an acquaintance of mine, Andrew Freedland, had the task of going with William Burgoyne to look for his flat-mate's father, suspected of having committed suicide.

Once we had given the old man a handkerchief, there was an air of total certainty about the outcome. He quickly drew a line on the map which led across the moor outside Dartmouth. We drove as close as we could, and then when we started walking he knew exactly the direction. We found the body of the father after half an hour or so beneath a cliff. It was a harrowing experience by any standards, but what left its mark on me was the complete absence of doubt in Burgoyne's work. The next day, because my friend wanted to find out something of his father's state of mind, the three of us went looking for all the places he had visited on the day before he had died. He had been into various pubs and shops; Burgoyne established the starting point, and then took us without hesitation to every one of them.

Such sensitivity is mindbending – perhaps too much to take at first reading. But then, perhaps that has been dowsing's problem for thousands of years: it makes possible the kind of feat that in the past led to charges of sorcery and witchcraft, and it is to these ancient accounts of dowsing that we can look now.

2 The Ancient Tradition

The literature on dowsing is truly monumental. Sir William Barrett's and Theodore Besterman's classic investigation of dowsing for the Society for Psychical Research in London, conducted in the 1920s, lists nearly 600 printed references, which, even so, are said to constitute less than one quarter of the total. They range from obscure German and Swiss texts of the sixteenth century, to highly personalized accounts by great dowsers of their day such as the Wiltshire dowser who wished to 'draw attention to the fact that J. Mullins has been before the public as a water-finder for upwards of 30 years, and together with his two sons, has located over 5000 springs, and in the same time has carried out works in connection with 700 water supplies for Mansions, Breweries, Factories, Farms, etc., by sinkings, shafts, boring Artesian wells, laying on Water Mains, and the fixing of Windmill and other Pumps . . . to dispel any suspicion of trickery the authors have annexed a few testimonials out of the many hundreds that have been received.'[1]

In 1917, Arthur J. Ellis, of the United States Geological Survey, was even more comprehensive. At the end of his essay *The Divining Rod: A History of Water Witching*, he published 650 references. But his purpose was diametrically opposed to that of Mullins – he wished to discredit dowsing. His chief in the Bureau, O. E. Meinzer, wrote an introduction whose tone of intemperate impatience is typical of most scientists when confronted with this 'enormous volume of uncanny literature': 'It is doubtful whether so much investigation and discussion have been bestowed on any other subject with such absolute lack of positive results.' From this judgement has stemmed much of the scepticism that characterizes subsequent American accounts of dowsing.

But what Meinzer and Ellis were unable to deny was that the literature proved the great antiquity of belief in dowsing; the spontaneity with which the dowsing reaction traditionally appeared; and that, throughout history, dowsing had been applied in a large number of ways.

Long before man learned to read and write, there is pictorial evidence that dowsing probably existed in the same form as today. Rock paintings in caves near Tassili in the northern Sahara desert, dated at *c.* 6000 BC, show a cattle herder walking behind his beasts, a forked stick in his hands held in the way that most dowsers do, with the rod pointing upwards. He is surrounded by interested spectators, and the painting has been interpreted as the world's first known portrayal of a dowser; so it may be, although a sceptic might say that he was simply holding a stick to urge the cattle on. Similarly, South African bushmen in a cave near Platsberg in the Orange Free State have drawn a figure which almost unquestionably represents a dowser; but it has not been dated with any great accuracy, being termed 'neolithic', which in Africa can be taken as a period several thousand BC right up to historic times. By Egyptian times, dowsing was certainly established – sculptures show a priest holding a forked twig, and it is also possible to interpret a bas-relief of the twelfth century BC, in the Hittite Kingdom, as being a mining official using a rod to divine for ore. Rock carvings in ancient Peru show the practice to have been widespread at a very early time – certainly in a period BC.

But finding unambiguous references in Biblical, Greek and Roman times is not easy, one of the problems being that then, as now, there were two ways in which the art was practised: in the narrow sense of water-finding, and perhaps mineral-finding too; and in the much broader sense of divination in general, in which the rod could be used to gain unlimited knowledge. The Greeks covered both applications with their word rhabdomancy (from ράβδος, the rod, and μαντεία, divination), which the *Shorter Oxford English Dictionary* defines as divination by means of a rod or wand, and specifically the art of discovering ores, springs of water, etc., in the earth by means of a divining rod. In Roman times King Theodorus the Great, *c.* AD 500, commanded his minister Cassiodorus to bring him some water-seekers.[2]

However, it is difficult to believe that during classical times dowsing, in its limited sense, was widely or commonly used. The Roman writer Pliny, in his multi-volume *Natural History*, does not include it in a long list of magical arts, nor among the methods of discovering springs or metals; and these books are so exhaustively thorough that one would expect at least a mention. Even the most-quoted Biblical incident in dowsing literature, when Moses smote a rock to obtain water for the children of Israel wandering in the Sinai desert (Exodus xvii, 4, 5 and 6, and Numbers xx, 8–12) is open to much doubt. For a start, dowsers don't smite things – at least, not while they are working. Also, it is sometimes literally possible, on certain kinds of limestone in the desert, to crack off the hard, polished surface and find underneath a much softer, porous rock from which water rises up in a funnel.

However, there is no doubt of ancient belief in the other, more magical, definition. The gods and goddesses Hermes, Mercury, Minerva and Circe all used rods which had a mystical power to protect or to heal. The augurs of Rome, of whom Cicero was one, used an arched rod called a *lituus* with which to divine the future. An early American account of dowsing by Rossiter Raymond says that Scythians, Persians and Medes, all had priests who used rods for divination.[3] But perhaps the most striking ancient account, and one which foreshadows many of the almost mystical aspects of modern dowsing, is contained in the *Cabbala*. This book, which enshrines early Hebrew oral tradition, passed on from generation to generation since the time of Abraham, was first written down around AD 1275 in Spain. The relevant passage deals with Solomon's Rod, by use of which he made himself the richest and most powerful man in the world, and one translation of the instructions of how to make the rod reads:

Look for a peach tree or walnut tree or olive tree which has not been planted by the hand of man.

The tree must be so young as to have never yet borne fruit.

In the morning of the day, just before the sun peeps over the horizon, cut a forked branch not less than fifteen inches nor more than twenty inches long.

While cutting the branch, repeat these words: 'I cut thee in the name of Eloina, Miraton, Aldonay, and Semiplaras, whom

I plead to bestow unto thee the magic qualities and virtues possessed by the rods of Jacob and of Moses, and of Aaron, and to impart unto thee *the gift and the power to reveal that which is hidden.*[4]

The *Cabbala* became a forbidden text, known only to secret societies, alchemists, and similar practisers of the magic arts. It may be more than a coincidence that at the same time, dowsing seems to have gone underground. During the centuries that followed the decline of the Roman Empire in the middle of the first millennium AD, there is no direct reference to it. Why this should have been is an unsolved mystery, but probably, just as the knowledge contained in the *Cabbala* was passed on orally and secretly, dowsing became a clandestine activity. It was a period when the whole of Europe was being converted to Christianity, and it is clear from Church literature that many forms of pagan worship continued to flourish in spite of the efforts of early missionaries. It may be that dowsing was absorbed by other occult sects, for St Theodore of Tarsus, in his *Penitential*, which is typical of many books instructing early British converts during the Dark Ages, condemns 'augury and divination' among other practices they must no longer pursue. Dowsing would certainly have been included in this category, and in 1518 Martin Luther specifically included the use of the rod in his list of acts that break the first commandment.

Mining and the wand
By then, however, the subject was reappearing in literature – not in its mystical sense, but in its highly practical application as an aid in discovering metallic ores. The place where dowsing surfaced was Germany, probably in the Harz mountains. As early as 1420, there is a Viennese manuscript by a surveyor stating that 'metallic exhalations' had led to a mine being discovered by use of a divining rod. By the beginning of the sixteenth century the art was commonplace, and a German scholar, Georgius Agricola, first of all in an essay in 1530, expanded into his book *De Re Metallica* in 1556, wrote a lengthy description of its use by miners in their search for metal. Reading this nowadays, there is a sense of timelessness about the issues he discusses. In the thous-

ands of treatises that have been published since his day, it is remarkable how the questions he posed remain basically the same: Is there some unknown magical force involved? Does the rod move of its own accord, or is it the operator who makes it move? Does it matter what the rod is made of? And above all, does it really work?

So far as magic was concerned, Agricola had no doubt that 'the application of the inchanted or divining rod to metallic matters took its rise from magicians and the impure fountains of inchantment'. Astutely, he observed that since the rods did not seem to work for everybody, there was thus no direct causal link between the vein of ore and the rod; but he nevertheless noted that different rods were used for finding different kinds of ores – hazel twigs for silver, ash for copper, pine for lead and tin, and rods of iron or steel for gold. As for whether it worked, the ambiguity of his conclusions also anticipated countless other investigations to come: 'Truly the twigs of the miners do move . . . some say this movement is caused by the power of the vein, others say that it depends on the manipulation, and still others think that the movement is due to both these causes . . . There are many and wide differences of opinion amongst miners about the rod for some say they have been of the greatest use, but others deny it.' Finally, a dutiful Christian, he retreated into a bland piece of moralizing which let him avoid taking sides: 'A miner, since we think he ought to be a good and serious man, should not make use of an inchanted twig, because if he is prudent and skilled in the natural signs, he understands that a forked stick is no use to him.'

But to the bafflement of the scholars and the fury of the Church, belief in dowsing refused to go away, and one can only assume that then, as now, the simple fact was that it sometimes worked – often enough, at any rate, for Queen Elizabeth I, at the end of the sixteenth century, to import German miners and diviners to Cornwall to look for tin (which was about the time when the word 'dowsing' first emerged). How it worked was less important than the fact that it delivered results.

During the seventeenth century, the practice proliferated. Acceptance of dowsing's usefulness in detecting underground veins of ore grew to the point where dowsers became, first, members of the staff of most mining explorations; then, in 1670 in Germany, given a rank equal to that of official surveyors; and by 1709, given precedence over surveyors – a progressive testimony, surely, of practical results. Shortly after the First World War, in the region of Erbenbach near the Operfalz mountains in Bavaria, there was remarkable confirmation of the powers of these early metal-divining dowsers. A map dating back to the seventeenth century showed a dowser's plan of two groups of lodes invisible beneath the surface, and inaccessible by mining techniques of the day. Modern drilling and excavating equipment showed the dowser, 300 years earlier, to have been precisely accurate.

In fact, the latter half of the seventeenth century and the first half of the eighteenth century was a period during which dowsing, particularly in connection with mining, was probably more respected and accepted than at any time before or since. A special diploma was granted to German professional dowsers, evidently much coveted – a petition from two certificated dowsers to the Bavarian Mining Office in 1738 requested that the authorities should not employ unqualified dowsers. There is considerable evidence from the period of the esteem in which dowsers were held. August Beyer, the Freiburg Mine Commissary and Surveyor, wrote: 'It is undeniable that with careful procedure and proper use much good can be obtained with the rod.' His cousin Adolph gave a vivid description of the master dowser Hans Wolff, who 'pressed his hands together and walked over the fields with his arms hanging down. As soon as he came near to a lode, his arms began to shake, and when he was directly over it his reactions were particularly strong, which then made him so feeble, that he had to rest for a while.'

In other parts of Europe, it seems that dowsing was equally accepted. Dr William Borlase, the Cornish antiquarian who described the folk-lore and local customs of the eighteenth century in his *Natural History of Cornwall*, makes it clear that miners relied on dowsers to locate their sites; one of the dowsers, the Quaker William Cookworthy, wrote in the *Gentleman's Magazine* of 1751 that 'metals have different degrees of attraction: gold is strongest, next copper, then iron, silver, tin, lead, bones, coals, springs of water, and limestone.'

Early water-divining

It is perhaps curious that during these hey-days of dowsing, so little attention was paid to what later became the commonest application of all: water-finding. Was it that the need for water then was less than the need for mines? Or was it that dowsers then, as now, tended to learn by imitation, so that it occurred to few that dowsing could be used for other purposes than the discovery of underground veins of ore? Whatever the reason, early references to water-divining are scant, credit for recording the first incident probably going to Teresa of Avila. Offered a site for a convent in 1568, she was about to abandon it because there was no water. Along came a certain Friar Antonio, armed with a twig with which he appeared to be making the sign of the cross. St Teresa is reported to have said: 'I cannot be sure if it were a sign he made, at any rate he just made some movement with the twig and then he said: "Dig just here".' She did as he asked, and the resulting pure water spring satisfied the convent's needs from then onwards.

The first person to have made a systematic attempt to apply dowsing to water-finding seems to have been the Baroness de Beau-Soleil around 1630, although it still took second place to a search for mines. Her husband was one of the foremost mining authorities of his day, and with him, she decided that to preserve the wealth and eminence of France among European nations, mineral-finding ought to be made more reliable; so she laid down a set of methods to be used. It is interesting that, as with much modern site-dowsing, the first thing she suggests amounts to an appreciation of the site with all the normal senses – observing herbs and plants and the way they grow, tasting the water in the streams, smelling 'vapours' in the misty air at dawn; only after this does she suggest using sixteen 'scientific' instruments, among which was the forked rod. In two books, she enumerated the successes of her husband and herself in finding gold, silver, copper, lead, iron and other mines and water veins, and most of these claims are nowadays accepted.

Alas, the couple fell into disfavour in royal circles, and the connection between their use of the rod, and contemporary alchemical practices, led to a charge of sorcery. They were placed in separate prisons, he in the Bastille, she in Vincennes, and died around 1645. Indeed, in spite of the evident success and localized acceptance of dowsing in relation to mining, all dowsers had to face up to the difficulties presented by the ambivalent disapproval of the Church. After Martin Luther's condemnation in 1518, the action of the rod was widely ascribed to the work of the devil, and to overcome this, many dowsers were careful to take steps to purify their activities. In Germany, it was common for the rod to be 'Christianized': having been placed for a while in the bed of a newly baptized child, it was then addressed by the child's Christian name in a formula such as: 'In the name of the Father and of the Son and of the Holy Ghost, I adjure thee, Augusta Carolina, that thou tell me, so pure and true as Mary the Virgin was, who bore our Lord Jesus Christ, how many fathoms is it from here to the ore?' – after which the rod, held in the hands of the diviner, would dip a certain number of times just as when dowsers 'depth' a stream or a vein today.

One of the problems for the Church was that so many of their priests were themselves natural born dowsers. Nevertheless, a learned meeting of academics in Wittenberg in 1658 decided that, in the cases where dowsing could be seen to have provided accurate results, this was the result of a pact with the devil. These findings were supported the following year in an important book, the *Magiae Universalis Naturae et Artis*, by the Jesuit Father Gaspard Schott, which started off a century of debate within the Church, and during which time, according to Sir William Barrett, 'dowsing, like so many other misunderstood practices, seemed about to wilt and disappear beneath the priest's frown.'

In fact, it didn't. Before long, Schott himself had changed his mind and come to believe that the movement of the rod might not, after all, be caused by the devil, because 'monks of great piety have used it with really marvellous success, and affirm positively that the movement is entirely natural and that it does not at all proceed from dexterity or from the strength of imagination of him who uses it.' By 1674, the Jesuit priest Dechales was able to write: 'There are two things which astonish me in this experience: Why this rod turns only in the hands of certain persons, and second, why this rod serves equally well to locate both underground streams and mines.'

It perhaps says something for the effectiveness of dowsing to find it emerging from now on so frequently, in so many places, in spite of the generally hostile intellectual climate which has persisted right up to today. It is impossible even to guess how many active dowsers were operating in Europe during the next hundred years; certainly hundreds, some of whom were emigrating to the New World and using their skills to locate water wells in New England. But as the practice of using dowsers in German mines gradually died out (the last official dowser was discharged in 1778 after a dispute with the mining authorities), interest moved to southern France where, in the region of the Dauphiny surrounding Lyons, there was a succession of remarkable dowsing feats that for many years captured the imagination of a wide public, culminating in the career of one of the most renowned water-diviners in history, Barthelmy Bleton.

Bleton, a peasant's son, born about 1740, was brought up near Bouvantes in a religious charity, and by the age of seven was earning his living in the fields herding the cattle and goats. It was said later that even as young as this, his gift of dowsing was fully developed, and there is a famous account, in a letter written in 1781, of how it first came to be noticed:

Bleton, when seven years of age, had carried dinner to some workmen; he sat down on a stone, when a fever or faintness seized him; the workmen having brought him to their side, the faintness ceased, but each time he returned to the stone, he suffered again. This was told to the Prior of the Chartreuse, who wished to see it for himself. Being thus convinced of the fact, he had the ground under the stone dug up; there they found a spring, which at the time of writing was still in use to turn a mill.

What makes Bleton particularly interesting in the context of dowsing history is that he is the first man who underwent prolonged and relatively successful series of tests, in some cases performed under what would now be known as 'double blind' conditions – that is to say, with neither himself nor the experimenter knowing the location of what he was trying to discover. The man responsible for this was one of Louis XVI's doctors,

Pierre Thouvenel, who while still in his twenties was appointed inspector of France's mineral waters, and was highly esteemed by the academic world until, when thirty-two, he took up the investigation of dowsing. Even then, almost exactly 200 years ago, it was enough to earn him the scorn of his fellows, and he died a disappointed man, semi-exiled in Italy after a long retirement. However, his two books *Mémoire physique et médicinal* (1781) and *Seconde mémoire* (1784) are invaluable records of early scientific experiments. Sir William Barrett records a typically sophisticated test, in which Bleton was kept in ignorance even of the fact that he was being tested:

> Over a stone bridge, of one arch, pass four small wooden aqueducts, carrying water to Nancy. Only the engineer, who had never seen Bleton, knew the exact position of these four rows of pipes, their distance apart and depth underground, the whole being well covered by earth and vegetation. He gave Thouvenel secretly information on this, of which Bleton was entirely ignorant. The latter was then taken across this bridge as though to return to the town, after various experiments had been made in the neighbourhood, and without being told that fresh experiments were to be made. Just before reaching the bridge he asserted water was flowing beneath him, and the sensation continued with slight gaps, while crossing and in front of the bridge to a distance of five or six feet. He retraced his steps several times before finding distinctly the four channels, and was much astonished to find them so near. He was then told that they were simply four hollow tree trunks made to serve as aqueducts.

On another occasion, a French Archbishop buried water pipes beneath the ground, and (in anticipation of many tests of this sort in the twentieth century) arranged for them to be secretly switched on and off. Whenever there was a flow of water, Bleton infallibly traced the paths of the pipes; when there was no flow, he had no dowsing reaction.

Bleton dowsed for more than forty years, and some of the innumerable commendations for his work are included in Thouvenel's books. Reading them, it is impossible to believe that all these successes could have happened by chance, as his critics at the time constantly upheld. Not only is the sheer number impressive, but also the documentation. One example stands out, because it involved a court of law. Ancient title deeds of Vervains Abbey mentioned springs of water that had once existed; but they were no longer visible, and according to Thouvenel, the result of a court action hinged on whether they could be found. After many unsuccessful searches by local priests and farmers, Bleton was brought in. He showed their exact position, which drilling substantiated – a classic case of a dowser succeeding where others had failed.

Bleton was the forerunner of a select group of master dowsers who, geniuses in their own way, became near-infallible in their ability to find water. Reading through accounts of the feats of these men and women becomes almost monotonous, because in essence they describe much the same thing: the dowser was called in to do a professional job of work, and did so. They often failed under experimental conditions, but when it came to working in conditions of genuine need, the list of satisfied clients far outweighed the few complainants. On the whole, those who wish not to believe in dowsing tend to dismiss this evidence as proving nothing – there is so much water everywhere, they sometimes say, that an experienced observer of the lie of the land would be bound to sink successful wells more often than not. Arthur Ellis, for instance, in his report for the US Geological Survey about the divining rod and the search for water, wrote that 'in the very nature of things, its successes must have outnumbered its failures, just as, taking the country over, successful wells outnumber unsuccessful ones.' D. H. Rawcliffe, in his long book about the supernatural *The Psychology of the Occult*, wrote:

It is significant that the cult of dowsing, at least in Western Europe, flourishes at its brightest in those parts of the country where it is rather more likely than not that water will be found at random. In such districts 'success' is virtually assured if the *soi-disant* dowser has some idea of the conditions under which water is usually found locally. Relatively few dowsers will be found in areas where water is scarce. Dowsing flourishes mainly in districts in which water exists in sheets of water-bearing strata, where almost any bore which is excavated below a certain depth will find water; the water from the saturated strata surrounding the bore simply percolates into the bore . . . the great fallacy of dowsing lies in the dowser's general tendency to think that almost all underground water is confined to running streams.

Now as geological observations these statements are generalized, doubtfully accurate, and unsupported by any figures. Accounts kept by the best dowsers are often the opposite: precise and provable. From Bleton onwards there have been a succession of dowsers whose consistent success in finding water has been more than 90 per cent of all wells sunk; most of them could also successfully predict the depth and the flow with about the same percentage of accuracy -- something at which Bleton confessed himself less than adequate.

It is from Britain's West Country, the birthplace of a number of great dowsers (just as Dauphiny was in France), that some of the best of these documented accounts have come down to us. In the nineteenth century, the supreme British dowser was John Mullins, born at Colerne, near Chippenham in Wiltshire, in 1838. Trained as a mason, he discovered his dowsing ability when he was twenty-one, but did not concentrate on it full-time until he was forty-four. From then until his death twelve years later he carried out an extraordinary number of successful water-findings and well-sinkings – by his own reckoning more than 5000 – recorded in two small privately published books, and checked posthumously by Sir William Barrett. A photograph taken two years before he died shows him to be a cheerful, rubicund, waistcoated figure, and many of the testimonials pay tribute not just to his successful dowsing, but to the matter-of-fact spontaneity with which he approached his job. 'He has the look of an honest John Bull master mason,' wrote one, 'and is of a quiet manner, but answers any questions he is asked promptly and in the most straightforward manner.' According to another, 'Mullins made no pretence of magic.'

In account after account, Mullins is given credit for succeeding where expensive attempts by geologists and other experts had previously failed. General Sir Mildmay Willson, who had sunk a

350-foot well on his estate at Raunceby, Yorkshire, without finding water, sent for Mullins – then earning half a crown a day as a labourer – in 1867 after hearing of his reputation. Mullins told him bluntly that if he went on drilling to 1000 feet he would still get no water, but provided several alternative sites nearby where water could be found within twelve feet of the surface. General Willson straight away tried three, all successfully, and subsequently recommended Mullins to many other landowners. He concluded: 'Personally, I cannot call to mind a single instance where Mullins proved himself wrong.' Mullins told employers that while he had often been to places and found no water, so far as he knew he had always been proved right when he had found a positive indication. 'He made no boast of this, said only he could not account for it,' wrote one satisfied customer.

In many of the accounts, there are descriptions of quite unnecessary precautions against fraud taken by those employing Mullins, but still unable to believe wholeheartedly in his reputation or his abilities. 'To prevent him gaining any local information Sir Henry met him at the railway station,' says one account; another, 'The clerk who accompanied him from the steamer, a reliable man . . . was warned to answer no questions as to wells, water, or strata.' In fact, such steps were unnecessary, almost ludicrously so. Mullins was known never to bother with such trifles as maps of geological strata, relying instead entirely on the evidence indicated to him by his hazel rod. On a typical occasion, he 'came to a spot over which the rod bent slightly and quite spontaneously, as well as could be observed. This spot was marked and the search continued. Similar indications appeared at two or three other places. At one, the effect was so manifest that the rod twisted completely round and broke! – also of its own accord. The firm sank at one of the places indicated and obtained a copious supply of water.'

His most famous and best-documented case, investigated with great thoroughness by Sir William Barrett for the Society for Psychical Research, involved a firm of bacon-curers at Waterford, Ireland. In 1888, needing a much greater supply of water than at the time existed, they took considerable professional advice, including that of G. H. Kinahan, senior Geologist to the Irish Geological Survey, and author of several technical books and manuals on the subject. In all, three bore-holes were sunk at a total cost of £1324, without any success. Mullins was sent for, and within minutes of arriving from the boat, had marked a point where he said there would be at least 1500 gallons per hour at a depth of 80 to 90 feet. The result of a drill showed him to be, as usual, accurate – on the initial sinking, 1672 gallons per hour obtained at 79 feet. Kinahan's subsequent report was extremely generous to Mullins. He conceded that the well had been sunk on what was later discovered to be one of the only two geologically probable water lines in the area, 'both of which our friend Mullins found by instinct, due either to his being able to smell water, or that water has such an influence on his nervous system that he can tell the distance and quantity when he is near it . . . As far as actual results went I failed, and the diviner "wiped my eye".'

Official acceptance

Then as now, a general air of incredulity surrounded the activities of dowsers, and there was a reluctance by official bodies to make use of their potential. Indeed, local authorities often sheltered behind the mistaken belief that it was illegal to do so, and Mullins makes no record of working for other than private employers.

Nevertheless, the twentieth century has seen some cautious advances by responsible Governmental bodies, and these are helpful in evaluating dowsing because on the comparatively rare occasions when dowsers have been so employed, they were carefully scrutinized, and put to work in difficult areas where other methods were failing. For several years after October 1925, Major Charles Aubrey Pogson, whose family had lived in India, was appointed official Water-Diviner to the Government of Bombay. There was famine in the area and a chronic watershortage in the farms and villages. The Bombay Legislative Council, at the time of his appointment, underwent a good deal of criticism, for the salary he demanded was a high one.

But he was triumphantly successful. In spite of the fact that the district was dotted haphazardly with wells that were complete failures, or had dried up shortly after being sunk, Pogson's early results were so good that the Bombay Government was confident enough to offer to repay half the cost of sinking a well on a site chosen by him, should it prove to be dry. In the first ten months, they had to pay up only once, and even here, according to the official report, 'water was actually tapped but dwindled down to a small quantity when further blasting was resorted to'. The *Indian Journal of Engineering* commented: 'Major Pogson can find water, it appears, when the machines specially designed for the purpose have failed. It is an interesting situation. Out of 49 wells which have been sunk upon spots indicated by Major Pogson only two have failed to produce water. It is a notable achievement.'

During the few years that he was in India, Pogson successfully found water at 465 sites, 199 of them suitable for drinking water, and 266 for irrigation purposes; the success rate was calculated at 97 per cent. On his return to England, his reputation and his military career helped considerably in changing the climate of opinion towards dowsing, and he was subsequently employed by many local councils and authorities.[5] By then the Australian Government, too, was officially employing a dowser in its arid continent, and in 1931 the Government of British Columbia in Canada embarked on a similar enterprise with an Englishwoman who became one of the most famous dowsers of the century: Evelyn Penrose.

During the years in which she worked in Canada, finding not only water, but copper, silver, lead and gold mines, and rich deposits of oil, she was calculated to have a success rate of more than 90 per cent. Of the occasional criticism of her work, she wrote that one of the problems for dowsers was, that they were expected – unreasonably – to be infallible in every detail. 'Suppose I suggest the sites of two wells at a depth of 30 feet and 60 feet respectively. If they struck the water at 29 or 59 feet, they thought I was a marvellous diviner; but if Providence had put it at 31 or 62 feet, they wrote furiously abusive letters to the Government about me.'[6]

Her work paved the way for many others. The German Government sent a dowser named von Uslar to help find water and set up farmsteads in the extremely dry colony of German South-West Africa. He was recorded as having an 81 per cent success rate in his locations. During World War II, Rommel used dowsers in North Africa, the Italian Army in Abyssinia. Publication of Kenneth Roberts's book on the dowser Henry Gross during the 1950s has led to an 'explosion' of interest in dowsing in the USA, according to Ray Willey.

Yet for all the successes in water-finding, any honest summary of dowsing's place in the history of water supply must conclude that it has remained a fringe activity that has always been looked on with scepticism and even hostility by most paid geologists and Water Board officials. As recently as the drought-stricken summer of 1976 in Britain, one such official was interviewed on television at a time when most of the reservoirs in his area were at a critically low level, and severe water restrictions were in force. What about dowsers? he was asked. Can't they find water for you? Somewhat reluctantly, he admitted that the Board had on occasions used a dowser – but only to confirm what 'experts' knew already. 'And in any case,' he added, 'dowsers are really only good at finding small amounts of water, enough for a farmyard, that sort of thing.'

It is on record that Evelyn Penrose, in an otherwise arid district, successfully predicted and found a well that produced *324,000 gallons a day*; and in the same area in England from which the Water Board official was speaking, John Mullins once found a well that produced *100,000 gallons an hour*.

Crime detection

Although until well into the twentieth century, dowsing literature concerned itself almost exclusively with the search for minerals and water, there are nevertheless glimpses to show that some of its other applications surfaced from time to time. The ancient alchemical formulas for the production of magic wands, in which many of the authors of alchemical treatises write of dowsing in approving terms, are probably the first published accounts. But there is no sensible record of successful results.

The unambiguous beginnings of the conscious, wider applications of dowsing lie in the career of Jacques Aymar, born near Lyons in 1662 (and thus preceding Barthelmy Bleton in the same area by nearly a century). While still in his twenties he was recognized locally as a water-finder, and it was while looking for an underground source that he showed the talent that put him into dowsing history. His rod had twisted violently in his hands, and he had given instructions for the well to be sunk at the point where he stood. But the drillers, instead of finding water, uncovered the head of a murdered woman. Aymar was then taken to the house where the woman had lived, and inside, a number of people were gathered; he pointed his rod at each of them in turn, and it reacted only to one person, her husband. He immediately fled, thus apparently admitting his guilt. So extraordinary was the incident that Aymar subsequently became much in demand for tracing other criminals and murderers.

His most important case, which caused a sensation in France at the time, and brought Aymar fame and notoriety even in court circles, occurred in 1692. Because it was so fully documented, and also because it is on first sight incontrovertible proof of a good dowser's ability to trace recent events, it has been written up many times. In brief, what happened was that Aymar agreed to try to track down, on foot, and guided only by his rod, the path taken by the murderers of a Lyons wine-merchant and his wife. Starting at their house, a winding route took him to the walls of the city, where he had to wait overnight as the gate was closed. Next day, he followed the bank of the Rhône to a gardener's house, where he said the three fugitives had stopped and eaten – a fact which was confirmed by the children of the gardener (who had at first denied it).

This encouraged the magistrates to give Aymar a simple test to see if he could distinguish some belongings that the murderers had left behind them. He was successful, and then continued on his way accompanied by a guard of archers. A mile or so further on, still by the bank of the Rhône, came another tangible sign that Aymar might be on the right track – footprints of three men in the soft sand by the water's edge, where they had embarked to cross the river by boat. Aymar followed the directions of his rod for many days more than 150 miles to the town of Beaucaire, identifying numerous places on the route where the murderers had rested. Finally, in Beaucaire itself, the rod guided him to the prison. Inside, it reacted to a hunchback who had just been arrested for a local petty crime, and who at first denied all knowledge of the murders. But when he was taken back to Lyons along the route that Aymar had traced, and accurately shown the various places which he had visited, he broke down and confessed. In later written statements he corroborated all that Aymar had found, including the involvement of two other men who had escaped over the border through the Pyrenees to Spain. (Aymar also traced their route, but too late.) The hunchback was condemned to death by being broken on the wheel.

Trying, so long after the event, to evaluate Aymar's feat, perhaps the most striking thing is how extraordinarily similar were his methods to those of later dowsers, for instance William Burgoyne. With both men, it was as if a physical trace had been left behind, operating rather like scent to a tracker dog. Similarly, there is the uncannily accurate recognition, in the proper chronological order, of the interiors of buildings visited. Both men liked to be able to hold some object or piece of clothing previously handled by the person they were tracking. Both felt a physical reaction – in Aymar's case, 'violent agitations' when he was searching for murderers.

Their shared experience strengthens the case that Aymar was indeed the world's first great dowser to spread his horizons beyond water and mineral-finding. For although his feat was widely acclaimed at the time, and witnessed in many of its details by many people, as total proof it does not quite stand up to the rigours of modern investigation. For instance, both the cases quoted depend, finally, on the confessions of the murderers. And although the hunchback's confession was made publicly as well as to the secret courts, some people say that any confession made in a time of torture and superstition is so dubious as not to be worth including. It has been suggested too, less convincingly, that because Aymar was present in Lyons during the time of the murders, and some time elapsed before he was appointed to the case, it would be 'quite possible that the diviner had obtained important clues before he was publicly set to work . . . the subsequent tracking of a hunchback would be no very difficult matter.'

Aymar subsequently enjoyed some fame in Paris, where he was apparently able to carry out successfully various parlour tricks very like those suggested to trainee dowsers today, such as choosing, from a number of hats placed on a table, the one under which a coin had been hidden. He was also put through some complicated and confusing tests by the Prince of Condé, at which he was less successful.

The nature of the witnesses and the documents means that we shall never know just how good a dowser Aymar was. But there is one other aspect of his work which again has a striking parallel with modern dowsing. For the only other activity which gave him as violent a reaction as when tracing murderers was when he was asked to trace 'criminally misplaced boundaries', and there is evidence that he could do this from plans as well as on site. In a time when there were many disputes over land ownership, this ability brought him much business, though once again the documentation is so scanty that it is impossible to work out a success rate. However, the fact that he was employed at all suggests a degree of accuracy, and probably also gives Aymar the title of the world's first map-dowser. In another curious parallel with our times, the Church authorities made a distinction between this work and other forms of divining. Rather in the way many modern observers have divided theories of the causes of the dowsing reaction into 'psychic' or 'physical' categories, so the Inquisition thought that the use of the divining rod in boundary disputes impinged on 'moral' questions, and in 1701 the practice was banned.

Origins of the pendulum
The use of the pendulum in dowsing seems to have grown naturally out of its ancient use, world-wide, among priests and seers to divine the future and receive messages from the world of the spirits. Documents from early Chinese dynasties describe a ring, hung from a silk thread, which could be used to indicate good and bad auguries; the Roman Emperor Valens *c*. AD 370, arrested and condemned to death a number of men for trying to divine the name of his successor. But it is not until the end of the eighteenth century that there are references to its use in locating well sites in France; from then on, its growth in popularity among dowsers was matched by those who suspended it above the letters of a ouija board to obtain answers to questions from supposed departed spirits, or to hold it by a glass, where a code of tapping movements would be interpreted by the operator to give answers to occult questions.

Undoubtedly its first significant practitioner was another of the great European cleric dowsers, the Abbé Mermet. For more than forty years until his death in 1937 at the age of seventy-one (when he was privileged to become the only dowser in history to have been given an obituary in *Nature*), he followed in the footsteps of Jacques Aymar by specializing in tracing lost or missing people. His book on the subject, *Principles and Practice of Radiesthesia*,[7] which he wrote to encourage students and researchers, contains details of method and instruction that would nowadays be considered over-rigid by most dowsers. But there is no denying the accounts and testimonies of his successes, and his basic method foreshadowed the way the pendulum is used by nearly all dowsers in similar cases – he needed a photograph of the missing person, or some piece of clothing or other object that he had recently handled; and two maps, one small scale and one large scale, of the area where the person went missing. From these, the Abbé located during his career dozens of missing or dead people – up mountains, in rivers, in hospitals and hotels. In one case in 1934, apparently even more unbelievable than the rest, he said his pendulum indicated that a six-year-old boy, missing from his home in Switzerland, had been carried off by an eagle. But he was right – the boy was found, dead, high up a mountain in an eagle's nest; and from the undamaged state of the boy's shoes and clothing, it was virtually impossible that he could have walked and climbed there. As with all dowsers who come into the public eye, the Abbé Mermet had his detractors. The few mistakes he made were widely criticized, and the case of the boy and the eagle was so sensational that it was minutely examined to discover whether or not the boy could have gained access to the nest without being taken there by the eagle – as if the principal discovery of the location were not a sufficient feat by the Abbé on its own.

The overwhelming evidence is of a large number of extraordinary successes. More than that, the Abbé's career coincided with, and helped to inspire, a much wider knowledge of the possible applications of dowsing. Besides finding mineral and water veins (in respect of the latter he was certified by one engineer to have been absolutely accurate in the location of 119 wells, with not more than 5–10 per cent error in estimates of depth), he could diagnose illness from a distance by using his pendulum over a photograph or medical diagram. In 1912 and 1913 came the publication of three massive books by Henri Mager,[8] whose blend of fact, speculation and pseudo-scientific language exactly fitted the mood of the period, and greatly helped to expand interest in the use of the pendulum.

In 1920, German dowsers formed themselves into a union for the investigation of divining, the *International Verein der Wünschelrutenforscher*. In 1930 in France, the Abbé Alexis Bouly invented the word *radiesthésie* to describe the use of the pendulum in dowsing, and formed the first dowsing society, *L'Association des Amis de la Radiesthésie*. Its new President, later to write another standard work on the subject, the Vicomte Henri de France, suggested the formation of a British Society of Dowsers, which came about in 1933, followed by Germany in 1937, then Belgium, Switzerland, Italy, and many other countries, and lastly, the Americans in 1961.

Compared with the hesitant and confined beginnings of the mineral-finding dowsers of the Harz mountains back in the sixteenth century, most dowsers in these societies today would say that the potential of dowsing is literally unlimited. The achievements of Aymar, Bleton, Mullins and Mermet, remarkable as they were, represented only the beginnings of the possibilities that dowsing offers. There is also another question mark over the history of dowsing as it has come down to us through contemporary records – it notes only the feats of the recognized masters of dowsing; almost nothing is known of whether, alongside them, there were many other less skilled or less sensational dowsers. It is rather as if the history of music had been written exclusively about the great composers, and soloists, and failed to mention the musicians who played with them. So the next question to look at is this: given the successes of great dowsers in the past, just how widespread may the aptitude be today?

3 Dowsing for All

Historical accounts of the great dowsers are full of instances of how, when they were on a water-finding job, one or two people among the crowd of onlookers found that they, too, had the gift. Thus Lord Winchelsea, writing about a visit by John Mullins: 'My brother, the Hon. Harold Finch Hatton, is present while I write, and confirms what I say. It is true that one of the Misses Wordsworth tried the twig and was surprised to find that an influence of similar nature, though not so strong, was imparted to it. I merely give facts, without attempting to explain them.' It is also fairly common knowledge that if a bystander holds one branch of a divining rod, and the dowser the other, and the two people walk together over an underground stream, the rod will turn just as if the dowser were holding it on his own. This is an apparent mystery which has been demonstrated in almost every television programme about dowsing, and which most dowsers are happy to show.

It was not until recently, within the last two decades at most, that the implications of this were realized: nearly all of us, with some help and guidance, are potential dowsers. It is becoming increasingly clear that most people can achieve a dowsing re-action, and also that this can be trained and focused like any other ability. John Mullins, for instance, is on record early in his life as saying that only he, in his family, had the gift of finding water. But over the years his sons learned it to the extent that though they never became, like him, almost infallible, they were successfully able to carry on his business after his death.

Of course, some people are naturally more gifted than others, particularly in the traditional area of water-divining; a few people seem to be marked out from the rest of us in the way that a divining rod turns violently and uncontrollably in their hands the very first time they use it. Nearly all the great professional dowsers say that their introduction to the art came when they were offered such a rod, and instantly found that they had a reaction as strong as the dowser who lent it to them, the rod sometimes flying right out of their hands. There are a number of families, too, where this sort of super-dowsing seems to skip a generation and is passed on from grandparent to grandchild. For such people, there is absolutely no doubt in their minds, right from their first experience, that they can dowse. From then on, all that happens is that they become more experienced, and learn to widen the range of what they can achieve. Raymond Willey has written evocatively of how such an experience feels:

> You feel a twist you must meet with all the strength of your grasp. Under many conditions you cannot prevent the arms of the rod from twisting out of your grasp. Dowsing greets you as some sort of unknown force in nature, a force you must master with positive physical exertion if you wish to carry through your full dowsing response. Combating this force for the first time can produce an exhilaration, a sense of being in tune with one of life's mysteries. The memory of this first encounter may easily stay with you the rest of your life.

This class of dowser is fairly rare. Willey thinks that no more than 5–10 per cent of the population are natural dowsers at such an exceptional level (even so, this means a minimum of 15,000,000 potential top-grade dowsers in the United States alone). Officials in the British Society of Dowsers would choose from just a handful of names in whom they have sufficient confidence to recommend to anyone wishing to spend £1000 or more on a well-bore. To become a master dowser in Germany and use the professional title *Rutenmeister* you have to be more than thirty years old, and have at least eight years of consecutive and successful dowsing work, three of which must have been under the tuition of another professional dowser; also, you have to pass two sets of examinations, oral and written, with attestations of success in water and 'biological' dowsing (which includes diagnosis for healing). There are only about a dozen such dowsers in all Germany.

US Marines in Vietnam
However, the story of how the US Marines came to use dowsing

rods in Vietnam is a particularly good example of a growing awareness at a popular level that dowsing works for many people, in spite of official scepticism. Christopher Bird, author, biologist and anthropologist, is a trustee of the American Society of Dowsers who taught himself Russian in order to be able to learn more about the extensive research into dowsing that takes place there. He told the First International Congress of Parapsychology and Psychotronics in Prague in 1973 how Louis Matacia, a Virginia land surveyor and dowser, had suggested to Marine officers that dowsing methods could readily be used to detect underground mines and tunnels. Matacia was taken to a defence base where, said Christopher Bird, he found 'a mock-up of a typical South-East Asian village complete with thatched huts, pig pens, rice paddies, wells, sampans floating on a river, bridges, trails and even graves, used for tactical training of young marines on their way to Vietnam. Below the ground ran the unseen world of the village: a network of tunnels, secret rooms, weapon caches, stores for supplies and hiding places for the "enemy".'

Matacia, using angle rods cut from wire coat-hangers, successfully mapped all these features, to the amazement but growing belief of the officers. However, since no scientists inside or outside the Defense Department could come up with any reason as to why he was successful, they came to the cautious conclusion that he must just have struck lucky, and wrote a letter to him saying that 'because of excessive false alarms, your technique would not find ready acceptance by field commanders.'

However, the letter was already out of date. Word of what Matacia had achieved had already reached Vietnam unofficially, and by the time his dowsing suggestions were officially rejected, they were already being put into practice in the field by many Marine patrols, and the fact of this was widely reported in the Press.

Two important scientific surveys (described in detail on pages 115–18) now seem to have shown conclusively that most of us can dowse to a surprisingly sensitive level. Professor Yves Rocard in Paris found that nearly 70 per cent, and Professor Zaboj Harvalik in Washington, DC, found that nearly 90 per cent of all people tested were able to obtain a dowsing reaction when asked to identify a small change in the earth's magnetic field.

General Scott Elliot thinks that dowsing may be not much different from the distribution of other gifts in a community, with a handful who are geniuses, a handful who are backward, and the rest of us capable of improvement with teaching and practice. 'We can't all be Michelangelo, and a few of us are unlucky enough to be colour-blind or unable to see at all; most of us see things with varying degrees of perception. Similarly with music, or sport, or any other art. We can't all be composers or record-breakers, but we can get better if we try. I see no reason to place dowsing in a different dimension from other human skills which we don't fully understand.'

Tom Graves, who conducts a course on dowsing at Kensington Institute, a further education college run by the Inner London Education Authority, is even more emphatic: 'Anyone can dowse. It's just a skill which, like any other, can be learnt with practice, awareness and a working knowledge of basic principles and mechanics – a skill which you can use as and when you need.'

Unconscious muscle movements

The first time you get a dowsing reaction, it is likely to be a very odd feeling. The rod or the pendulum seems to take off spontaneously, moved by some force which you can't understand or control, and like anything supposedly inanimate which seems to have a will of its own, it can be unnerving. For anyone new to dowsing, their first response to the rod twitching or the pendulum gyrating is likely to be a series of exclamations: 'Look! What's happening! It's moving! What's making it move! What have I found! It's weird!'

So initially, a good teacher will help you overcome this feeling of strangeness by explaining that the only thing which is making it move is – you. For of all the imponderables, the hows and whys of dowsing, it is almost universally agreed nowadays that it is an involuntary and unconscious muscular movement that makes the dowsing instrument start to move. Out of respect for some extremely sensitive dowsers, such as Raymond Willey, there should perhaps be a caution about this statement, for he and a few others believe that some force outside the human body is acting directly on the pendulum. But there have been many laboratory tests on dowsers to show that there are marked physiological changes in the body during a dowsing reaction, including decreased skin resistivity and a change in muscle tone, and the consensus is that these alone are quite enough to cause all the manifestations of dowsing. Arthur Bailey told the 1976 Congress of Dowsers in Scotland: 'The instructions that come from the brain to a certain part of the body for the muscles there to tighten up and trigger off a dowsing reaction may be quite different from one person to another. If you try angle rods or forked rods and they don't work, don't assume you can't dowse. You may be able to get it by a tingling in your fingertips or a tensing of muscles in your stomach. The vast majority can dowse, and people get an enormous variety of differing reactions.'

The various tools in dowsing have evolved over the centuries because, when held, they are in a delicate state of equilibrium, responsive to the smallest movement by the dowser. And it is precisely because they are so sensitive that they work as amplifiers and as indicators of something happening in our bodies that we would otherwise not recognize. If you want to check for yourself just how finely in balance our muscles are, here is a simple experiment suggested by the late Tom Lethbridge,[1] an archaeologist specializing in the Anglo-Saxon period, who used to take great pleasure in annoying established academics by being right time and again, using dowsing methods, in telling them where to dig for archaeological remains.

First, get hold of a makeshift pendulum. Almost anything fairly light, and attached to a short length of thread (or similar) will do – a medallion on a jewellery chain, a piece of cotton tied to a key or key-ring, a piece of string in a child's wooden bead. Next, pinch the string (or whatever) between your thumb and forefinger two or three inches from the bob at the end of the pendulum, and wrap any spare string round your fingers, so that it doesn't get in the way. Bend your elbow so that your forearm is approximately parallel with the ground, and comfortable. It doesn't matter if you are sitting down or standing up. The main thing is to let the pendulum hang freely. Now gently swing the pendulum about: to and fro (oscillating), clockwise and anti-clockwise (rotating, gyrating), using as little movement in your thumb and forefinger, or wrist and arm, as possible. If you play with the pendulum for a few minutes, adjusting the length of the string up and down, you should find that quite soon a natural, or optimum, length will emerge. This will have to do with the weight of the bob (the heavier the bob, the longer the string), and your own personal, unconscious, automatic rhythms. Don't struggle to achieve this; it's important, but will come with practice of its own accord, and it may vary a little from day to day. The only thing that matters is that you should feel happy with the length, so that the pendulum moves about smoothly and with almost imperceptible effort.

Now take three coins and put them on a table. Two should be the same – the same value, and better still, the same date; say, two pennies. The third can be any other coin, of different value and different date. Put the two pennies in front of you, one three or four inches further away than the other. Keep the different coin in reserve, a foot or so away. Now suspend the pendulum a little above and between the two pennies. Let the pendulum oscillate from one to another; a rhythm will set up on the line between them, as if the pendulum was being attracted first to one and then to the other. Next, have a friend replace the penny furthest from you with the different coin (you might do it yourself with your spare hand, but it's difficult not to disturb the rhythm of the pendulum).

Now comes the surprising part. Keeping your thumb and forefinger, hand and arm as still as you can without going tense or rigid, watch the pendulum. As if it was being repelled by the different coin, it will change its motion: either the oscillation will become diagonal, so that it is swinging away from the line of the coins; or it will rotate, either clockwise or anti-clockwise. Whatever the change, do nothing to prevent it or help it; just observe it.

Then have the penny put back where it was, and the different coin removed. And again, without any conscious movement on your part (indeed, you should consciously try to be motionless, providing you stay relaxed), the pendulum will gradually resume its up-and-down oscillation directly between the two pennies.

That's all. Don't ask why it happens, and for the moment you don't need to read further. If you want to have a brief glimpse of what it feels like to dowse, try it.

Now show a few relatives and friends what happens, and get them to do the same thing. Watch if the pendulum variation is the same for everybody (it probably won't be).

The point of the experiment above is only to get the feel of things; dowsing comes naturally, providing you don't shy away from it. What it should have demonstrated to you is that without trying, you can use a dowsing instrument to indicate something that is otherwise undetectable (in this case a minute physical signal that the coins were different). It is not dowsing in the true sense of searching for something and then finding it, but many people have found it a useful first step: for until you have learned to recognize a dowsing reaction personally, it is impossible to move forward.

The most important thing at this early stage is to maintain an attitude of neutrality, or psychological detachment. Don't be especially surprised at what is happening; just let the reaction occur. When the volunteers in Dr Harvalik's experiments were trying to detect a magnetic anomaly, they were told: 'Think of something trivial, of something dull or unexciting.' General Scott Elliot says it is simply a matter of letting 'Mind' take over, as opposed to the brain or the five normal senses. 'Just let the subconscious mind do the work, and don't interfere.'

Dowsing tools

The point is that these unconscious thoughts are working their way out to the surface through minute neuro-muscular reactions, and these in turn are amplified through the dowsing instrument. As well as the pendulum, there are three other basic types of tool that do the same job in telling you something of which you would not otherwise be aware: angle rods; the traditional forked stick, and a straight, pliable wand. Each has its own way of staying in equilibrium, and then of signalling information.

As people progress in dowsing, they generally acquire a selection of all types for use in different situations – indoors, outdoors, map-dowsing, site-dowsing, windy weather, hot weather, and so on. It may be convenient to buy some or all of them to start with. There are kits on the market, and the dowsing societies either sell pendulums and rods themselves, or will give you suppliers' names. There is something to be said for having a 'professional' tool. A good pendulum will be evenly lathed and balanced, so that it will not tend to wobble about as a home-made one might; and some dowsers are only happy using sensitive whalebone rods, which keep their spring even after long use.

However, since dowsing is such a personal activity, there is just as much to be said for making the tools yourself, and adjusting them until they suit you. Angle rods (or 'L' rods), it seems generally agreed, are the most sensitive of any of the four types, and therefore the most suitable for anybody beginning a dowsing search. They are also just about as easy to make as pendulums, since a wire coathanger is an ideal material. Simply cut off the long bottom rail of the coathanger to its full length, and the attached short side about five inches along. Then bend the two sides away from each other until you have a right angle – and there is your completed angle rod. You need two of these, one for each hand.

The way to use them is to hold them steadily but lightly in your hands, the thumbs on top, your elbows in to your sides and your arms out parallel in front; the long parts of the rods should also stick out horizontally forwards and parallel. If you stay motionless, so will the rods. In motion, they can move in three ways, and you can simulate these (as with the pendulum) before you start. If you turn your wrists over in a vertical plane towards each other, the rods will swing inwards and cross; if you turn your wrists over outwards, vice versa; and if you turn your wrists together in the same direction, the rods will move in parallel to point in a new direction. All three of these movements will happen unconsciously when you are using the rods in a dowsing search, and they can all be interpreted as giving different sorts of information.

Many dowsers feel no need to go beyond this simple manu-facture – indeed, they like the direct feel of the short arm of the angle rod twisting against their skin, which they can then control to a certain degree to prevent the rods being affected by a strong wind or by a particularly strong dowsing signal. However, most people prefer the refinement of having some kind of a sleeve in which to put the short part of the rod. Around the home, the casings of a couple of discarded ball-point pens would probably do the job; or three cotton reels glued together – anything, in fact, which enables the rods to swing more freely than friction from the hands allows. Or you can make rather more professional angle rods by buying straight 3/8-inch steel, brass, welding or brazing rod from the ironmonger, bending it into a right angle, and sticking the short (about 6 inches) end into a similar length of copper or brass piping with the swivel end suitably smoothed. The heavier and longer the rods, the more powerful the dowsing reaction will have to be to make them move; but at the same time the more positive will be the indication that you have really had a reaction. It is a matter of trial and error to find what suits you best, and initially, there is nothing wrong with coathangers in a casing.

Forked rods (divining rods, 'Y' rods, 'V' rods, spring rods) are usually a little more difficult for a beginner to get the hang of. The traditional way of making them, of course, is to go into the hedgerows and cut a rod of hazel. Many experienced dowsers would still never do anything different, and from personal experience hazel has a feel to it, almost of independent life, that is hard to match. It keeps its spring and tension, too, for some time after being cut, whereas most other woods quickly become brittle and breakable. Nevertheless willow, hawthorn, rowan, apple, privet, rhododendron and many other kinds of tree or shrub will work well enough; the important thing is to know from experience which jointed twig to cut. It is best if both branches are about the same thickness, and if the angle between them is not too great. The length and thickness depends on whether you prefer to dowse holding the rod with your fingers or your whole hands. You will probably need to try several until you find one that suits you, for difference in characteristics between one forked rod and another is remarkable. In the countryside, it is a deeply satisfying way to dowse, redolent of tradition, and reassuringly natural.

However, not all dowsers can be countrygoers, and the truth is that much longer-lasting forked rods can be made of many materials other than wood. The technique is either to take two

71

springy pieces about eight to twelve inches long and fasten them together at one end (plastic curtain rod, for instance, or two plastic knitting needles stuck in a cork), or to take a single resilient strand and bend it back on itself, tying it tightly close at the bend. This can be done with copper and brass wire, or lengths of plastic; one of the neatest I have seen was a tiny, light, and almost everlasting rod made from a tough strand of nylon taken from a roadsweeper's broom, doubled backwards, and kept in place with an elastic band.

The point is to hold any rod of this kind in such a way that you open the branches outwards and thus create a highly unstable tension. Getting the rods into this position needs practice – if they are particularly lively, they are capable of springing out of your hands while you are trying to adjust them and set them steady. Once you have found the knack of doing this, you will have a highly sensitive indicator that is poised to spring up or down as soon as you receive a dowsing signal. Probably the easiest way is to start with a longish rod, with each branch at least a foot long. Put your elbows in to your sides and your forearms parallel to the ground and to each other, just as if you were map-dowsing, and then turn your wrists over backwards as far as you can, so that your palms are facing up. Clench each fist over one branch of the rod, pull backwards and outwards, and adjust the tension on the rod by pressing your thumbs into it. Try to hold the rod steady and horizontal, with the joint of the rod pointing away from you.

As with the other dowsing tools, the physical key to use of the forked rod is to learn how to combine a relaxation with enough muscular effort to keep the rod in equilibrium. The unfamiliar feel of the forked rod, and the difficulty of keeping it temporarily stable, makes almost everyone initially too tense. It's essential to relax sufficiently to let the rod react freely when the dowsing signal triggers off its movement. If you have the position right, it is possible (as with a pendulum or angle rods) to simulate this movement. By tightening your grip, or pushing with your thumbs, you can make the rod begin to move. After that, its internal torsion takes care of the movement; some rods will rotate through 180° and more of their own accord, once you have started them off.

There are so many types of forked rod, and so many ways of holding and handling them, that there is really no substitute for attending a meeting of dowsers and seeing them demonstrated. But basically, the only thing that any forked rod can do is to whip suddenly up or down as soon as its unstable equilibrium is upset. To achieve this, most dowsers seem to need to be on the move in some way – either walking, or turning, or (especially in the United States) moving the body rhythmically backwards and forwards while standing on one spot. There seems to be no universal reason why the rod moves up with some people and down with others. Bill Lewis thinks it has to do with whether it is held above or below the solar plexus, and this may be generally true; but there are exceptions. Unlike other dowsing tools, it will not return to the neutral (horizontal) position on its own – you have to re-set it after each dowsing reaction.

It is the most dramatic and in many ways the most pleasing of the tools to use, and if you're lucky enough to come quickly to a forked rod that suits you, the dowsing reaction is unmistakable. But be prepared for a considerable period of trial and error while you accustom yourself to its use.

Least used of all the tools is the single straight wand. You can cut it, three to four feet long, from a hedgerow; or use a piece of aerial for a car radio. In either case, most dowsers hold it by the thin end, and let it vibrate gently up and down. A dowsing reaction makes it gyrate like a pendulum. It is sometimes used in the field for finding water because dowsers find it less tiring over a period of time than the other instruments. For beginners, it has no special merit.

Finally there are the many variations on these tools, homemade or manufactured, that whirl, bob, vibrate and react according to their kind. If Willie Donaldson, a Yorkshire dowser, puts a penny in the palm of his hand, it flips over when he moves above an underground stream. Zaboj Harvalik has experimented with a springy looped rod that can be held upright between the hands which is even more sensitive than angle rods. So long as such contrivances work for their owners, they're fine. But there seems no justification for spending tens or even hundreds of pounds on devices that are advertised to be particularly sensitive to water, oil, gold or treasure – because they

73

aren't. Only the dowser is sensitive to anything, and the simpler the indicator he uses, usually the better. Good dowsers regard expensive tools as at best a joke, and at worst a confidence trick. Some of the best dowsers manage to dispense with tools altogether. For fundamentally, dowsing is not in the hands or the equipment; it's a process that happens in the mind.

Tuning the mind

So finely balanced are the tools that most beginners will quickly have a reaction of some sort. Even walking across a room with a pair of angle rods is likely to cause a deviation from the horizontal – and outside, if there is any wind, the effect will probably be even more marked. You can check whether this is just accident by tilting the long arms of the rods down a few degrees, so that they become more stable, then walk to and fro two or three times over the place where you had the reaction, and see if it is repeated. Sooner or later you will almost certainly find some place where you get a reaction consistently – at a certain point on a lawn, or in a room, or on a pavement. But the question is: what have you found? A drain? Underground water? An electric cable? Ground disturbance? For any of these things and many more (including wishful thinking), are enough to trigger off a generalized and unfocused dowsing reaction. This sort of aimless practice is useful to familiarize someone with the dowsing tools, but is otherwise of limited help. It is very important, all dowsers say, to move on to a positive and concentrated search for something identifiable and real.

The secret of good dowsing is to be able to hold something in your mind – a lost object, an underground tunnel – clearly enough for you to be able to identify just that, and nothing else. It is a curious state of mind, about which thousands of words have been written without anyone having come up with an all-embracing, totally satisfactory description; for it involves a series of paradoxes and contradictions, a balance between two opposing moods. You have to concentrate on what you are looking for, but at the same time be relaxed and uninvolved. You must have a need to find the object of your search, but not anxiously or obsessively so, for this, too, upsets balance. Many dowsers believe that greed prevents successful dowsing, as does too technical or analytical an approach. It has been compared to a mild state of hypnosis, or trance, or meditation; and certainly most dowsers, even if they talk to you, when they are working, give the appearance of having temporarily removed part of their mind from normal consciousness. It is a state that involves harmony, instinct and simplicity. Another adjective often used is 'receptive'. I know of no better description than that given in the eighteenth century by William Cookworthy from Plymouth, who wrote in the *Gentleman's Magazine*:

> The rod must be held with indifference, for if the mind is occupied with doubts, reasoning, or other operation that engages the animal spirits, it will divert their powers from being exerted in this process, in which their instrumentality is absolutely necessary: from whence it is that the rod constantly answers in the hands of peasants, women and children, who hold it simply without puzzling their minds with doubts and reasonings. Whatever may be thought of this observation it is a very just one, and of great consequence in the practice of the rod.

With familiarity, dowsing becomes as much an automatic and unconscious a process as writing letters on a page, hitting a tennis ball, or riding a bicycle. But some part of your mind, deep down, always knows what you are looking for. This aim, or focus, need not always be conscious. Traditional water-diviners are often apparently able to dispense with an explicit need to focus on their search for water – a Welsh water-finder, Sidney Thomas, is typical of those who say that no matter what the interruptions around him or what conversation he was having, if he walked over an underground water vein when he was holding a hazel twig, it would bounce up nevertheless. But the point is that he – and others like him – may be unconsciously looking for water. They are so used to doing so that the search is automatic.

So an overly direct effort to look for something may not always be necessary. As long as you know basically what you are looking for, and you settle your mind into a state where it is comfortably receptive, the reaction will happen anyway. Dr Harvalik's subjects, besides being told to think of trivial, dull, and unexciting things, were also told to try to relax the arm and hand muscles without influencing the parallelism of the angle rods. 'Let the twist of the arms occur when it occurs, and let the magnetic field do the twisting of the arms,' was the instruction. In this way it was suggested obliquely, almost surreptitiously, that a magnetic anomaly was the object of their search.

It may even be best to pretend that the pendulum or the rod has an independent existence, its movements willed from outside in spite of your rational brain saying that this is impossible. Tom Graves puts it: 'Treat the instrument as if it has a life and mind of its own – which in most senses it hasn't, but that's beside the point. I sometimes think of instruments as being like cantankerous children: they won't work unless you ask them to, and certainly won't work if you try and force them to; they occasionally lie, and sometimes sulk and refuse to work at all; so you have to use a little guile, a little ingenuity and a little wit to get the results you need.'

I like the way Steve Bosbach puts himself in the right frame of mind for dowsing. He settles himself with his rod comfortably poised in the neutral position, and asks quietly: 'Please indicate when I am ready to receive positive answers to dowsing questions.'

Then he waits, contemplating.

After maybe ten or twenty seconds, the rod stirs faintly to life and then flicks quickly up in to his chest. Now, he is ready to work.

Although dowsing becomes richer and more complex as you delve more deeply into the experience of it, in the early stages it is well to remember that there are a very limited number of indications that a dowsing tool can give. What every dowser does is to sort out these indications into a code of his own; and at its most basic level this code is simply giving a yes/no answer to a clearly phrased question. 'Is there water underground here?' – a stationary forked rod means no, a flip of the rod means yes.

So the first job is to discover what code suits you personally for each instrument. It's up to you whether to begin with a pendulum or with angle rods; as a suggestion, whichever has given you the strongest and most spontaneous reaction. But as a pendulum is relatively straightforward and convenient, and can be used indoors, outdoors and over a map, General Scott Elliot invariably starts his pupils with that.

The pendulum can do only four things: remain motionless; oscillate to and fro, in any direction; rotate clockwise; or rotate anti-clockwise. Out of these, you have to sort out which means yes, which means no, and which means maybe.

General Scott Elliot believes it doesn't matter which. He asks his pupil to hold the pendulum over a flex leading to an electric light. Then he switches it on and tells his pupil to ask the question: 'Is there current running in this cable?' After a while, the pendulum begins to rotate in one direction or the other. Whichever way, it is indicating the answer 'Yes'. Then he switches the light off, and the same question is asked. If things go well, the pendulum will reverse the direction of its rotation. From now on, after repeated practice, this will be the dowser's code: a rotation one way will mean yes, and the other way will mean no; a stationary pendulum will be neutral, and an oscillation can be taken to mean neither yes nor no (a sort of 'maybe', or perhaps 're-phrase the question').

Few dowsers would disagree with him on the general principle that it is very important, early on, to learn what naturally means 'yes' and 'no'. However, it is worth putting one or two reservations at this stage. First, a large number of dowsers feel that for a right-handed person, clockwise should be positive, and anti-clockwise negative; and certainly, those for whom this is not the case are the odd ones out at a dowsing congress, however successful their method is in practice. This feeling, which is intuitively held by some of the best dowsers in the world, is a spin-off from arcane theories that every single thing in the universe, from fundamental particles to heavenly bodies, is polarized. I think that the achievements of good dowsers are so remarkable that their insight should be respected, even if it is unprovable; and so if without strain you can encourage your reaction to work in this way, so much the better. Secondly, many dowsers ignore the stationary pendulum as being a waste of time (rather like having to re-position a forked rod after every flip); as we shall see, there are ways of constructing question-and-answer sessions where the pendulum keeps almost constantly on the move. And finally, if you feel that an oscillation of the pendulum ever 'draws' you in a certain direction (for instance if you were to ask the question 'which way is due north?'), do your best to co-operate, for this is a rare and barely understood phenomenon sometimes called 'attraction', and akin to automatic writing, that can be of immense value in map-dowsing.

Assuming from now on that clockwise means 'yes', the next thing is to practise some genuine searches. There are innumerable tests which you can set yourself, rather like party tricks, in order to become accustomed to the idea of letting a pendulum find something for you – for instance, you could shuffle half a dozen black playing cards, and one red one, place them face down on a table, and then find the red one. One way to do this is by holding the pendulum over each card in turn, and asking (silently or aloud) the question: 'Is this the red card?'; better still, you could use the widely-applicable technique known as scanning, which means placing the palm of your left hand, or your left forefinger, over each card, and asking the same question. According to Bill Lewis: 'You receive with your left hand, and the reaction is signalled in the right.'

Try to get yourself into that state of mind which combines indifference with curiosity. You may find it useful to adopt Steve Bosbach's tip and let the pendulum tell you when to start by first saying: 'Please indicate with a positive reaction when I am ready to find the red card by dowsing.' Watching the pendulum rock gently to and fro, and then after a few moments change into a clockwise rotation, is remarkably like a small dose of self-hypnosis; it induces an agreeable sensation that you are looking at the whole operation as an observer – as if it was happening to someone else. This state of semi-detachment is no bad thing.

Then, as you scan, try to picture as clearly as you can what the red card looks like. Wait long enough with your finger over each card to see what is happening to the pendulum. Anti-clockwise will indicate a black card, clockwise red; you may be surprised, when you move from a black to a red, just how quick and marked is the change in the pendulum movement.

Don't be bothered if you get the answer wrong at this stage – you're only practising. Regard the whole thing as inquisitive fun. Above all, don't try to 'prove' dowsing to yourself or anybody else in tests of this sort; there is an artificiality about them which would prevent any dowser, however experienced, achieving 100 per cent correct responses. What you are doing is acclimatizing yourself to the dowsing reaction, learning what it feels like, and whether it feels different when you get the answer right. Nor should you persist at any one test more than a few times in a row – it is pointless to become discouraged, and there have been many statistical experiments which show that the dowsing reaction quickly becomes dulled or confused when set to one task for too long. As soon as you get an answer right, move on to another exercise. There are many which will occur to you, and General Scott Elliot listed some to a meeting of the British Society of Dowsers in 1975:

Put four similar coins and one different under a cloth, and seek the different one.

Take three or more cups. Put water or a coin in one. Cover up and seek the one with the water or coin.

Fill a large but shallow box with sand. Place a metal object in it and shake up. Seek the metal object.

Get someone to hide a note or object in the shelf of a bookcase. Work along the bookcase with a pendulum and locate it.

Get someone to take a leaf from a hedge or a plant. Take the leaf in your hand and find the plant from which the leaf came.

Work over your own house drains, electric cables, water pipes, to establish their run, in and around the house. Then try your friends' pipes and drains.

Fill three or more glass phials with similar-looking liquids (e.g., diluted coffee, meat essence, tea; or water, salt water, sugared water) and get someone to mark secretly which is which. Then identify them.

Binary questions

Once you gain confidence in identifying a true dowsing reaction, a search for something that is genuinely lost or missing is better than any exercise. It can be a search for something as trivial as a bunch of keys or a family photograph – the point is that an element of genuine need has been introduced, and just about every dowser believes that whatever process may be involved in dowsing, it is more easily triggered in a real situation than an un-natural one. Also, a search for a lost object is a good intro-duction into the wider possibilities of question-and-answer techniques.

So far, the searching exercises have asked only one basic question: 'Is the playing card (or coin, or leaf) *here*?' Searching for, say, a lost wallet demands more extensive questioning. Just as if you were programming a computer, it is essential to keep the questions simple, precise, and capable of a yes/no answer. Otherwise, the technique is the same:

Is the wallet in the house? Yes (clockwise motion).
Is the wallet on the ground floor of the house? No (anti-clockwise).
Is it in an upstairs room? Yes.
Is it in a bedroom? No.
Is it in the bathroom? Yes.
Is it in the bathroom cupboard? Yes . . .

And so on, narrowing the area of search until you know fairly precisely where it is – at which point you go and look for it, using the pendulum around the bathroom cupboard if you still have difficulty in tracking it down.

Fundamentally, all dowsing is just as simple as that; but for most of us, alas, it's not quite as easy as it's simple. For apart from the basic difficulty that most beginners have, of slipping into a receptive state of mind and then staying there without embarrassment or distraction, there is the constant problem of concentration and focusing. Now although all dowsers say that it is unhelpful to clutter up your mind with detailed theories about how dowsing may or may not work before you have gone out and proved it as a physical reality to yourself, I believe that it is reassuring to know in general terms what may be happening. When you have a dowsing reaction that indicates yes or no, you must be picking up information from *somewhere*; from your sub-conscious mind, as sceptics would say; from some 'ray' or emanation given off by the object you are seeking; or from some cosmic pool of knowledge, as many believers in ESP would explain it. Now whichever of these three sources it is (or whatever combination), you are trying to distinguish an almost insignificantly tiny signal from an overwhelming mass of regular stimuli – sights, sounds, sensations. So it is hardly surprising that to begin with, inexperienced dowsers make many mistakes.

Most people find (and Zaboj Harvalik has produced some statistical confirmation of this[2]) that as they learn to dowse, the mistakes become less and the reaction more positive; and one way of moving on is by making sure that all the questions asked are absolutely unambiguous. According to Arthur Bailey: 'Once people have learned to obtain a dowsing reaction, and then to work out their personal code of interpretation, most inaccurate dowsing is caused by them not having a clear enough mental picture of what is being looked for, and not asking sufficiently precise questions.'

Thus in the case of the lost wallet, it may not be good enough to finish with the question 'Is it in the bathroom cupboard?' You should certainly check with another question such as 'Is *my* wallet in the bathroom cupboard in this house *now*?' – for it is one of the inexplicable facts of dowsing that it seems possible to pick up information about where an object has been in the past, even if it is no longer there. (This is known as remanence, and is used to explain the many times that treasure, for instance, has been map-dowsed only for an exploration of the site to disclose that what the dowser has found is a well or a cave from which the treasure has been removed. Asking the question 'Is it there now?' helps, but is seemingly not foolproof.)

Under the right circumstances, however, and properly phrased, the possibilities of this sort of question-and-answer dowsing may be limitless. It is just as if you were plugging into a computer with an infinite amount of knowledge – the only thing being that a computer can do no more than answer yes or no, and the question must be clear, specific and exact. This method of dowsing also goes a long way to de-mystifying the two phenomena that are initially so hard to accept – map-dowsing and number-dowsing. Both are just a logical extension of the normal question-and-answer technique. For to take the example of the lost wallet again, a dowser might as easily have taken a sketch-plan of the house and asked 'Is it here?' With a positive answer, he could then have map-dowsed the various rooms in the house until he again had a 'yes' over the plan of the bathroom.

The map, in other words, acts as no more than an aid and a focus in his search. And if, to continue the example, the first pendulum answer had indicated a negative – that the wallet was not in the house – then work over smaller-scale maps of the area might have indicated whereabouts the wallet had been lost.

The principle remains the same with number- and date-dowsing. A dowser wanting to know the age of an archaeological artefact usually asks 'Is it AD?' (and then, to double-check, 'Is it BC?'). Having established which, he then counts backwards – 'Is it at least 100 BC . . . ? 200 BC . . . ? 300 BC . . . ?' The pendulum will rotate clockwise until quite suddenly, if he is experienced, calling out a certain figure – say, 600 BC – will make it change direction. So the object was made between 500 and 600 BC, and the exact year can be pinned down by the same method: 'Is it at least 510 BC . . . ? 520 . . . ? 530 . . . ?'

Of all the suggested methods of finding dates by dowsing, this system of working down through steadily decreasing numerical factors – from millions or hundreds of thousands, if necessary, through to tens and units – is probably the simplest, and therefore the best for beginners. But some experienced dowsers find it too time-consuming: when Bill Lewis looks for a date, he envisages it coming up on a scale, and the dowsing reaction happens when the mental 'pointer' reaches the right figure. Other dowsers have made up packs of cards with a number on the binary system written on each – 1, 2, 4, 16 and so on up to 8192 – in all, fourteen cards. Any number up to 16,383 can be extracted from a combination of them; all the dowser has to do is to scan each card in turn asking the question 'Should this card be included in the total?' and putting into one pile those for which there is a positive indication. The sum of these cards will give the required number.

Once again, experienced dowsers warn that the questions must be framed very carefully, or error will creep in. Handling a small stone sculpture, or a piece of pottery, it is necessary to ask when it was first carved or first fired; otherwise, they say the age of the material itself may confuse the answer.

If all this, at first reading, strains belief, you may be reassured to know that there isn't a dowser alive who has not gone through a period of amazement and scepticism. It is mind-boggling, contrary to all rational teaching, to conceive of somebody wobbling a paper-clip on the end of a piece of nylon thread and thereby divining accurate information from the other side of the globe. It is almost as difficult to believe that people can detect not only underground water, but its quantity, its depth, and its mineral content. But the fact is that some people manage to do this accurately, nearly every time they try.

The now generally accepted rationale of dowsing methods above at least gives, for the first time in dowsing history, a step-by-step progression that encompasses all forms of the art, so that map-dowsing and number-dowsing is neither more nor less strange than traditional site-dowsing. Until World War II, map-dowsing was hardly known – and even then, there was only a handful of people on both sides working secretly for the intelligence services (their results have not been published). After the war, dowsing literature scarcely ever mentions it as a reliable method. Yet by 1967, when the research committee of the British Society of Dowsers carried out a survey into methods used by members, no less than 86 per cent said they were using it successfully. Today, few professional dowsers would be prepared to waste time on a site without first having narrowed the area of search by dowsing over a sketch-plan.

General Scott Elliot's advice is for his pupils to be confident and bold – in his quaint phrase, 'to be prepared to chuck their hats over the windmill'. There are plenty of opportunities for doing so: find out what sex a friend's baby is going to be (in Japan, dowsers work all day with near-100 per cent accuracy sexing baby chickens as they pass through on a conveyor belt); try to find the month and day of birth of somebody whom you know slightly; trace somebody's movements for a day on a map, and find out how right you were afterwards.

Nobody suggests that a beginner will come up with the right answers all the time, or even most of the time. Idle curiosity may not trigger the correct response. But sooner or later there will almost certainly be a success which demonstrates conclusively that dowsing works – and that point marks the breakthrough.

Practice and improvement

For anyone who can accept that, under the right circumstances, a potentially limitless amount of hidden information is available through dowsing, all else follows. The two best modern definitions of dowsing contain the same thought. Ray Willey: 'Dowsing is the exercise of a human faculty which allows one to obtain information in some manner beyond the power and scope of the standard human senses.' James Scott Elliot: 'Dowsing is the ability to use a natural sensitivity which enables us to *know* (by some means we do not understand) things that we cannot know by the use of the day-to-day brain, by learning, by experience or by the five senses.'

Of course, this sort of sensation is not exclusive to dowsers. All languages have commonly-used phrases which implicitly accept that experiences beyond our normal senses happen occasionally. In English they would be such remarks as 'I felt it in my bones', or 'I had a gut-reaction', or even, quite simply, 'I *knew* something (awful/extraordinary/coincidental) had happened'. Dowsers would say that their special ability is to call at will on these inexplicable yet instinctive feelings – and that the first time anybody manages to do this, voluntarily, he has taken the crucial step to becoming a dowser.

In other words, no matter how well you are taught, there is no substitute for finding out the ways that dowsing works for you. Reading how to do it is no more than an introduction – like trying to learn how to drive a car by just studying the manual, or expecting to play championship golf after looking at an illustrated book of instructions.

Arthur Bailey told a meeting of dowsers in 1975 how he first experienced a dowsing success, and because the story exemplifies what must happen to many people as they make a tentative initial attempt, it is worth repeating in his own words:

I came into dowsing originally by getting Asian 'flu. If I hadn't been desperate for reading matter I would probably never have looked at a book on dowsing, and at first it all sounded terribly far-fetched. I forget which book I read, but it had a picture of a rather sombre-looking Frenchman in a top hat holding a pendulum that didn't exactly fill me with enthusiasm.

However, there was an illustration of angle rods, and I made a pair for myself with wooden handles. With these I wandered round my garden, feeling rather idiotic. It was the limit of what I could do at that time. I found that whenever I went over things I knew were there, such as gas pipes and main drains, the rods moved, but they didn't move very far.

Some people seem to think that dowsers are born: they pick up the rod, it reacts, and everything is wonderful. It didn't happen that way with me. I started very gently, and when I went over something which would give me a mighty reaction nowadays the rods hardly moved – just a little way. I kept going backwards and forwards and rechecking. Now I knew enough about psychology to realize that this could be auto-suggestion, which can be extremely powerful, so I proceeded to go a bit further. I found out that there were other areas in my garden where the rods crossed which had nothing whatever to do with anything I knew about.

To cut a long story short, I discovered the cold water supply to our house, which was not where it was shown on the plans. We had never known where the cold water stop tap in the road was, and I also found that. The line of the pipe came diagonally out of my house, and whenever I went over it my rods swung in. I pegged it out to where the pipe apparently stopped abruptly. I got my wife to keep an eye open for anyone from the Council seeing me knock holes in the road, and took a hammer and chisel and went straight down to the stop tap cover. There was about an inch of Tarmac on top of it.

Now that was what convinced me that there was something in dowsing, because I had no means whatever of knowing that it was there.

I think once you have discovered one thing like that, which is against all the known laws of probability, you realize that you are dealing with something which does exist, that it is not just a figment of somebody else's imagination or inspired writing in a book. That is when the whole thing suddenly takes off, and that is where I took off originally.

After that first experience, dowsers say there is no substitute for practice; and that at the same time it makes sense to broaden your use of dowsing tools. Even though you may in the end finish up with a pendulum as your most versatile and convenient piece of equipment, angle rods are at the same time so sensitive and positive as to reassure you that your practice is achieving results. They are particularly useful out of doors, where the kind of way they are used by Arthur Bailey and many professional dowsers can usefully be copied by beginners. In this kind of search – site-dowsing, it is often called – it seems that we are all sensitive to certain kinds of unseen anomalies beneath the earth: underground running water, especially, but also ground disturbance created by the laying of drains, electric cables, and so on. Some of this can be measured by good scientific equipment such as proton magnetometers or echo-sounding metal detectors, but as we have seen, a good dowser can generally do the job more quickly and just as accurately. So it is worthwhile practice to look around where you live for the water, electricity or gas supply, sewage drains, or other kinds of ground disturbance which can be subsequently checked either on maps and plans, or by reference to manholes and inlets.

For people living in areas where a large number of radio stations can be picked up, Zaboj Harvalik invented an intriguing and repeatable experiment that has been shown to work for nearly everybody. He tunes in a transistor radio to a frequency chosen at random, and asks the dowser to listen. Then he switches off, and asks the dowser to scan 360° to find from which direction the signal originated. Switching the radio on again, without altering the dial on the frequency tuner, he turns it this way and that until the sound is loudest – so that the aerial inside, being directional, is aligned with the beam from the station.

At an early stage of his own training in dowsing, he devised a more complicated feed-back device to help him distinguish between various background 'noises' which were making the angle rods move, and the emanation which he was deliberately trying to pick up – in this case, the magnetic field effect caused by underground electricity. The device consisted of a sensitive frequency detector which triggered off a visual signal on a dial, and an audible signal through headphones, as soon as he walked through a magnetic field of sufficient strength. After a while, he found that he was able unconsciously to programme himself to recognize the field by dowsing methods alone, so that the angle rods indicated to him the presence of the field whether or not his feed-back device was switched on. He also deliberately carried out the process in reverse, so that he could programme himself *not* to react to the field. 'The secret of good dowsing is to know what you are looking for, and to ignore everything else,' he says.

Many dowsers also find angle rods useful because of their versatility – the way that they can be used to indicate direction. Someone coming into a field where he wants to find the right spot to sink a well for water, will first of all turn slowly round in a circle, holding the rods parallel before him, asking the question: 'In which direction is the nearest substantial supply of potable water?' At one point in the compass, the rods will come together and cross, and that will show him in which direction to head off looking for an underground stream, the rods again pointing parallel in front of him. (If he wants to check the approximate area of the stream, he often uses a triangulation method, taking an additional bearing from another corner of the field.) When he reaches the stream, the rods will cross once more, showing that he is now directly above it.

So far, this is exactly the technique that a professional dowser might normally use with the traditional forked rod. However, Arthur Bailey has found additional advantages with angle rods. If, when walking towards the stream, the rods begin to veer off in another direction, it is an indication (to him) that there may be something else worth looking for there – perhaps another source of water. Also, he finds that the amount the rods move towards each other is an early indication of the quantity of water flowing beneath the ground: if the tips barely deviate from parallel, the stream is not worth bothering about; if they touch, it is a medium-sized stream; and if they cross right over he would assume a flow of at least 1000–2000 gallons an hour.

Other dowsers have worked out their own form of code with the rods so that they can quickly identify the direction of an underground stream, or the perimeter of a buried archaeological site, by the way the rods swing outwards, away from each other, coming to rest in a straight line in the same direction as the edge of the stream or ancient building beneath the earth. Or the rods can be programmed to move one at a time to indicate a crossing of underground streams and the directions in which each stream is flowing.

Aids and techniques

In the end, dowsing comes back to the two fundamentals of working out how to interpret your own individual code, and of focusing. Among the aids sometimes suggested for beginners is the use of samples. These consist of a specimen of the object you are looking for, whether it is a certain kind of rock, oil, a piece of clothing belonging to a missing person, a photograph, a lock of hair, pure water . . . the more exactly similar or more closely associated to the original, the better. Some good dowsers can't, or won't, work without samples; most people tend to find less and less need for them as they become more experienced. Probably, they have a restricted use as a help in concentrating and focusing. But they can bring complications too – there are many cases of dowsers finding the wrong object because the sample was not exactly matched. Enid Smithett, wife of the secretary of the British Society of Dowsers, tells the story of the West Country dowser who was asked to find a lost boy. 'They gave him the boy's cap and he picked up something which was going round in circles. It was not the boy he was picking up at all, but a dog which was rushing about everywhere and which had recently had the cap in its mouth.' In other words, you must be prepared to over-ride the use of a sample, and check with normal dowsing methods as well. Many dowsers feel that the name (perhaps with a description as well) of what they are looking for clearly printed on a piece of paper, is much better as an aid to concentrating the search. It is a method that is also frequently used for a question-and-answer session about an unfamiliar subject.

Another device much used is the Mager rosette, a small disc consisting of V-shaped segments coloured white, black, grey, red, yellow, green, blue, and violet; it is named after the French dowser Henri Mager, who invented it to 'prove' a complicated set of rules about a resonant relationship between colour, harmony, vibrations, the dowsing ray, and such. Its first practical use was to test the potability of water – what kind of water was underground, how drinkable it would turn out to be. Thus if Enid Smithett holds the violet segment between left-hand finger and thumb, and the pendulum reaction is positive, then this means, for her, pure water; with a reaction to the grey segment, the opposite; and to black, a dangerous water combining minerals such as lead, arsenic and copper. Other colours give other indications that have been observed and correlated over a period of time. All dowsers have to work out their own colour code, and for those who use it regularly, the Mager rosette is a useful short cut to discovering the nature of something unexpectedly causing a dowsing reaction outdoors. Working round the archaeological site of Cadbury in Devon, Clive Thompson was infallibly able to predict where there would be bones or pottery because, for him, yellow on the Mager rosette meant the bones, and green indicated pottery.

Various short cuts are used in map-dowsing, too. Rather than try the pendulum over every quadrant of the map in turn asking 'Is it here?' you can run your finger down the side of the map and ask 'Does it lie on a line east/west of here?' As soon as you get a positive reaction, double-check from the opposite direction (bottom to top), and mark the point with a pencil. Then run your finger across the map, from side to side, asking 'Does it lie on a line north/south of here?' Again, double-check and mark the reaction point. The place where the vertical and horizontal lines cross will be the right area in which to pin-point the location exactly.

Another warning to beginners is that, because their dowsing reactions usually happen more sluggishly than those of experts, they will tend to overshoot the area they are looking for. Thus the need to check upwards as well as downwards in the map-dowsing technique above; and in the field, the need to approach an underground stream or pipe from both sides, and to put in pegs or stamp out a heel-mark where the dowsing reaction occurs. Mid-way between the two marks should be the centre of what you are looking for.

You may find, too, that there are a number of marks outside the line of the pipe or stream, apparently occurring at random;

these will have been caused by 'noise' giving a false dowsing reaction, and should be eliminated from your interpretation. As people become more experienced, less and less of these spurious reactions crop up, and dowsers learn to programme themselves so that the tip of their shoe, or the pointed end of a forked rod, or the end of a pencil, gives them the exact position they want.

Beyond these simple but quite sophisticated suggestions about how to learn a basic dowsing technique lie dozens of hints and tips and methods that work for some people, but not for all. The dowsing journals are full of them, and conversations with experienced dowsers throw up even more. No two people dowse in exactly the same way, and fortunately this doesn't seem to matter. In general, what has happened to dowsing over the past twenty years or so is a move away from rigid and dogmatic statements about dowsing technique, towards a general recognition that it is within each person to find his own method. Early pioneers used to debate hotly about the respective merits of various pieces of equipment. Should pendulums be heavy or light? How long was the thread to be? Vicomte Henri de France wound his on a short stick, the Abbé Lambert waved his wrist to make the pendulum move, the Abbé Mermet moved not only his wrist but his thumb and first finger. Which of these methods was correct?

In the same way, it was vehemently argued that wearing rubber-soled shoes inhibited the dowsing reaction; or that unless a pendulum were made of a 'natural' substance it would not give a true response; or that it was dangerous to dowse when the moon was on the wane. Nowadays, most dowsers would say that if people believed these and other rubrics to be true, then they were true – for dowsing is sufficiently intangible and ghostly a gift for any mental blockage or preconception to interfere with it.

The mechanism of dowsing is still so little understood that whole areas of mystery and wonder lie within its operation. Many of the greatest dowsers are indeed sensitive to the phases of the moon or slight changes in barometric pressure, so that they feel they work better on some days and in some seasons than others. When working, they sometimes suffer from inexplicable feelings of terror, or shivering cold, or cramps, or a nauseous dizziness – all symptoms that show just how volatile and un-predictable are processes set in motion by the dowsing force.

Alongside the tolerant acceptance that each person must be free to suffer his own idiosyncracies and to practise dowsing in his own way, has come a greater insistence that positive results are the only things that count. General Scott Elliot told the American Society of Dowsers at their Danville congress in 1973: 'I think we must be more professional in our approach to our work. I am not talking about money. If we are professionals, we *must* deliver the goods. Gone are the days when we feel we have been "lucky" when we find water, or minerals, or an archaeological site. We must expect to do so, accurately, and be upset if things go wrong. When they do, we must want to know why, and how the mistake happened.'

Delivering the goods, nowadays, means more than walking out into a field and telling a landowner where to sink his well, and what quantity and quality of water will emerge at what depth. It means, for a new generation of dowsers, looking at the way in which these traditional abilities can be applied to wider uses. For instance, there has long been a method, known as the 'Bishop's Rule', of depthing a stream. This involves walking away from the stream at right-angles to it, rod in hand, until a dowsing reaction happens. The distance of this point from the stream, says the rule, is the same as the depth of the stream.

The method has worked for many years now, and is still used. But what also works, much more conveniently, is the straight-forward method of counting down: 'Is it more than 10 feet . . . 20 feet . . . 30 feet . . .?' If you watch Arthur Bailey do this, a pair of angle rods in his hands will gradually converge as he reaches the crucial figure, and then move back to parallel again when he has passed it. It's a system which saves his time and his leg muscles – but more importantly, he can adapt the same yes/no technique to working on maps, to finding missing people, to discovering which herbal remedies will suit which ailment . . . in fact, to demonstrating that, for a believer, there is almost no theoretical limit to the information that can be gained through dowsing.

In practice, the limits are set only by an individual dowser's ability to concentrate and set the right questions. For General

Scott Elliot, 'there is no such thing as a universal dowser'. For Steve Bosbach, 'questioning seems similar to programming a computer – the more accurate the facts fed in, the more accurate the answers will be. You should dowse in your most knowledgeable field.' But over all, the approach to dowsing has become near-scientific, with a basically unified method providing repeatable results.

It may be wondered, then, why dowsers and science have been such uneasy bedfellows for so long; and it is to this troubled relationship that we now come. But before trying to disentangle the mistakes, evasions, half-truths and failures that mark this next part of the story, it is as well to bear in mind the summary of one eminent scientist, the physiologist and Nobel Prize-winner Professor Charles Richet:

'Dowsing is a fact we must accept. Don't experiment to find out whether it is so. It is so! Go ahead and develop it!'

Part Two: the Scientific Search

The reason why thinking and scientific people reject psychical phenomena is not because they lack the power of discrimination, but because of the innate pull of nature back towards the sensible world. They intuitively feel that the facts of psychical research will no more mix with the beliefs of common sense than will oil with water, and fear that the dissonant facts, if admitted, will disrupt the scheme of the known and the familiar.

– G. N. M. Tyrell, *Science and Psychical Phenomena*, 1938.

4 Dowsing versus Science

It was 1913 when Professor Richet exhorted his fellow-academics to carry out his advice; he might as well have shouted at a mound of cotton wool. For throughout the twentieth century, what has characterized the attitude of scientists in general towards dowsing is the way in which they have persistently ignored it, dismissing it as a delusion or a fraud, and justifying their lack of interest by reference to a small number of studies which supposedly 'prove' that it does not work. It is not hard to understand their attitude. Most aspects of dowsing, even the physiological ones, are notoriously hard to measure under experimental conditions, and if you are a scientist, you are taught to believe that unless you can measure something repeatedly, it probably doesn't exist. Even more is this the case with odd-ball phenomena whose strange claims apparently fly in the face of the known laws of physics.

However, there have always been a small number of properly qualified people who have been prepared to look at the subject in spite of its difficulties and paradoxes, most commonly because, like Charles Richet, they were unable to deny that for them personally, dowsing was a demonstrable fact, or because, however mysterious and however near the frontiers of disbelief, it evidently had a potential practical value. Somewhat against the odds, it is in Russia and Eastern Europe where, currently, much the biggest research effort is taking place – a gigantic programme, according to some reports, attempting nothing less than to discover, once and for all, the basis on which dowsing works.

The Russian approach
This impression gained wide currency in the West in 1970 with the publication of *PSI: Psychic Discoveries behind the Iron Curtain*,[1] a book based on a 1968 research trip by the two

journalists Sheila Ostrander and Lynn Schroeder, who came upon a lucky dip of largely unrelated findings in the field of parapsychological investigation which, when strung together, tended to look like a vast, co-ordinated plan to bring these matters within the area of respectable science. The book's section on dowsing was received with not much less than delirium by some dowsing circles, being held to demonstrate that at last their talents were being harnessed and properly recognized, and that the governments of the West must surely now, if only in self-defence, provide similar facilities and recognition. However, a few years have passed since then and, alas, it hasn't happened. From a fresh perspective, it is not at all clear that the Russians are offering any new solutions to the fundamental difficulties of finding out what happens when somebody dowses,[2] nor that the broad mass of Eastern scientists are any less cautious than their Western counterparts about either the fact or the foundation of dowsing.

The background to their current research is that, somehow, a very few researchers managed to continue their studies of extrasensory perception during the Stalin era, despite his insistence that the great bulk of scientific effort should be devoted to areas that had a military application, and also despite the continuing stricture that all theories must be explicable in Marxist and materialist terms. We still do not know just how much work went on, but it is now clear that the most renowned ESP researcher in Russia, the physiologist Dr Leonard Vasiliev, holder of the Lenin Prize, was able to continue surreptitiously from the 1930s right through until Stalin's death in 1953, and that during this time he produced significant evidence of telepathy.[3] There was also, in 1944, an isolated article on dowsing in the reputably orthodox *Journal of Electricity* in Moscow, by the hydrology professor, G. Bogomolov, followed by a mass experiment involving geologists and soldiers to find out if his claims were justified: on balance, they were.

By the time Vasiliev died in 1966, with four of his books published towards the end of his life, parapsychological research in his country was being freely discussed. Within this context, the study of dowsing was playing its part. In April 1966, a paper was presented to a biological seminar in Moscow entitled

'Research into Electro-Physiological Effects of the Dowsing Rod', and later the same year, a similar paper on the 'Physiological Reaction of Man to Water and Minerals in the Earth – The Problem of the Dowsing Rod'. In 1967, Moscow saw a number of parapsychological seminars attached to larger conferences, and then in 1968 came what seems, in retrospect, to have been the peak of interest: in April, there was the first international symposium on dowsing, held at Moscow University; and in May, the first Moscow International Conference on Parapsychology. At both, there was a high expectation that a breakthrough, both politically and scientifically, was about to be made – indeed, was being made; now, nearly a decade later, they seem to have been exaggerated hopes.

This is not to deny that there are still important differences in the approach to such matters as dowsing between Russia (especially) and the rest of the world. Their first symposium on the subject was chaired by Professor A. Ogilvy, head of the Department of Geology in Moscow State University, and there has been nobody of such stature in the West who has been prepared to go on record with the statement as unequivocal as his announcement that his country 'stood on the eve of a new birth in the ancient field of prospecting – discovery of the scientific basis of dowsing. Dowsing will be used to solve problems and may supplant many contemporary geophysical methods.'

The second seminar, in 1971, in which he also took part, was attended by more than 100 scientists representing some forty research, geological and planning institutes from many parts of Russia. Not even the most distinguished parapsychological conferences in the West can command such an attendance of officially approved academics, even though the conferences may cover a range of subjects far wider than dowsing.

On the experimental level, too, for sheer volume the work in the USSR leaves the combined work of all other countries far behind. The 1971 seminar was told of a methodical dowsing search for gold, tin and other minerals, statistically checked against orthodox geological methods, from the borders of Finland in the north to the shores of the Caspian Sea in the south. Reports of this research indicate that literally thousands of people have been observed in an attempt to find out just how dowsing works, how often, and how well.

But Chris Bird, whose painstaking translation of the proceedings and resolution of this second seminar has made it possible to put all this work in proportion, pointed out in a lecture to the Washington branch of the American Society of Dowsers that the tone of the seminar was 'not all that self-congratulatory. In one part it refers to the lack of research into the physiological and neurological causes. In another, it criticizes the lack of co-ordination between various research groups. In a third, it takes to task those interested in dowsing for having undertaken only fourteen of sixty-six research tasks recommended at the 1968 seminar.'[4]

The resolution of the seminar, after making a formal request to the Ministry of Geology to organize an expert commission to evaluate the results of dowsers in the field, then goes on to propose that any such investigation should be limited to the 'disclosure and tracing of tectonic disturbances on a scale of 1: 50,000 and larger for dowsers both airborne and on the ground'.

In other words (if it is possible to extract a meaning from such opaque officialese), to test dowsers only on whether they can distinguish gross underground anomalies – for instance, magnetic anomalies – which also show up on scientific measuring devices.

Map-dowsing is never mentioned, and there is a constant pre-occupation with the movement of the rod that marked so many previous European enquiries. Dowsing itself is called the 'Biophysical Method' (BPM), and the dowsing reaction becomes the 'Biophysical Effect' (BPE), presumably to legitimize its study.

Reading translations of the work of the geologist Dr Nikolai Sochevanov, who is directing much of the research, it is impossible not to feel that compared to the subtle – even if vaguely mystical – rationale of dowsing that has lately been emerging in Western Europe and the United States, he is taking an unnecessarily mechanistic approach. For instance, he has designed a standard type of dowsing rod, to be made out of a certain grade of wire, bent into a certain shape, so that it can be used identically by all his subjects. He is able to attach an automatic recorder that counts how many times the rod turns over when the person holding it passes through a 'dowsing zone' (a typically loose phrase that seems to embrace underground water, volcanic disturbances, oil, minerals, or archaeological sites: you might say, anything which the experimenter cares to designate). Then he meticulously records whether different people obtain a differing number of turns of the rod (they do), whether the number of turns varies when the dowser is on foot, in a car, or in an aeroplane (it does), and whether there is a correlation between the number of turns and the type of object being sought, taking into account the speed with which the dowser passes over it (he says there is, but most Western scientists would argue that his statistics are meaningless).

From what we have seen of the way that Western dowsers work, it seems certain that the different neuro-muscular reactions in each person would be bound to defeat any such attempt at standardization. Moreover, other unlikely findings such as the reported fact that Russian dowsers are 'insulated', and fail to get a reaction, if they wear leather gloves, suggests that nothing like enough effort is being made to avoid self-fulfilling mental blocks of the kind that plague historical literature on the subject; as we have seen, if you *believe* you can't dowse while you wear leather, then assuredly you won't be able to.

However, the sheer quantity of research being done must in time illuminate certain aspects of dowsing, and in one respect the Soviet scientists take a very different approach from the Western one: they believe in dowsing, and are concerned only to discover the basis on which it operates.

For while their straitjacket is that they are confined within their own kind of scientific orthodoxy, the problem for Western scientists has in some ways been even more constraining: their accepted methods demand that they must obtain a certain kind of statistical proof before even considering it as a subject worthy of investigation. It has led to a sporadic and largely fruitless encounter between scientists and dowsers from which, it must be said, neither side has emerged very well.

The elusive phenomenon

Looking at the history of tests of dowsing ability held under

99

controlled experimental conditions, it is clear that none of them has unambiguously proved dowsing to be a repeatable faculty to be summoned at will. Once you depart from the kind of anecdotal case-history recounted so far in this book, you move into a treacherously sticky area of claim and counter-claim, proof and half-proof. Trying to demonstrate dowsing by statistical methods is like trying to photograph a ghost – you may see it, but the moment you try to operate the camera, the shutter jams and the ghost disappears. (Therefore, a scientist would say, there wasn't a ghost.) Maddeningly for dowsers – even those with years of experience – theirs seems to be a slippery and elusive gift that wilfully slides away at the moment they would most like to show it.

Which, of course, is why it is so suspect to a classically-trained scientist, most of whom even today would say that there has never yet, anywhere, been a satisfactorily demonstrated example of dowsing. What they actually mean by this is that there has never been a satisfactory demonstration in front of their own eyes and under their own conditions, which is a rather different matter; and it is in this profoundly different approach to two kinds of 'proof' that one can trace the basis of the generally hostile relationship between them and dowsers.

The gap between the two was well summarized in 1952 in an exchange between the New Zealand research chemist P. A. Ongley and the British dowser J. C. Maby, a physicist who spent most of his life attempting to discover a workable radiation theory for dowsing. Ongley, having tested seventy-five dowsers in his country and judging them no better than geologists in finding water, wrote: 'The nuisance value and the menace of dowsing is not sufficiently realized. A water- or mineral-witcher can cause an awful waste of private and public money. The medical-witcher can cause a waste of public life.'

Maby responded: 'Ongley shows no sign of having properly examined the very large body of positive instrumental and physiological data, or the excellent records of a few accredited dowsers, before drawing dogmatic conclusions . . . a vast body of evidence by numerous competent engineers physicists, physiologists and others has securely established the basic facts of radiesthesia and dowsing.'

Unfortunately, the evidence and the basic facts do not include very much in the way of statistically positive results – at least, statistics in the form of tables of values, graphs and diagrams which are the basis of all modern scientific work. From the earliest days of Jacques Aymar undergoing a series of blind-folded tests in the Luxembourg Gardens of Paris in front of the Prince of Condé, the results have been unpredictable and un-repeatable. Nobody has yet tried to compile and evaluate a com-plete record of them (perhaps because under the different cir-cumstances of each test, the comparisons would not be valid), but those which can readily be traced show dowsers to have per-formed much better than chance, much worse, and about average, in a disconcertingly random manner.

Most tests either ask a dowser to identify hidden objects, or to discover the existence of underground water. The largest number seem to have taken place in the first two decades of the century, such as that conducted by Professor G. Wertheimer in 1906, using well-known dowsers who all believed, he said, that it should be well within their powers to tell whether water in a pipe beneath them was switched on or off at the main; he con-cluded that the 'experiments do not answer definitely the ques-tions of whether or not dowsers have the power to find water.' Another test, also negative, took place in 1913, when a group of scientists (including some sympathetic to dowsing) were thoroughly sceptical after the failure of seven professed dowsers to discover the positions of sewers, a known underground water source, and another spring capable of delivering 50,000 gallons per hour. According to the author John Sladek, whose book *The New Apocrypha* is devoted to a prosecution of fringe beliefs, there have been 'dozens of such tests, which would certainly indicate that dowsing has had a fair trial, and that whenever test conditions are scrupulously fair, dowsers do very poorly.'[5]

The most recent of such negative tests took place in 1970, when the engineer R. A. Foulkes, on behalf of the British Ministry of Defence, attempted to find out whether dowsers, including untrained ones, could be of genuine help in detecting unexploded shells. A careful series of experiments was carried out in countryside north of London and under the guidance of Colonel K. W. Merrylees, a past president of the British Society of Dowsers, using himself, other selected dowsers, and volunteers from the British Army.[6] The results were published in *Nature*, one of the most authoritative of all scientific journals and have been quoted ever since as having 'proved' that dowsing does not work: for on this occasion, there is no doubt that it didn't – nobody, either individually or collectively, performed significantly better than chance would predict.

Positive tests

On the other hand, there is also a history of tests with positive results, although until recently these have usually involved individual dowsers, rather than the statistically large samples which scientists prefer. Early this century, the University of Paris conferred the degree of Doctor of Veterinary Medicine on Dr Abel Martin for his thesis on the use of the pendulum in diagnosis of animal maladies. In one controlled test, it was established independently, by orthodox methods, that a particular herd of forty cows contained thirty-eight that were infected by TB, one that was possibly infected, and one that was clear. Martin, with his pendulum, quickly and accurately came to the same diagnosis. More recently, the *Journal of Parapsychology* has occasionally reported on experiments in US universities, particularly in California and Utah, where above-chance scores have been obtained by groups of dowsers finding missing coins, or predicting the results of horse races. The success rates, however, have not been spectacularly significant.

A number of individual dowsers, too, like Major Pogson in India, have classified their results over a period of time – for example, A. C. Williamson, who from 1952–7 matched his water-divining against the results of the Water Development Department of Tanganyika, which was using orthodox geological water-finding techniques, and beat them 76 per cent to 30 per cent.[7]

Even more rarely, there have been occasions when somebody has been prepared to risk his reputation and undergo a controlled and publicized experiment. In Britain, easily the most satisfactory of these was when – typically – Robert Leftwich, alone of all members of the British Society of Dowsers (as a general rule, the society frowns on such tests), agreed to take part in a televised attempt to distinguish a can of water buried underground from other empty cans, and to discover five other hidden targets. He was completely successful in the first test, and scored (somewhat to his disappointment) 'only' three out of five hits in the second.[8]

The results astonished Professor John Cohen of Manchester University, who was overseeing the experiment: 'I didn't expect him to get anything like this degree of success. I must admit I'm amazed . . . every effort must be made to explain the results in terms of natural science.'

But this and other isolated achievements do not, in scientific terms, add up to a body of proven fact. Taken as a whole, the negative results probably outweigh the positive ones, and scientists, from a distance, generally explain away individual successes by saying that over a period of time, the law of averages would predict that some dowsers are bound to be right some of the time. Now this is in many ways a superficial and patronizing attitude; but I think it is important to remember that it exists in the scientific community largely because dowsers have been unable to provide, on the occasions when it mattered most, incontrovertible evidence to back their claims – and this is the main reason why science has stood away from dowsing for so long.

The other main reason for the gulf between the two is the persistent unwillingness, or inability, of dowsers to present their material in a way that makes any sense to science. The accepted format for any scientific paper is to outline the purpose of the experiment; to give a detailed account of methods; to discuss the results; and to state what is the conclusion. In the thousands of papers published in dowsing journals, scarcely one would follow that pattern: nearly all are personalized and subjective. Thus *Nature* was able to comment on one of Cecil Maby's books:[9] 'In presenting facts and theories to the scientific world, there is a well-established and necessary procedure. It is to be regretted that the author has not followed this procedure, thus making the position of the scientific reviewer impossible.'

Worse, in the eyes of such scientists, dowsers often borrow scientific language and mis-use it. Traditionally, the dowsing reaction has been said by them to arise from a 'fundamental ray', or a 'ray of attraction', which although physical in its

103

nature was perhaps divine in origin; in any case, it was a radiation unaccountably not yet known to science. Even today, in the space of a single issue of one of their journals, one can read of 'microvibratory-physical fields', 'oil radiations', 'radio-active resonance', 'aluminium deflection of noxious earth rays', and a dozen other examples of pseudo-scientific terminology that might have been deliberately phrased in order to put up the hackles of orthodox scientists.

So, briefly, scientists have two main grounds to justify their lack of interest in dowsing. Firstly, it can't be shown to work consistently in laboratory conditions. Secondly, its proponents put up naïve theories to suggest how it might work, many of them contrary to the whole structure of modern physics. As the psychologist D. H. Rawcliffe wrote comprehensively in 1952: 'Their basic assumptions possess no internal consistency, lack anything approaching a logical foundation, and are generally flatly contradictory to one another.'[10]

Needless to say, dowsers have their answers.

Attitudes of investigation

First of all, they will readily admit that the test results are disappointing, and explain this by saying that the atmosphere of doubt, tension and anxiety, and the presence of an audience, are simply not compatible with the state of mind needed for successful dowsing. D. M. Lewis, a scientist who is also a dowser, and who shares many of his colleagues' dissatisfaction with the way that dowsing results are usually published and presented, has pointed out that this nervousness during a demonstration is far from unknown to scientists themselves. 'All of us have seen, many times, delicate scientific experiments in front of a critical audience that simply don't happen in the way they should. Scientists will always attribute this kind of failure to nervous tension, and I believe they should apply the same kind of tolerance to a dowsing test.'[11]

Certainly, the inevitable scepticism that surrounds a test does not mix happily with the kind of psychological detachment that people are taught to acquire before they start dowsing. Zaboj Harvalik has found that in his experiments, it is often novices who initially do better than professional dowsers, who, he says, 'seem to feel that they must be on their mettle and compete with the newcomers, with the inevitable result that a block sets in and they do a lot worse.'

In the past, too, many of the dowsing experiments were carried out in conditions of extreme artificiality, with the dowsers being blindfolded, strapped up, manhandled, wired to electrical meters, asked to perform at precisely regular intervals, and so on; on the face of it, any one of these things would be enough to upset the fragile equilibrium needed to dowse successfully. It says quite a lot about the extrovert nature of Robert Leftwich that he actually *enjoys* dowsing blindfold for demonstration purposes, and has done this several times on television.

Of his 'failure' in picking out only three of the five buried objects, he says: 'In the first test, involving cans of water in a field, I was 100 per cent right. But then it was said that as the cans had been buried some time previously, there was a remote chance that somebody could have cheated and told me where they were.

'So they decided to set up another test straight away, and this time they chose an abandoned rubbish tip as the site. It was full of all sorts of junk just under the surface, and I had the devil's own job trying to distinguish the targets from everything else that I was picking up.'

However, there is still a residue of a few carefully-prepared experiments where the conditions were approved in advance, or even designed, by the dowsers, who were reasonably sure that they would be able to achieve what they set out to do – and failed. The most notable of these was the experiment reported in *Nature*, of which Colonel Merrylees now says: 'We said we would have a go, that's all. I was never totally certain that we would succeed, because we were looking for objects – bits of concrete, empty mine casings – that we weren't accustomed to seeking. Nearly all my experience has been in finding water, and I know I can do this best for small villages, hospitals and so on where there is a real need. I never accept payment for this sort of thing, and I am pretty well always successful at it.

'But it doesn't necessarily follow that proficiency in one type of search is followed automatically by an equal success in any other. There are three necessary conditions: sensitivity of mind, experience, and confidence. In any test, all three are likely to be adversely affected, and in the case of this particular test, the experience simply wasn't there.'

So, you might conclude, dowsing sometimes works, dowsing tests usually don't. Dowsers may be on firmer ground when they complain that most scientists have a bias, conscious or unconscious, that leads them to reject or ignore successful tests of dowsing, or well-attested dowsing achievements, because they do not fit neatly within the grand scheme of agreed knowledge. I think there is some justification in this charge. Scientists are taught to explain all unusual matters according to the philosophic principle known as Occam's Razor, named after the fourteenth-century British scholar William of Occam (or Ockham), whose main dictum is taken to mean that you should work through all known or likely solutions to a problem before suggesting a new or magical one. This is, on the whole, a thoroughly sound way to approach reports of paranormal events, but it has the disadvantage that when taken to extremes, the likely solution tends to become even more strained and improbable than the magical one.

Thus the 'likely' solution to dowsing is that the dowsers unconsciously interpret surface clues through greatly heightened powers of observation – clues that to the ordinary person (or even the trained geologist) are so minute as to be unnoticeable. In this respect, the tracking ability of Australian aborigines or North American Indians is often noted (although, as we shall see, this ability may need more than a physical explanation). Some of the indications, according to D. H. Rawcliffe, would be: slight modifications in the colour of the soil and vegetation; scarcely perceptible changes in the health and growth of grasses, plants, shrubs and trees, particular attention being paid to the spread and direction of their roots; the type of vegetation; texture and dampness of the soil, including 'feel' of the ground underfoot; differences of temperature in the atmosphere. He also suggests that good dowsers must have well-developed olfactory senses – a good 'nose' – so that they can smell water from a distance, like some animals seem able to do; also, since 'many underground streams are audible to the normal ear', particularly good hearing. As for map-dowsing, he says that tests never succeed (quoting one that didn't) and that 'against thousands of map-dowsing failures' (unspecified) we must expect an occasional chance success.

He concludes: 'Such rational explanations as the above are anathema to most of the divining fraternity, and there is little doubt that many years will pass before the march of reason ousts the present naïve conceptions which brighten the lives of so many!'

In fact, it is difficult to imagine a more far-fetched or less rational explanation than the one he gives. He summons up a picture of some hyper-sensitive person in perfect health, presumably armed with a trowel with which to dig up the roots of plants, that is totally at variance with the observed behaviour of most dowsers, and which would be regarded as absurd by the working dowsers themselves. He makes no attempt to explain how it is that a dowser, as opposed to a geologist, will correctly insist on a well being sunk exactly, to within two or three inches of where he says, for fear of missing the narrow underground stream beneath, which was, for instance, the proven basis of the success of Major Pogson in India (whose career there Rawcliffe describes and then abandons without explanation). Nor, by any standards of probability, can there be surface indications of moisture effects where a well has to be sunk through perhaps 200 feet of solid rock before striking the vein below. In other words, he is indulging in armchair theorizing from a philosophical standpoint, rather than logical explanation based on scientific observation and enquiry into all the facts.

It is also, at best, a partial explanation. Only a small fraction of the cases which I have come across, themselves only a minute part of the total, would lend themselves to this kind of interpretation. Even in the traditional, and nowadays somewhat narrow field of water-finding, Rawcliffe makes no examination of a dowser's ability to predict depth, quantity and quality. But more than that, he utterly ignores claims by dowsers to discover other things hidden underground – minerals, buried artefacts, and so on; he also disregards, except briefly to dismiss them as chance events, the many documented cases of missing people being traced.

This tendency to exclude *prima facie* evidence, to pretend that the more extraordinary and difficult case-histories simply did not happen, is the basis of the second main charge by dowsers against scientists (and vice versa): that in spite of protesting that they cannot examine something without a core of statistics on which to work, they themselves often unscrupulously mis-use and select from statistics if it happens to suit their case.

It is not hard for an outsider to find instances of this happening, and it seems to me that it does so in the two enquiries in the United States that have done most damage to official confidence in dowsing: the book *Water Witching, U.S.A.*,[12] by Evon S. Vogt and Ray Hyman, and the introduction to the 1917 US Geological Survey report on dowsing written by Professor O. E. Meinzer. Vogt and Hyman, one an anthropologist, the other, like Rawcliffe, a psychologist, go along with the general theory that it is unconscious muscular twitches that trigger off movement in the rod; but to them, these twitches are set off by the dowsers deluding themselves into imagining that, through ESP or some other paranormal source, they are truly receiving occult answers to their search.

In support of this theory of theirs, that it is a dowser's gullibility and suggestibility that allows him to claim he is undergoing a genuinely inexplicable reaction, they quote many examples of how good magicians can trick people into believing that supernatural events have occurred. Although the link between such tricks and dowsing is tenuous and not well argued, it is a point worth making. There is no doubt that many dowsers claim to be able to achieve more than, in the end, they are able to deliver, because of an element of self-delusion in their makeup.

But this leads the two authors to the premise that dowsing *never* works, and in support of this they are ruthless in selecting, overwhelmingly, from the individual records of dowsers, cases where dowsing has failed, and ignoring times when they have spectacularly succeeded. Thus the man who is probably the best-known dowser in United States history, Henry Gross, about whom the Pulitzer Prize-winning novelist Kenneth Roberts wrote three books,[13] is dismissed as of no consequence after they managed to trace a single customer who was dissatisfied because he dug for water on Gross's instructions, and found none.

Yet Roberts, who became Henry Gross's partner in a water-finding business, and was meticulous in chronicling his development from traditional water-divining to more advanced techniques of map-dowsing for other substances, was able to quote hundreds of successes, all fully documented – and none recounted in the Vogt/Hyman book. Nor is the single failure examined in such a way that one can discover whether it was the result of an aberration by Gross, or – as can readily happen – if the drill was slightly out of position, or the drilling operation itself mishandled in such a way that it blocked the water vein.

This partiality, in the case of the Geological Survey report, degenerates into a sneer. Meinzer's introduction makes no attempt to support its argument with facts; instead, there are such phrases as 'the outline of the history of the subject presented in the following pages will probably enable most honest enquirers to appreciate the practical uselessness of "water-witching" . . . It is difficult to see how for practical purposes the entire matter could have been more thoroughly discredited . . . It is by no means true that all persons using a forked twig or some other device for locating water are intentional deceivers. Some of them are doubtless men of good character and benevolent intentions. However, many of the large group of professionals are deliberately defrauding the people, and the total amount of money they obtain is large . . .'

Now all this is assertion, not a balanced scientific finding, and it is difficult not to feel sympathy for dowsers when they are told: (a) that their talent doesn't exist, (b) that it is the result of self-delusion or fraud, (c) that it is nothing to get very excited about, because they are only using their five basic senses in a special way. For dowsers are certain that none of these explanations is sufficient, and many of them would say that there is not much point in continuing to try to prove themselves to scientists. They argue that the gap between the two sides is now too big, and dogged with a history of mutual mistrust; and that in any case there is almost certainly nothing in the framework of orthodox science that can provide an explanation of dowsing.

However, not everybody feels like that. An increasing number of dowsers are themselves scientists, and in spite of the troubled background, when they first come to the subject they are all fascinated with the possibility of a physical explanation. But the puzzle is this: science has identified four basic forces which govern the behaviour of the minute particles that make up the universe, and most physicists agree that no new force is needed to complete what is already a deeply satisfying picture; yet none of the forces seems fully capable of solving the basic mystery of how the dowser gets his information.

Only in the last decade or so have come the first few encouraging pointers. The main one of these, which will occur again and again in the next two chapters, is the gradual recognition by scientists that somewhere within our bodies we are capable of sensing and processing minute signals about changes in our environment. It seems that all of us can, quite unconsciously, detect tiny differences in such things as barometric pressure, electrical activity, temperature, magnetic fields, radio beams – a whole host of shifting influences that, because they are invisible and so small, we have long ignored.

What dowsers of old instinctively recognized as their much-derided 'ray of attraction' has become tantalizingly close to being measured.

5 The Attraction of Magnetism

The search for dowsing's 'fundamental ray', pursued from the turn of the century onwards with sporadic and mostly amateurish vigour, was almost completely ignored by reputable scientists. They had a number of apparently sensible reasons why. Amid the emerging picture of physics during the 1930s, no such ray could be seen to exist, or even need to exist. At the time, it also seemed ludicrous to suggest that humans could perceive and interpret something as intangible as, say, a radio beam – scientific receivers and amplifiers were needed for this purpose. But mostly, it was a question of measurement. Dowsers were claiming a special sensitivity and affinity to this so-called ray – but how on earth could this be quantified? With such normal senses as sight and hearing (though not reliably touch, taste or smell), this could be done; with the dowsing sensation, it could not.

Nevertheless a few dowsers, and even fewer scientists, were undeterred. The obvious existence of the dowsing reaction, however caused, was sufficiently strange and enticing for them to continue to research. Cecil Maby and Bedford Franklin produced their immensely complicated theories about the interaction of various forms of energetic waves which would combine to form a signal which the dowser recognized.[1] They also proved some physiological side-effects of the dowsing reaction, such as decreased skin resistivity. But this was a long way from showing that dowsers had a definite and measurable skill compared with other people.

One way through came from steady improvements in the design of magnetometers, devices which measure the strength of the magnetic field created by magnets. The Dutch geologist Professor Solco Tromp, in a 534-page book called *Psychical Physics*,[2] reporting on experiments that took place in 1946–7, showed that blindfolded dowsers were able to detect a sudden, but small change in the gradient of such a field. But it was not until the

111

arrival of the proton magnetometer during the 1950s that sufficiently sensitive and repeatable experiments became possible. Since then, two scientists have come up with findings that, because they are so surprising, are still greeted in many academic circles with incredulity. First, in 1963, Yves Rocard, Professor of Physics at the École Normale in Paris, the leading French college of teachers, was able to suggest in his book *Le Signal du Sourcier*[3] that the magnetic field gradient changes identified by dowsers were not just small, but almost inconceivably tiny. And now Dr Zaboj Harvalik, a scientific adviser to the US Defense Department, and for twenty-five years Professor of Physics at Arkansas University, has shown in a series of experiments from 1968 to the present day that even Rocard grossly underestimated the capacity of nearly all of us, and good dowsers in particular, to sense minute changes in our environment.

For a non-scientist, it is perhaps as difficult to grasp the concept of magnetism as it is to comprehend the infinitesimal amounts of energy being talked about. However, it is crucially important to make the effort, for in both Rocard's and Harvalik's findings may lie a vital key to understanding how dowsing works.

Magnetism is one of the two components of electromagnetism, which is the second strongest of the four fundamental forces known to physicists (the others being nuclear, radio-active, and gravitational). Yet we cannot, in normal circumstances, feel it as we can feel, for instance, gravity (which we notice every time we take a step or lift an arm) or other environmental factors such as temperature, pressure, atmosphere and light. On the contrary, the static magnetic field has hardly any apparent effect on the human body; put your finger inside a child's horseshoe magnet and you sense nothing. Yet the effect is there (as you could tell at once if the same finger wore a metal ring), and the fact is that we all live perpetually under the influence of a giant magnet – the earth itself.

For, although nobody has agreed on the details of how it happens, the earth produces a magnetic field, probably created by the flow of molten metals at the earth's core. Compared to a child's magnet, it is very weak – but it is remarkably constant, even if unnoticeable in day-to-day life. The standard unit of measurement for static magnetic field strength is a gauss. The strength of the field created by the whole earth varies somewhat from the equator to the poles, but averages about half a gauss. A child's magnet would be, typically, about one thousand gauss. So, remembering how difficult it is to feel the force of a child's magnet, consider that it will be two thousand times more difficult for you to recognize the power of the earth's field. Nevertheless, we are all living under the influence of this half gauss of magnetic field strength all the time (*Diagram 1*).

Most of the time, we are so well adjusted and accustomed to this influence that we simply don't notice it. However, work by a handful of scientists suggests that when there is a sudden change in the field strength, we unconsciously sense this.[4] The approach of magnetic storms causes the earth's field to reduce suddenly, and studies in America, Denmark, Switzerland and Israel have shown that this has a marked effect on human behaviour. Psychiatric admissions to hospitals increase; there is a strong correlation with certain pathological states and suicide. What is more, people are known to be able to anticipate the arrival of such unpleasant winds as the mistral in the Mediterranean, or the khamsin in the Middle East, two or three days in advance, and this is because they are reacting to the associated magnetic change. Animals can detect the imminence of an eathquake by sensing the magnetic changes built up by pressure in the underground rocks. Experimentally, people have been placed for ten days in a laboratory from which the influence of the earth's magnetic field was artificially removed (to simulate conditions on other planets). At the end of the period, they were unable to distinguish whether an electric light bulb was flickering or constant.

Dowsing sensitivity

An electric storm, if it is a powerful one, decreases the earth's field by a factor of about 100, and one might predict that the human body would notice the difference. But these are, relatively, gross effects. What Yves Rocard reported about the sensitivity of dowsers was far more astonishing. His results suggested that they – and many ordinary people as well – could detect a change in the level of a magnetic field gradient of only three ten-

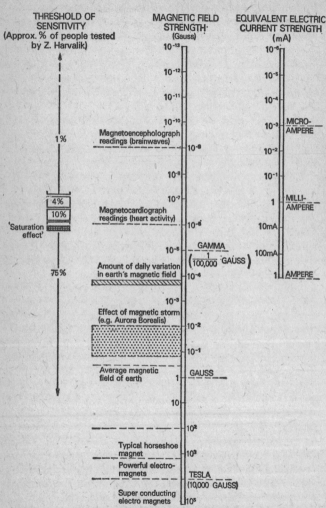

HUMAN SENSITIVITY TO MAGNETIC FIELD GRADIENT CHANGES

Diagram 1

thousandths of a gauss. This tiny amount was measurable only by the latest magnetometers, and it was beyond any scientist's suspicion, let alone belief, that the human body and brain could accurately sense a variation as minute as this.

If it was true, it meant that these same dowsers could probably detect the tiny drift in the magnetic field of the earth each day, which the new equipment was now establishing as also being around thirty gammas (a gamma being one hundred-thousandth of a gauss). So incredible did the whole idea sound that scientists on the whole ignored the findings, or ascribed them to faulty laboratory work.

It was certainly true that some elements of Rocard's experimental methods could be criticized; also, that he had used only a very small number of experienced dowsers, compared with his untrained pupils. So what Zaboj Harvalik wanted to do in America was to try to repeat Rocard's results on a larger scale, and without the problem of temperamental equipment. As a Trustee of the American Society of Dowsers he had access to many volunteers, and the solution he came up with was both simple and effective. He decided to create a controllable weak magnetic field in his own garden.

First he used a magnetometer to survey the ground, to find an area relatively free from the magnetic anomalies caused by overhead power lines, buried cables, drains and so on. (In the light of his previous experience with dowsers, he was cautious enough to have a good dowser check the site; as a result, it was moved a few yards, and rechecked with the magnetometer.) Next, he drove two iron pipes, each three feet long and three-quarters of an inch in diameter, into the ground twenty metres apart. Finally, he connected these pipes to a DC electric power supply, one to the positive and one to the negative, arranged the cables so that they would not interfere, and switched on. As the power leaked through the slightly damp earth from one pipe to another, a weak magnetic field appeared around and above it.

Zaboj Harvalik says he used this method of soil conduction, instead of the copper wire coils of Rocard, because he knew that dowsers were sensitive to all manner of spurious signals from natural and man-made electromagnetic fields such as those from power lines, and radio or television transmissions. While these could affect the copper wire coils even when they were switched off, the soil in his garden minimized them to a level where they were no longer noticeable, and therefore could not interfere with the dowsing experiment.

By varying the voltage of the power supply, he could increase or decrease the strength of the field. A meter capable of measuring as little as one-millionth of an amp – the standard unit of electric current – monitored the amount it was going up or down. He used his magnetometer to correlate the change in levels of electric current to different strengths in the magnetic field. All that any volunteer had to do was to walk between the two electric poles with a dowsing instrument, and say from their dowsing reaction whether Harvalik, hidden out of sight, had switched the current on or off. Most people used angle rods, which swung outwards or inwards as they crossed the line between the pipes. Harvalik in turn was able to reduce the power progressively (or at random) until the dowser was unable to recognize the signal.[5]

A summary of his findings, using more than 200 people over three years, many of whom had not dowsed before, is shown in diagrams 1 and 2. In brief, not only did he confirm and extend Rocard's description of the sensitivity of dowsers, but he has also been able to show that the threshold lies beyond the best portable magnetometer yet made. His most sensitive subject, the German master dowser Wilhelm de Boer, was still identifying a weak signal at a micro-ampere (one-millionth of an amp, or $1 \mu A$) and below. To most people, this is barely credible. In the conditions existing in Dr Harvalik's garden at the time, $1 \mu A = 10^{-10}G$ (0.0000000001 gauss). In plain language, de Boer recognized a change in the magnetic field gradient *one billion* times weaker than the earth's own weak field. When the results of the experiment were put to Dr Paul Fatt, head of the Department of Neurophysiology at University College, London, he said with an air of defeat: 'How does that man live on this earth?' For as we shall see, it has always been held theoretically impossible that such a tiny signal could be identified and singled out from the mass of background radiation that bombards us all the time.

But just as important as this exceptional result has been his

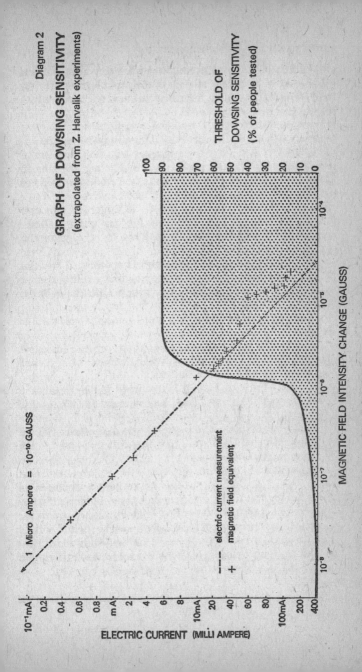

Diagram 2

GRAPH OF DOWSING SENSITIVITY
(extrapolated from Z. Harvalik experiments)

THRESHOLD OF
DOWSING SENSITIVITY
(% of people tested)

1 Micro Ampere = 10⁻¹⁰ GAUSS

- - - electric current measurement
+ magnetic field equivalent

MAGNETIC FIELD INTENSITY CHANGE (GAUSS)

ELECTRIC CURRENT (MILLI AMPERE)

finding that up to ninety per cent of all people can sense changes of as little as half a gamma. This compares with around fifty per cent of those tested by Rocard in a much stronger magnetic field, and Harvalik ascribes the difference mainly to the use of angle rods instead of the traditional forked rod.

'More or less all of us can tune in, if we let ourselves,' he says. 'On the other hand, there comes a point in the graph, around half a gamma, when most of us stop registering the anomaly. After that, I think we have to leave it to the professionals. About five per cent of people can get to recognize a gradient change of one-millionth of the earth's magnetic field. So far I've only come across one man – de Boer – who can go a long way beyond that. His sensitivity is phenomenal, nothing less. It makes you feel he could achieve almost anything.'

So far, Harvalik's work is probably less appreciated even than Rocard's. In part, this is due to the obscurity or inaccessibility of his material – out of thirty-four papers which he published between 1970 and 1976, thirty were for the *American Dowser*, the journal of the American Society of Dowsers, which is neither highly regarded nor widely read in established scientific circles. Also, scientists who have taken the trouble to read his papers criticize them for not including enough data on which to check the statistical validity of his findings.

However, Harvalik himself is unworried (although quick to point out that all the raw data is kept carefully on file).

The important thing was to get down on paper the work I was doing, and the way I was doing it. Anybody is now free to repeat my experiments, and I'm sure that their results will not be significantly different. However, after my experience with de Boer, I would say it is essential to have a 'double-blind' system for switching the current on and off. I have shown how to make a cheap randomizer that will perform this way, so that neither the operator nor the dowser knows the switch position until afterwards. It is now clear to me that many dowsers can pick up your thoughts, perhaps even your subconscious ones, and this can affect the results.

Fatigue effects

In fact, having established, to his own satisfaction, the general principle that we are all extremely sensitive, and some dowsers extraordinarily so, Zaboj Harvalik's interests have turned to other aspects of his experiments, which have turned up as by-products. Why, he wonders, is there a 'saturation effect' from about 1·2 to 2 gamma? The results show that in this narrow range, many dowsers become confused, and cannot recognize whether the current is switched on or off (*Diagram 3*).

Again, he has noted that fatigue sets in much faster than can be explained purely by the physical effort of walking several times backwards and forwards – results quickly become extremely unpredictable:

If you move about holding dowsing rods for between quarter and half an hour, which is the length of time it takes to do a series of fifteen or twenty walks backwards and forwards across the magnetic field, there is bound to be a certain amount of physical tiredness – your muscles don't react quite so sensitively. But I also think that the monotony which so many dowsers have complained about in tests in other places, also plays a considerable part. Anyway, I insist nowadays that nobody has more than a dozen test runs in succession, even if they say they want to go on. We get much more consistent results by leaving off and resting for a while.

He has published a limited set of results to back up this belief. Testing four dowsers over the familiar artificial magnetic field in his garden, he found that they were correct 88 per cent of the time during the first five runs; 72 per cent in the second five runs; 40 per cent in the third. (Predictably, he found he could 'wake' them by pumping up the current in the fourth run.) One detail of the test was even more striking: during the first ten runs, not once did a dowser say the current was on, when it was in fact cut off – 100 per cent success; during the second ten runs they were wrong 90 per cent of the time – almost as if the dowsing reaction had gone into reverse.

Other curiosities that have come out of the experiments include the fact that Wilhelm de Boer could increase his sensi-

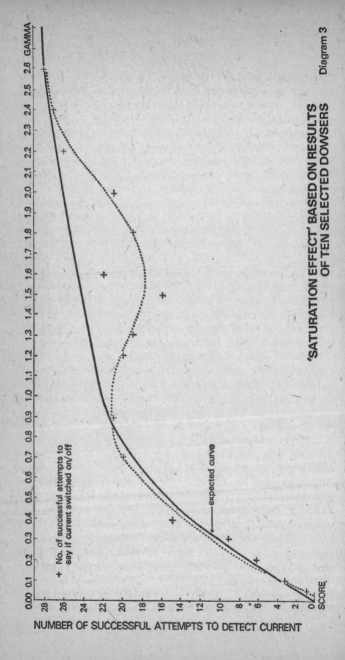

'SATURATION EFFECT' BASED ON RESULTS
OF TEN SELECTED DOWSERS

Diagram 3

tivity tenfold if he drank two glasses of water before he dowsed – and that after a good lunch his sensitivity dropped by a factor of 1000. On another occasion, a volunteer who had at first been unable to get a dowsing reaction, drank a large Bourbon and shortly afterwards was cheerfully and accurately saying whether the field was on or off at a level of less than half a gamma.

Trivialities apart (if that is what they are), the implications for dowsing of the over-all findings are highly important. They do nothing less than indicate a possible explanation for much of the mystery of site-dowsing – because although Harvalik's experiments were carried out in artificial conditions, it may be highly significant that magnetic field anomalies occur naturally in many of the areas in which dowsing has traditionally been successful. Underground water, for instance, as it flows along a channel, creates tiny amounts of DC electricity which would be recognizable as a magnetic disturbance on the surface of the ground; so would water seeping through porous rock, or a slowly-shifting table of water next to, for instance, a bed of clay.

Similarly ground disturbance creates magnetic anomalies. Archaeologists using proton magnetometers can detect the position of former ditches, walls, and so on, which leave a magnetic imprint at the surface of between half a gamma and 40 gammas – easily within the detective reach of a competent dowser. The tunnels, caves and mineshafts in North Vietnam (see p. 65) produced the same effect. So does buried treasure, electric cables, sewers, drains . . . in fact, a large proportion of the artefacts that dowsers are called upon to seek.

Searching for the sensors

But the problem immediately arises as to how the dowser distinguishes between one anomaly and another. Dr Harvalik looks for the answer in recent research which has shown that different artefacts throw up different three-dimensional 'signatures'. Like the difference between two people's handwriting, no two magnetic signatures are exactly the same – there is a broader magnetic pattern for underground water flow than for a buried cable, for instance. If we were able to perceive these signatures visually, they would look rather like individually shaped mountains, or molehills, sticking up from the otherwise flat countryside. Just like seeing, the whole process might take place in a dowser unconsciously and almost instantaneously. To continue the analogy, we are all able to concentrate visually on one face in a room crowded with people, or to separate one conversation from another at a cocktail party in what sounds like an unintelligible cacophony when heard later in a tape recording. Similarly, a dowser might be able to sort out one magnetic signature from another.

But if this is so, Zaboj Harvalik knew that it was necessary to discover whether enough parts of the human body were acting as sensors to detect the minute differences of pattern, which are three-dimensional, being vertical, horizontal and perpendicular to the plane formed by the first two. As with two eyes, the dowsing centres had to be in separate parts of the body, so as to be able to perceive in perspective.

One riddle presented itself at the beginning of his tests – the mysterious fact that in a magnetic field produced by DC electricity, the dowsing reaction occurred only when the dowser's left side (heart side) was towards the pipe/electrode carrying the negative flow of current. In other words, the dowsers could detect the magnetic anomaly only one time in two; when they turned round and walked back to where they had started, the reaction disappeared. Harvalik puzzled about this, particularly as one set of results, when volunteers used the traditional forked twigs instead of L rods, seemed to contradict his findings. But with Wilhelm de Boer it was conclusively true.

In de Boer's case, the normal dowsing reaction is an upward flick of his forked wire rod. Before and during the tests, Harvalik deliberately refrained from telling de Boer about the polarized signal suppression. Nevertheless, it occurred invariably. Harvalik reported: 'With his heart side towards the negative electrode, and with the current switched on, he showed a reaction 100 per cent of the time; facing the other direction, there was 100 per cent signal suppression. The only odd effect was that occasionally, when he had his heart side towards the positive electrode, he had an abnormal dowsing reaction – his rod flipped downwards instead of upwards.'

By accident, Harva'ik was able to identify the part of the body where this suppression takes place. He noticed that of all the dowsers tested with angle rods over the artificial magnetic field, one man was able to dowse with equal accuracy in both directions. In other words, this dowser alone did not experience signal suppression. Discussing the matter with him, Harvalik discovered that he had once suffered a severe multiple fracture in his upper left arm, which had been mended with the aid of an eleven-inch-long stainless steel pin in the marrow cavity. Harvalik therefore simulated this condition by attaching metal rods to the left arms of other dowsers, including de Boer. As soon as he did so, the signal suppression disappeared for them also.

'I have no explanation for this at present,' says Harvalik. 'But it was such an oddity that it made me continue in my search for other parts of the body that were related to sensing magnetic or other signals.'

Already, in 1967 and 1968, he had made an experimental study using a highly effective magnetic shielding material known as the Co-Netic AA Perfection Annealed Sheet. Although his paper on the subject does not give the transmission characteristics of the sheet, he says that the attenuation was considerable. He took a piece about a foot wide, and wrapped it twice round himself loosely so that it formed a cylindrical barrel that could be moved up and down his body. Then, blindfolded, he moved in and out of the magnetic dowsing zone, with the barrel covering various parts of his head and torso; an observer noted when his angle rods indicated a dowsing reaction. As a result, he came to the general conclusion that when the area between the seventh and twelfth rib was shielded – roughly between the navel and the sternum – the ability to dowse weakened or disappeared. This was consistent with much dowsing literature, and a certain amount of scientific research in Switzerland, which suggested that the solar plexus might be one of the dowsing sensors in man.

Later, with Wilhelm de Boer, he was able to refine his experimental methods by watching him dowse through a carefully-oriented high-frequency electromagnetic beam (usually radiating at 58·55 megahertz with a strength of one watt), switched on and off by the randomizer. Instead of the crude approximation given by his earlier barrel shield, he was now able to form a shield with an aluminium belt only two inches wide, or two-inch square metal strips, to narrow down the area where the magnetic radiations were being perceived. After many tests, with de Boer walking across the beam at various angles, Harvalik was able to report:

Two magnetic sensors exist in the kidney region, perhaps more accurately in the area of the renal gland of each kidney. This region does not include the solar plexus, although it is fairly close.

I know of two cases, at least, which seem to confirm this. A good Australian dowser, an engineer who lives in Sydney, had his right kidney removed when he was eighteen years old, but not his renal gland, and it has left him unaffected. But a Swiss dowser has completely lost his ability after having his right kidney and renal gland removed. Some dowsers have complained to me of decreasing dowsing sensitivity when they have had what they call 'kidney trouble'. I am now certain in my own mind that this is one of the key sensory areas in the human body.

The other area that most dowsers feel to be important in receiving signals is the head (or brain). Robert Leftwich, for instance, can demonstrate this by leaning forward at an angle over an underground stream or pipe; when his forehead is directly above the centre, his rod flips upwards. Swiss research includes the case of a soldier-dowser who lost his dowsing ability when wearing his Army steel helmet. So Zaboj Harvalik, operating the same methods of shielding, but this time using 3·5 mm aluminium wire as well as the two-inch belt, attempted to pinpoint the area precisely. Tests seem to show that it was somewhere along a line taken through the brain just above the ears and behind the temples.

It is too early to be certain just how accurately Zaboj Harvalik has identified these two sensory areas for dowsers, or if there may be more. He himself has drawn attention to one confusing, and possibly contradictory piece of evidence, which is that if both areas are shielded simultaneously, as opposed to just one or the other, the dowsing reaction not only reappears, but increases in strength. But what excites Harvalik is that if he is right about there being two or more centres, this provides a theoretical model of how a dowser can sense, in three dimensions, the difference between one kind of magnetic field and another. He has summarized his thoughts on this a number of times:

If three-dimensional perception of dowsing patterns is possible – that is to say, if a dowser can recognize and react to vertical as well as horizontal components of the magnetic field – then this would enable him to discriminate between the 'signatures' of the various disturbances. He could programme himself (or dowse) for specific features such as water, minerals, and so on, all of which have different signatures. A subterranean cavity shows a different magnetic field pattern from a buried power line or water flow.

The process of dowsing would then be described as a search to identify a particular magnetic signature. As soon as the search was successful the brain would give the order for the arms to twist, the blood flow would increase through the finger capillaries, the skin moisture would increase, and all the other minor physiological changes that make up the dowsing reaction would take place.

Put succinctly like that, it sounds as neat an answer to the problem of dowsing – at least, of site-dowsing – as could be found. But alas, it isn't – as Dr Harvalik, after yet more experiments, is the first to agree. Static magnetism may well play a role, and a very important one, in the mystery of how we sense the unknown. But it forms only a small portion of the ocean of other unseen forces that influence our lives; and of these, electromagnetism is another one which, scientists are now discovering, has an unsuspectedly large part.

The electromagnetic spectrum

The importance of electromagnetic waves to dowsing is, quite simply, that somewhere in their infinite spectrum there may be a frequency, or a series of frequencies, which can carry enough information for the dowser to be able to perceive what he is looking for. Here may lie the dowser's 'fundamental ray', by which he interprets information radiating from deep beneath the earth or far beyond the horizon in somewhat the same way as a radio receiver is able to. Of course, this is not a new theory; but in the last fifteen years, scientific experiments with sophisticated and highly sensitive equipment have shown that, as with static magnetism, human beings may be far more receptive and responsive to electromagnetic waves than anyone had believed possible.

Again, in order to understand the theoretical possibilities, it is necessary for a non-scientist to make the effort to visualize broadly just what electromagnetism is: in essence, waves travelling at the speed of light that carry information about disturbances in the fundamental particles of the universe. All bodies at above absolute zero temperature (0°K) in our known physical universe emit electromagnetic radiation. The theories surrounding this were first proposed by James Clerk Maxwell in the middle of the nineteenth century; their true nature was discovered in 1888 by Heinrich Hertz, whose name has been immortalized to describe one of the most important properties of electromagnetic waves – the fact that they oscillate (pulse, vibrate) at different frequencies. This oscillation takes place in inverse proportion to the length of the wave. Thus a wave one metre long oscillates more than one hundred million times a second (10^8 hertz); a wave one hundred kilometres long oscillates at a rate of three thousand times a second (3 kilohertz) (*Diagram 4*).

This range is literally infinite. At the low end of the scale, at around one hertz (that is to say, one oscillation per second, when the electromagnetic wave is so slow that it is virtually indistinguishable from static magnetic or static electric fields), the length of the wave equals approximately 50 times the radius of the earth. Astronomers think they have discovered waves that last for forty seconds, which would give each wave a length of seven million miles. At the other end of the scale are the cosmic and gamma rays that bombard the earth from outer space, their wavelength so short that a million side by side could pass through the eye of a needle.

In between come the familiar frequencies that we have learned to use. Going upwards through the scale are the radio waves, long, medium, and short; the microwaves, now used for cookers and communications, and shortly to be incorporated in a host of

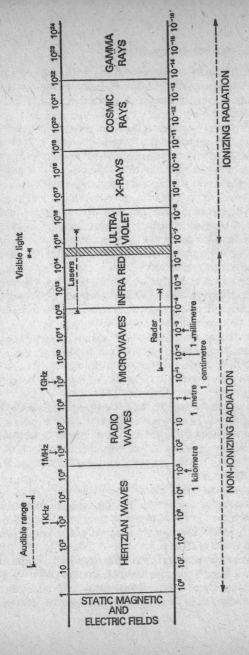

Diagram 4   ELECTROMAGNETIC SPECTRUM

new technological devices for the home; then infra-red rays' applied in physiotherapy; next the relatively narrow band of electromagnetic waves that make up visible light; and finally ultra-violet and X-rays.

Biological systems – including man – are known to generate low-energy electromagnetic fields covering a large portion of this spectrum. Since all other bodies also emit electromagnetic radiation, it would be simple and natural to assume that just as we can see in the visible spectrum and hear in the audible range, there might be a sympathetic area elsewhere that would give a dowser (or perhaps all of us) the means to interpret unseen information. Somewhere in the spectrum, perhaps in many places, would lie a frequency that was transmitting information to us just like a radio beam, used in telecommunications, while we used some hitherto unrecognized part of our body or brain to decode and interpret it. But unfortunately, there are profound theoretical objections to this, of which perhaps the most basic is that at the high end of the spectrum, radiations that penetrate the body can be lethal; while at the low end of the spectrum they do not have enough energy to upset the natural stabilizing processes in the body – they simply go unnoticed.

In spite of this, a few scientists, running the risk of ridicule and ostracism, have continued to search for a way of resolving the many difficulties and paradoxes. Their work has been exceptionally arduous, not just because many scientists are hostile or hidebound in this area of research (and therefore won't co-operate), but also because orthodox theory presents genuinely formidable, almost insurmountable, obstacles in the way of a rational attempt to establish just what wavelength a dowser, or a mind-reader, might use.

For a start, the so-called 'ionizing' radiations – those in the frequency spectrum above visible light, can almost certainly be eliminated. They are just too dangerous, and a combination of the nature of our environment, and the protective skin on our body, prevents most of them penetrating us. For instance gamma rays, the shortest wavelengths of all, were we not shielded by the layer of ozone in the atmosphere, would simply annihilate the tissue of all living things (which is why there has been so much concern about damage to the ozone layer by supersonic aircraft, or the action of aerosols).

Cosmic rays are almost as powerfully harmful in the way they cause genetic change and damage, but most of the time are kept out by the earth's magnetic field. It is known that from time to time in the earth's history this field reverses polarity, so that the north pole becomes the south pole, and vice versa. During the time in which this process takes place, there is for a while no magnetic shield, and this has been linked with genetic mutation and the extinction of various species of animals; some scientists even suggest that such reversals can be directly related to the emergence of man himself.[6]

The harmful effect of X-rays has been known since soon after their discovery in 1895. There were early signs in paint factories and mines where radiation in these frequencies was high, that people began to suffer from hair loss, burns, skin ulcers and cancers. The development of the nuclear bomb and then nuclear power stations has led to a colossal research effort into this area of the electromagnetic spectrum (in just one year recently, the US Atomic Energy Commission experimented on 783,615 rats and 111,084 mice). Yet people are still arguing about what is the 'safe' level of exposure; X-ray photographs in hospitals are now used as little as possible, and it may even be that prolonged viewing of colour television, which emits small quantities of X-rays, is enough to trigger off effects in the human body. Ultra-violet light, most of which is, like other ionizing rays, filtered out by ozone, carries similar hazards – sunburn, a link with skin cancer – though to a lesser degree.

So it is among the non-ionizing radiations, below the wavelengths of visible light, that the search for the dowser's 'information carrier' has been concentrated. But here too, orthodox scientific thinking would say that the range of frequencies is just as impossibly unsuitable, if for different reasons. The generally accepted view is that the only effect of these non-ionizing radiations on the human body is thermal – when directed with sufficient energy at people, they heat the molecules of the body and cause damage. The simplest example is the fact that you get burned by infra-red waves if you stand too near a fire. There is an eye disease known as glass blowers' cataract, caused by years of being exposed to the infra-red rays in furnaces that make glass; the skin and the cooling effect of the blood has protected the bodies of people suffering from the disease, but not the eyes, which have little blood and a poor cooling mechanism.

Similarly in the range of frequencies called microwaves, the effects on humans have always been thought to be purely thermal. As they have a greater capacity to penetrate tissue (the longer the wavelength, the more this becomes true), they have been used for 'deep heat' treatment of some illnesses; some frequencies will relieve soreness or sprained muscles, others have destroyed tonsils without the need for surgery, or have scarred parts of the brain in the treatment of Parkinson's disease. This ability to penetrate also led to the development of microwave ovens for cooking.

At lower frequencies than this – in the spectrum of radio waves, and below – scientists have been almost unanimous that, apart from the way in which we are able to hear sound waves vibrating in the air within a band of hertzian frequencies, they had no effect on the human body whatsoever, and that they were therefore irrelevant to the mechanism of dowsing, telepathy, or anything else. It was certainly true, as shown by the radio waves, that they could be used to transmit information. But it was obvious to everybody that broadcasting involved far more expenditure of energy than the tiny levels which the human body generates. Also, to make broadcasting work, you have to have an aerial and an electrical conducting system – and there was no way, according to orthodox theory, that the body could conceivably function in this way. So, since it was held to be theoretically impossible for low frequencies of radiation to be detected biologically, scientific research in this area was minimal.

But as we shall see, a number of strange effects, at first apparently unrelated, began to disturb this general view. Gradually, observations were collected to suggest that we all, instead of being inanimate sponges for all this radiation, are on the contrary finely balanced mechanisms somehow capable of reacting to almost every wavelength that reaches us. This steady accumulation of evidence has mostly been ignored or resisted by mainstream science, an attitude which was criticized at a high level in 1971 by Paul E. Tyler, of the US Navy Department's Bureau of

Medicine and Surgery, when he introduced a conference on the subject to the New York Academy of Sciences:

It has been said that present physical laws do not account for any non-thermal effects, and unless new laws are discovered, there can be no possible effects of electromagnetic radiation on biological systems. This statement is slightly contrary to good science. In general, our present laws have evolved after many trials and errors. Many so-called laws have been altered or discarded after scientific observations revealed that the concept or law would no longer account for new scientific facts. A classic example of this was the belief held for centuries that the earth was the centre of the universe. It was only after many observations were made which did not fit this theory that a re-evaluation occurred and the concept was discarded.[7]

A similar re-evaluation is taking place right now. Revolutionary and upsetting though it may be to the accepted concepts, there is already overwhelming evidence that low frequency electromagnetic fields and weak static magnetic fields can affect all life. According to James B. Beal, of the World Institute in New York: 'As a product of the Cosmos, we are all tuned in.' And with this increasing knowledge comes the hope among some scientists that it will at last be able to encompass the nature of the dowser's fundamental ray.

Magnetoreception
Electricity, even when it wasn't understood, has long been put to medical use. The Roman, Anthero, said to be a freedman of the Emperor Tiberius, accidentally discovered that stepping on a live torpedo fish alleviated gout. Later, Dioscorides, who was a surgeon in Nero's army, and a famous herbalist of his time, used the discharges of electric fish to treat gout, migraine, and other illnesses. The Italian physicist Luigi Galvani wrote on 'animal electricity' in 1791, speculating on the electrical nature of life processes, and it has always been popularly assumed that 'rays' from electricity might be harmful. In 1891, when electric lights were installed in the White House, they were at first not placed in

the rooms used most often by the President, because they were thought to be too dangerous. However, in spite of this early guesswork, almost no research was carried out until the invention of powerful electromagnets in the 1930s began to make it possible. Even then it was largely ignored, overshadowed by work in pure biology, and then later by the pressing need to discover more about the obviously harmful effects of nuclear radiation, which was so immediately important that nearly all available funds were devoted to it.

Nevertheless, a number of very odd occurrences, none of them attributable to thermal origins, were noted from time to time. There was the remarkable 'phosphene effect', discovered in 1898. This happens to most people when a bar magnet emitting electromagnetic waves at 30–60 hertz, and with a strength of 200 gauss upwards, is held against their temple; they believe they can see light, even if they are in a blacked-out room. Then, it was found that infra-red radiation at levels too low to give a sensation of warmth, could cause tiredness and headaches. When broadcasting was invented, it was found that some people could hear radio signals through the fillings in their teeth, which acted as amplifiers. But even stranger, many people who live near a strong radar beam can perceive it as a noise, generally described as 'buzzing like bees', and this happens both with deaf and normal individuals. Mental hospitals have patients who find the noise intolerable, for ear-plugs will not suppress it. Aurora displays have been heard by some people. So, too, have meteorites, usually in a form described as a buzzing or hissing. Since meteors travel faster than sound, through the upper atmosphere at levels where the air is too thin to transmit normal sound waves, these people must have been picking up an electromagnetic frequency.

Evidence of unsuspected sensitivity also accumulated from the animal kingdom. The electric fish *Gymnarchus niloticus* reacts to a change of magnetic field so weak that it is the equivalent to the disturbances caused by an electric light bulb at 1500 yards distance.[8] Birds and bees are thought to use the earth's magnetic field in homing and navigation – an experiment in which tiny magnets placed with the north and south poles pointing the wrong way round, were attached to pigeons so disorienting them that they were unable to find their way.[9] The British scientist Dr G. V. Robins has recounted how at the site of an ancient megalithic tomb at Pentre Ifan in Wales, constructed in such a way as to create a magnetic field anomaly, a normally docile cat became hysterical when walking under the main capstone.

Clues such as these have helped towards the growing conclusion that all creatures are in some way affected by a variety of frequencies, and it is in Russia where most of the scientific research has taken place. For more than twenty years there has been a huge effort in dozens of universities and institutes, and their experiments, tens of thousands in total, have been summarized in *Electromagnetic Fields and Life* by Professor Alexandr S. Presman,[10] of the Department of Biophysics in the Faculty of Biology at Moscow University ('biophysics' being a new word coined by him and his assistants to summarize the interaction between the physical forces that surround us all the time, and the normal working of our bodies).

This book, published in an English translation in 1970, is required reading in any modern bibliography on the subject. But even so, its findings are the subject of much caution and disbelief by Western scientists, including John Taylor, Professor of Mathematics at King's College in the University of London (and probably best known for his popular scientific book *Black Holes*). Professor Taylor, a friendly and readily-accessible man in his forties, is one of the few internationally-renowned scientists in the Western world who finds dowsing a subject worthy of serious research, and his own experiments (referred to on pages 152 and 226) are meticulously prepared and recorded. He thinks that generally far too many of the Russian experiments are not backed up by good statistical controls, and that in Presman's reports much of the evidence of, for instance, sickness, was obtained by subjective techniques such as interviews. Putting the US point of view, Paul Tyler has said: 'Soviet literature and standards have created a controversy in this country for several reasons: lack of personal contact with research personnel, difficulty in translating, and different basic philosophies on how research is presented in the open literature. The criticism has been that Soviet literature did not contain adequate details to permit the replication of the experiments. Although this is a valid criticism, our past publishing record is certainly not better.'

In spite of these caveats, the book was a milestone. Frank A. Brown Jr, Professor of Biology at Northwestern University, Evanston, Illinois, whose own work on circadian rhythms (see pages 137–8) is closely connected, introduced the translation with words showing that he, personally, was satisfied: 'The present convincing evidence is that living systems are steadily buffeted and stressed by the noisy fluctuations in the natural electromagnetic fields of their environment . . . organisms behave as specialized and very highly sensitive receptive systems for diverse parameters – strengths, frequencies, vector directions – of fields of the order of strength as the ambient natural ones.'

Again and again Professor Presman hammers home his point (although here, too, he is widely criticized for being both sweeping and vague). 'Organisms of the most diverse kinds – from unicellular organisms to man – are sensitive to . . . energy tens of orders [!] less than the theoretically estimated effective level.' 'Cumulative biological effects produced by repeated exposure to electromagnetic fields well below the effective threshold for a single exposure have also been observed.' 'Changes in tissues and organs are produced . . . in the absence of any significant thermal effect.' 'A very important feature of the biological effects is that they are often produced by fields of extremely low intensities.' 'Abundant experimental evidence directly confirming the role of environmental electromagnetic fields in life has been amassed in recent years.'

The experimental evidence quoted in his book suggests that there is virtually no organ or mechanism in the body which is not sometimes affected. Work on the brain, for instance, showed that structural changes took place in the brain cells of rabbits, cats, rats and guinea pigs when they were exposed to bursts of electromagnetic waves at a variety of frequencies. The affected areas included the crucial 'glia' cells that help conduct nerve impulses and are also possibly memory cells. Work on higher animals – monkeys – showed that their pulse rate, heart activity and central nervous system could be altered by strong constant magnetic fields; so were the embryos of frogs. A weak radiation at 2800 hertz caused the degeneration of a rat's testicles. In weak static magnetic fields, birds and fish became more alert and energetic.

So numerous and varied were the responses of all kinds of animals and humans to the experimental conditions that examples of this kind could be quoted from almost every one of the book's 275 pages. But perhaps the most extraordinary general finding is that often the effect on the nervous system is the exact reverse of what one might predict – Presman found time and again that weak fields had a greater effect than strong fields, and that over all the physiological changes were 'independent of electromagnetic intensity'. This was noticeably the case in a lengthy experiment with dogs, when there were significant changes in their conditioned reflex to salivate at a given signal.

Another paradox was the powerful evidence that exposure to low levels of radiation on repeated occasions had a cumulative effect, whereas the body seems to be able to adapt quickly to repeated 'doses' of strong fields. He speculated that each of these short bursts of weak electromagnetic energy had worked like a trigger within the body, setting off a chain reaction much stronger than the original impulse.

The other strange general finding is that the effects are often contradictory and irrational. With his dogs, for instance, those with so-called 'strong' personalities salivated faster when they had been exposed to radiation; those classified as 'nervous' salivated more slowly. Depending on the type of electromagnetic field applied, the rate of growth of mustard seeds was inhibited or increased. In fact, Presman's results are so all-embracing that it is too early for anyone to be able to make them the basis of any detailed hypothesis. What he has succeeded in demonstrating is that electromagnetic radiation at minute levels can have an effect on human life in many ways, for better or worse. It is a mark of how seriously this area of research is taken in Russia that their safety standards impose a level of microwave radiation strength on humans 1000 times less than that permitted in the USA.

Indeed, research in North America has only recently begun to catch up – but now it is doing so, it is confirming Presman's broad picture, and as the evidence grows, it becomes steadily less surprising that a dowser can, for instance, find true north, or identify the direction from which a radio beam is coming. Not only are these experimental results deeply fascinating, and perhaps revolutionary in their impact on the biological sciences, but through their complex analysis of the way in which the body reacts to minute levels of outside influences may come an understanding of the dowsing mechanism itself.

6 Rhythms of the Universe

Professor Frank A. Brown Jr, the biologist who introduced Presman's book to the Western public, is perhaps foremost among the handful of US scientists who have made pioneering discoveries about the way in which life reacts to minute levels of outside influences. Long convinced that unseen energies were playing a more important part in the behaviour of living things than anyone would recognize, he has performed since the 1950s an elaborate and careful series of tests which seem to prove that even under constant conditions of light, temperature, humidity and barometric pressure, all organisms have an internal biological clock and/or biological compass which enables them to maintain their regular rhythmic life patterns.[1]

The best-known example in man is jet-lag – the way in which we suffer if we are forced to change our normal pattern of waking and sleeping by moving quickly round the hemisphere. But as well as the solar day of twenty-four hours with which we must keep in tune, Frank Brown has discovered many more natural cycles that animals and plants live by: the sidereal day (the period of rotation of the earth relative to the stars) of 23·95 hours; the lunar tidal period of 12·4 hours and the lunar day of 24·8 hours; the lunar month of 29·53 days; and the solar year of 365·25 days. When he brought oysters, which feed and live according to a tidal cycle, from the coast of New England to his laboratories in Evanston, near Chicago, he found that after about a fortnight they were opening and closing according to the local phase of the moon. In spite of being kept in tanks of water too small for there to be a gross effect of tidal currents, they had somehow behaved like jet-plane travellers and adjusted themselves to their natural lunar rhythm.

If this was the first time it had been demonstrated that the passage of the moon could, by itself, affect a living creature, his work with potatoes was even more remarkable. These have been studied now for more than ten years in carefully controlled conditions that involve hermetically sealed rooms and no variations of atmosphere or light. Throughout this period, cut off from their natural environment, the potatoes have maintained the natural rhythm (for instance, growing and resting) of the sidereal day. Frank Brown has written how very small, but statistically significant biological fluctuations within that rhythm have been correlated with 'fluctuations of background radiation, primary cosmic radiation, and terrestrial magnetism'. It now seems certain that geo-electromagnetic forces, penetrating in small quantities into the otherwise sealed environment of the potatoes, are what enables them to keep to their sidereal rhythm.

Further work with animals has confirmed this view. Dr Brown has shown that mud snails can be drawn away from their normal paths by altering the strength and direction of the magnetic field around them. Insects orient themselves magnetically: cockroaches, bees, crickets and many flies always land, in calm weather, in a certain direction, irrespective of the position of the sun. Either increased or decreased field strength induces a change in the orientation of the bee dance on a honeycomb, and it generally takes about two hours before the bees are adjusted to the new strength. In another experiment, birds become livelier when placed in a stronger magnetic field than normal. It also upsets their circadian rhythm – instead of gradually decreasing their activity from morning to evening, there was a second maximum around 3 p.m.

In Germany, R. Wever studied the sleeping/waking circadian rhythms of 82 men in two specially constructed underground bunkers. In both bunkers, the normal environmental conditions of light, heat and so on, were kept constant; the only difference was that one bunker was shielded as much as possible from static magnetic and electromagnetic fields. While it is impossible to cut these fields out altogether, they were greatly reduced. The aim was to see if there was any effect on the sleeping/waking patterns of the volunteers.

They turned out to be considerable. In the control bunker, where magnetic fields still played their part, the main thing that happened was that the normal 24-hour daily cycle in men and women to which we are all accustomed, was increased by roughly an hour, probably because of the influence of constant light. The pattern remained remarkably steady throughout the experiment. But in the shielded bunker, it often took only a few days before sleep and activity patterns were grossly disturbed. In most cases, this could be corrected when a weak electromagnetic field of only 2·5 volts per metre oscillating at 10 hertz was introduced. According to Wever, this is 'the first significant proof that natural electromagnetic fields exercise an influence on human beings'.[2] The crucial importance of this 10-hertz frequency, naturally generated by the earth, was confirmed when experiments on rats and greenfinches at North Texas State University in 1972 showed precisely the same results. When the influence of the 10 cycles per second wavelength was removed, they became desynchronized just like humans.[3]

Electric healing

Another lone figure in the story of the Western world's belated recognition of the importance of electromagnetism in our lives is Dr Robert O. Becker, who joined the Veterans Administration Hospital at Syracuse, New York, in 1957, and since then has worked with spectacular success to show that, in his words, 'this field holds promise of containing the next great advance in biomedical science.'[4] It was his group which first related the disturbed behaviour of patients in mental hospitals with the occurrence of thunderstorms and the associated changes in magnetic field intensity. He says that, since he began 'the response to our reports has changed from complete rejection through amused disbelief to – at present – enthusiastic acceptance'.

His special interest is in the application of minute amounts of electricity, either DC or pulsed, to certain parts of the body, and he has listed some of the clinical effects that are currently being achieved. They include the more rapid healing of skin ulcers and bones, the promotion of anaesthesia and sleep, and an increase in the efficiency of acupuncture techniques. But his most astonishing work is to show that it may, before long, be possible to discover methods of electrical therapy that will enable humans to regenerate tissue in the same way as some animals – salamanders, for instance – can regrow an amputated limb.

He studied what is called the 'current of injury' – an electrical anomaly that always occurs at the site of a wound – and found that it was different in those species of animal which could, and could not regenerate a limb. The application of an almost unbelievably tiny, but very precise current (1–3m μamp) was able to correct this difference. When the current was applied to the amputated stumps of 21-day-old white rats it resulted, in a high proportion of cases, in them regrowing. In no case yet has there been a complete new leg, but on many occasions growth has continued to below the knee. Similar techniques are now being used to promote faster healing on broken bones in humans. Five New York doctors reported in 1971 how they had cured pseudarthrosis, a rare bone disease, in a fourteen-year-old boy by applying DC electrical current of less than half a volt continuously for 125 days. The alternative for the boy would have been amputation, and the doctors summarized: 'It is clear that electrical potentials play an important role in directing the architectural and structural development of bone.'[5]

With the increasing awareness of how delicate may be the equilibrium in which human life exists has come the worry that, because there is no immediately obvious or apparent effect caused by many of the electromagnetic waves to which we are exposed, we may be going beyond the threshold of safety without realizing it. Certainly, many dowsers find their reactions are confused or erroneous in the presence of power stations or rooms where there is electrical disturbance, which may be one reason why experiments in television studios so often go wrong. Robert Becker spends a great deal of his time nowadays preparing evidence for US Government commissions to warn of the potential danger of the too-fast development of more electronic or electric equipment. 'I feel great concern about the continuous exposure of the entire North American population to an electromagnetic environment in which is present the possiblity of inducing currents or voltages comparable with those now known to exist in biological control systems. I believe that it should be subject to the same types of controls imposed on the use of experimental drugs.'

Project Sanguine[6] is a space-age communications set-up that has been put under intense observation and criticism in the United States. Its purpose is to transmit high priority messages to submerged submarines and other US Forces anywhere in the world, in the event of a nuclear emergency. Operating at frequencies of less than 100 hertz, it involves transmission power of 20–30 megawatts, and a total antenna length (because the frequency is so low) of several hundred miles, split into segments. Wherever the Defense Department has tried to site it, there have been local protests. When a prototype was built and tested in an isolated area of the Chequamegon National Forest in Northern Wisconsin, there were complaints of psychological effects. In 1975, when the antenna was finally built and switched on, seagulls flying over it were observed to disperse randomly instead of heading off on their predicted migration path. Other observations on bird flocks have suggested that they fly unnaturally high over electric power lines, as if to avoid the electromagnetic field that they create. Russian caution about microwaves is also now being taken more seriously in the West. In 1972, some Italian workers in a furniture factory said they had become impotent after using machine tools operated by short-wavelength radiowaves. Recent experiments in the US have shown that the heart activity of chick embryos is affected by 24-gigahertz radiation, and that the development of insect pupae can be damaged by 10-gigahertz radiation.

Magnetism and life

The common thread of all this research is that there is some at present unknown mechanism within the body which is capable of reacting to many levels and frequencies of electromagnetic activity. The most comprehensive survey of this has been carried out by two former Hungarian physicists, Madeleine and Jena Barnothy, who turned to what they term 'biomagnetism' after fifteen years work in cosmic ray research was ended by the siege of Budapest, when the Russian soldiers used their cosmic ray telescopes for target shooting practice. After moving to the United States, she became Professor of Physics in the University of Illinois, and he became attached to the Biomagnetic Research Foundation at Evanston. Between 1961 and 1966 they arranged three international symposia on the subject, and Madeleine Barnothy edited an essential source book on the subject, *Biological Effects of Magnetic Fields*.[7] Like Harvalik and Rocard (the latter of whose work she published), they think that the solution to dowsing may come through a greater understanding of how humans sense changes in magnetic fields. Her work has concentrated on static magnetism, because she feels that with electromagnetic experiments, it is sometimes difficult to tell whether the effect is generated from outside or inside the body. 'Our aim was to find out whether magnetic fields affect biological functions, and I think we have shown that this is so. We purposely never used alternating magnetic fields (electromagnetism), because these alternating fields would generate induced currents in the biological system, and complicate thereby the evaluation of whether an observed effect is due to the magnetic field or not.'

Although it can be supposed that, in the work which they have described, the effects of weak fields have more relevance to the dowsing reaction than the strong ones, it is nevertheless worth reviewing the whole range because, as with Professor Presman, the sheer variety of results demonstrates once again the capacity of living beings to perform unsuspected wonders. For whether the whole body and behaviour of an animal is observed, or whether the effects are examined at a microscopic level, it is clear that something beyond the present knowledge of science is operating within us.

In experiments that have been summarized in a series of papers by the Barnothys, fields varying in strength from 1/1000 to 100,000 times the earth's natural level were used. Various physical effects are now indisputable. A field of 4000 gauss altered the haemoglobin count of blood in mice and rabbits. Very strong fields (100,000 gauss) produced major changes in the electrocardiograph readings measuring the heart activity in squirrel monkeys. In a 4200-gauss field, there was a drop in the body temperature of mice. A similar strength caused cellular changes in bacteria. Fish were trained to seek food on the application of a very weak field (10–30 gauss), applied for as little as ten seconds.

Already, the Barnothys have been able to identify some of the ways in which magnetism may be put to practical use in medicine before very long – and these are so remarkable that some scientists speculate whether they may be approaching the secret of life itself. For in a series of very careful experiments, it was shown that a strong magnetic field could retard ageing. Mice who spent the latter half of their gestation and their youth in a 4200-gauss field, at first appeared stunted and slow to grow. But by the time they had lived 400 days – the equivalent of 80 years in humans – they had a much younger appearance, with smooth, unwrinkled fur. Not only did they look younger, but they behaved younger – their activity level was on average 36 per cent higher, and they ate 26 per cent less food.

Just as promising, the rate of breast cancer, normally 98 per cent in this strain of mice, dropped to 40 per cent in the magnetically treated sample. This led to further experiments that show magnetism to have a dramatic effect in curing or minimizing cancer and leukaemia. Ten mice into which carcinoma had been transplanted were split into two groups. All five untreated mice died within fifteen–twenty-five days; four of the magnetically treated mice rejected the tumour completely within a few days, and the growth of the tumour in the fifth mouse was substantially slowed. In another experiment in the Barnothys' laboratory, cancer in mice was slowed down sufficiently to give the mice an extra two months of life. 'This finding raised the hope that although the magnetic field could not heal the animal, the time while the tumour growth was arrested could be used for the successful application of other known therapeutic methods, chemical or radiative,' they say.

In Chicago University's pathology department, fifty-seven mice were injected with leukaemia cells. All thirty-two untreated mice died from leukaemia within four weeks. Only seven of the remainder, all of which were treated in a static magnetic field of 32,000 gauss, died within that time, and two of these were for causes other than leukaemia. The remaining mice lived on, completely cured.

Yet more experiments have suggested that magnetic treatment may one day be applied to abortions (the foetuses of mice are resorbed into the uterus if placed in a strong field very early in pregnancy) and as an anaesthetic – the application to lizards of a field 5000 times that of the earth's has been shown by Robert Becker to reduce consciousness and alter the electroencephalograph pattern to one resembling moderate to deep anaesthesia.

Similar work with a variety of animals has shown an increase on the EEG tracings of the alpha brainwaves; these are the same rhythms that dominate in some states of altered consciousness, such as transcendental meditation.

This explosion of interest in electromagnetic radiation in all its forms – static, herzian, radio, microwave, infra-red and beyond – is now of such momentum that Paul Tyler has described the increase as 'more than a quantum jump'. Yet the over-all impression is that there is no coherence either to the research or the results. Many experiments cannot be replicated. And everywhere, there is a sense of tampering with the unknown – that the newly-discovered effects of electromagnetism are far-reaching, and even revolutionary, but as yet highly unpredictable in their effect. For instance, in one experiment, pigeons became livelier when the earth's magnetic field was increased; but when Robert Becker tested some mental patients in a similar field (10–20 times that of the earth, modulated at 0·1–0·2 hertz), their reaction time was slowed. In 60,000-gauss fields, monkeys stopped punching a lever for food. Mice placed in a much-reduced field of 100 gamma have been shown to become less active, more docile, to lie in unusual positions, develop alopecia (baldness), signs of premature ageing, and to die early – whereas with those in strong (4200 gauss) field, as we have just seen, the opposite happened. Moreover, carefully conducted as the weak field experiment was, it has not been successfully repeated. Similarly with research on the fish *Rhodeus ocellatus*: depending on which way the fish were placed relative to the direction of the magnetic field, contrary results happened – either very large increases, or similar decreases, in growth took place. The truth is that research into the area is relatively so young, nobody is quite sure where it will lead. For instance, a supposed break-through was announced in 1971, when it was found that application of microwaves to the nests of Leghorn chickens increased their egg production substantially; unfortunately, it was later also discovered that the death rate in the radiated hens was double that of those in their normal environment.

The receiving mechanism

The first great theoretical problem to be overcome is that of discovering just how the body can sense these weak fields and then transmit their information within the body. Orthodox science has taught that we have certain biosensors – eyes, ears, nerve-endings – on the periphery of the body, and that any stimulus which is noticed by these is transmitted through the central nervous system, which processes the information and dictates the appropriate form of action for the body to take. The central nervous system consists of two main parts – the spinal column, along which all the impulses track, and the brain, which recognizes the information and interprets it. The five normal senses are sight, hearing, touch, smell and taste; the stimuli which make them come to life include light, sound, pressure, gravity, vibration, injury, cold, heat, and acceleration.

It has long been apparent that some creatures have additional ways of communicating with one another, and perceiving information. The biologist J. Bigu del Blanco, working at Queen's University in Kingston, Ontario, Canada, says that among the more striking and unusual methods are 'sonar techniques (bats, etc.), electric field scanning and sensing (certain fish), temperature scanning (some snakes), sensing by means of chemicals (silkworms), sensing by movement, or ritualization (monkeys, bees, etc.). There are a variety of different known methods of communication but there are also a great number of cases in which the information transfer mechanism is far from being clear.'[8]

The principal difficulty here is that by all standard calculations, the information being radiated into the body by many of these unorthodox means – including electromagnetism – are much too feeble, in theory, to be noticed. Madeleine Barnothy has written how even a strong magnetic field – say, 50,000 times the strength of the field produced by the earth – transfers about 100 times less energy to a molecule than the energy formed by the normal heat of the human body. So, theoretically, any effect of magnetism on a molecule should be quickly over-ridden and randomized by thermal energy.

But we know, from all the experiments quoted above, that this is not so – weak electromagnetic fields have an undeniable effect on living beings. Therefore, says Bigu, there are only three possible explanations:

1. Electromagnetic radiation must interact directly with the

central nervous system, perhaps at the molecular level;

2. Our five known senses must respond to wider frequency ranges than they have yet been observed to do, through some mechanism that we do not yet fully understand;

3. There is a completely new kind of radiation, which science has not yet discovered, but which the body instinctively recognizes.

To most scientists, the third possibility is simply another way of asking them to look for a phenomenon that defies all the known laws of particle physics; moreover, one which so far has given no hint of its existence. So it seems to them fruitless to pursue a search for something that has not even given a clue as to where in the framework of knowledge it could one day, hypothetically, appear.

As for the second possiblity, Alexandr Presman has collected evidence of the effects of electromagnetic radiation on the normal sense organs of people. These include some of the experiments and observations already described, such as the phosphene effect of a bar magnet pressed against the temple, and the ability of some people to hear radar directly. He also mentions cases where people have described sensations of itchiness or soreness on the skin of their faces or arms when living near long-wave radio stations (14·7 kilohertz), and somewhat vague reports of drowsiness and weakness among people exposed to centimetre-long waves of very low intensity.

But generally, the way in which the peripheral sense organs function is now so well analysed and understood that almost every scientist interested in the subject looks to the first possibility for the answer. Non-ionizing electromagnetic radiation, carrying the relevant information and penetrating the barrier of the skin, must somehow act directly on the organs beneath. Nearly all the ideas involve suggesting how, just possibly, the molecular balance may be disturbed by weak radiation in such a way that the energy maintains or gathers momentum as it passes from nerve cell to nerve cell through the central nervous system. Madeleine Barnothy has summarized more than a dozen of these possible explanations; all of them are on the outermost fringes of knowledge of how physics, chemistry and biology combine.

Although none yet provides a complete model, probably the

most promising approach stems originally from the work of the Yale University Professor of Astronomy Harold S. Burr,[9] who discovered as far back as 1949 that each nerve is surrounded by what he termed a life field (or L-field), consisting of a measurable quantity of electricity. His work is still controversial in part, but other experimenters have repeated his results, and Robert Becker in turn has suggested that each cell may work like an electrical semiconductor, with biological transistors making the connections between them.

The hypothesis was put more technically at a congress on bio-communication held in Aspen, Colorado, in 1973:

> There is evidence for solid-state electron conduction mechanisms in living systems, which could easily be adapted to the reception of electromagnetic signals, both low-frequency and high-frequency. There is evidence for semiconduction in protein, which is involved directly in enzyme function in certain cases. There is evidence that p–n junctions in living systems are directly involved in photo-biological processes, such as photosynthetic processes and free-radical decay in the eye; these are at membranes and particle surfaces. There is also evidence for this kind of thing in pigmented nerves of invertebrates. In addition, there is evidence for superconductive junctions, which are known to be extremely sensitive detectors of electromagnetic radiation. So the framework of knowledge for detection by solid-state mechanisms already present in the body is available in present-day solid-state electronics.

> Another delegate had a theory of how genetic changes could come about by an exchange of information within a species or population: 'You can regard DNA molecules as radio-frequency signal generators, RNA molecules as amplifiers, the cell wall as a noise filter, and enzymes and amino acids as effectors of signals coded in various regions of the spectrum.'

In other words, every one of us may be a living, breathing wireless transmitter/receiver.

If that is the case, the next question that arises is on which frequencies we may function best, and here again profound theoretical difficulties arise. As we have seen, there is the problem of penetration – if organs deep within our body are indeed capable of sensing weak electromagnetic waves, then these waves have to be of sufficient length to pierce the barrier of the skin. This effectively rules out any that oscillate at more than about 10 gigahertz, where penetration at the kind of natural strengths being discussed would be only about 0·3–1 centimetre, depending on the type of tissue. Going down the spectrum from here, the longer the wavelength becomes, the more easily it can penetrate tissue – in fact at 1000 hertz and less, the human body is virtually transparent so far as electromagnetic radiation is concerned. But at the same time, and in direct proportion, the power drops, so that progressively less and less information is carried by these long wavelengths. There is the additional problem, when suggesting them as a partial solution to dowsing, that it is absolutely impossible for any frequency to carry information about an object smaller than the length of its wave – the radiation simply pulses round the object without noticing it. Suppose the dowsers were trying to pick up the minute level of electromagnetic radiation emanating from a gold ring lost in the sand: then, as shown in diagram 1, the frequency of this length would be around 20 gigahertz – and here, as we have seen, the radiation simply would not penetrate the skin, nor be emitted outwards through the skin (as would be needed in, for instance, telepathy). Nor has anyone yet found a sign of sufficiently sensitive sensors on the surface of the skin. So the whole question of just where in the spectrum may lie an effective frequency raises paradoxes – impossibilities, some say – that are nowhere near being satisfactorily resolved.

Nevertheless, in spite of the formidable problems, many ingenious solutions have been proposed. Some of the most fascinating concentrate on the lowest end of the scale – from 5000 hertz down to near-zero – since these are the frequencies that have been measured as emitting from various parts of the body. If it could be shown that information on these wavelengths were received, transmitted or exchanged between one person and another, or between one person and an object, it would be theoretically satisfying, since there is a law of physics which says that the maximum energy exchange between two physical systems happens when both have identical natural frequencies. When this happens, says Juan Bigu, 'they approximate the classical case of two coupled oscillators'.

Sympathetic resonance

A few clues are emerging that we are indeed sensitive and responsive within this frequency range. There is a particularly compelling frequency around 10 hertz, known as the Schumann resonance. It is here that the earth's own magnetic field pulses most strongly; and here that the dreamy, meditative alpha rhythms of the human brain predominate. A relationship between the two has been suggested by many researchers, including Professor Michael Persinger of Laurentian University. He made a study[10] of reported cases of telepathy and other forms of extra-sensory perception, and found that there was an above average incidence during the hours surrounding midnight; it is at this time (whatever the longitude) that the earth's field is strongest.

Two other scientists, the biologist Dr Francis Cole of the Alton Ochsner Medical Foundation in New Orleans, Louisiana, and Dr E. R. Graf, of the electrical engineering department in Auburn University, Alabama, have published another discussion on how a 10-hertz frequency may be the key to the evolution of life on this planet.[11] Noting the difficulty which biologists have had in synthesizing the macromolecules of living tissue that must have emerged originally from inorganic chemicals, they have suggested that at one time a giant earth-ionosphere resonance cavity pulsating at 10 hertz existed between the surface of our planet and the van Allen belts of radiation in space.

> For millions of years, evolutionary changes in protein structure would have had to conform to the dynamics of a 10-hertz external field . . . Proteins thus evolved would be remarkably sensitive to low frequency electromagnetic events in much the same way that a more complex evolutionary form, the eye, has evolved to be sensitive to that region of the electromagnetic spectrum to which it was constantly exposed, the visible region of solar radiation.

149

Thus, at the most fundamental level of life, they believe we and all other living things have an inherited sympathy to a wavelength on which we might send or receive signals. They say that the essential elements of this signal would be that it:

(1) is common to all, and between all, life forms, i.e., plant to plant, plant to animal, even cell to cell;
(2) is transmitted and received with energies available to life systems, again even with the energy between a single cell;
(3) is unattenuated between great distances, the atmosphere, oceans and the usual conducting materials;
(4) is not present in, but may be affected by, inanimate objects;
(5) can contain codified information.

Few scientists would disagree that these must be the hypothetical characteristics of such a signal. The difficulty comes in imagining how a sufficiently large amount of power, and a sufficiently large aerial to transmit or receive, could exist to make a low frequency communication system work. At 10 hertz, the wavelength is 30,000 kilometres (slightly less than the circumference of the earth). Professor John Taylor has suggested that somehow the brain may act as a folded aerial – if each of the thousand million nerve cells in the cerebral cortex, with their tiny projections known as axons, were laid end to end, they would total 1000 kilometres. 'Something of this sort must occur,' he says. 'Otherwise it is very difficult to imagine an aerial of body length, or even a few metres, being excited by these enormously long wavelengths.'

As for the power involved, and the ability of people and animals to distinguish such a signal from the noise of background radiation, all the recent evidence shows that we just do not know how sensitive we may be. Francis Cole points out that the human ear can react to a motion no greater than the diameter of a hydrogen molecule. 'We are aware of the fact that the system we are proposing would be radiating only minute amounts of radiation. However, when one has a very sensitive and highly evolved receiving system the signal does not have to be that strong. What we are proposing is that proteins evolved under the influence of this frequency, and thus both the transmitter and receiver are exclusively matched to one another and can discriminate this signal from random environmental noise.'

Nevertheless, even if some sort of communication between one being and another exists at the low frequency level, it still contains great limitations as to its use. Dr Bigu believes it may be confined to the mechanism used by primitive cellular forms to avoid collision, and perhaps partially to explain the phenomenon of simultaneous changes in direction by schools of fish. In these cases, weak electromagnetic signals carrying a small amount of information (very low frequency waves) would perhaps be sufficient for the purpose. But for anything more precise or sophisticated, a shorter wavelength is needed – and here, attention is beginning to be focused on the properties of the microwave region of the spectrum.

Animal sensitivity to the microwave frequencies is now well established. They can sense the microwave energy generated by a tornado well ahead of any physical change in the weather. It has been speculated that this, the use of microwaves, is how many species are able to communicate and find their way to one another over long distances – how a cat or a dog, for instance, can sometimes track its way over a continent to find its way back home.

Some of the most detailed studies have concerned the near-simultaneous turning and wheeling of huge bird flocks. Long a baffling phenomenon, the use of high-speed movie film has now proved once and for all that something more than a sound, or a visual signal, is involved. When the film is analysed frame by frame, it can be seen that as many as 50,000 birds can turn in synchrony in about 1/70th of a second. Were the birds playing follow-my-leader, either watching or listening for a signal, a wave effect would appear through the flock, and this is rarely the case. Also, when a flock reverses direction, the presumed leader would then be at the back, where any visual signal which he gave could not be seen by his 'followers' in front.[12]

So investigators began to wonder whether a form of instant communication using electromagnetic waves might be the answer. As long ago as 1931, the British scientist E. Selons wrote an article entitled 'Thought Transference (Or What?) in Birds'. The odd behaviour of sea-gulls over the aerial of Project Sanguine was an indication that they were more sensitive than had been thought; similarly in Germany, some native birds were observed to return to their natural nesting place near an airport only after the radar had broken down. Alexandr Presman speculated that there might be two ways in which electromagnetic orders from the leader of the flock might operate. In the first, the signal would go out, all birds would simultaneously receive it, then instantly process the message in their central nervous systems, and act accordingly. Alternatively, the signal might somehow act directly on the neuromuscular system, changing the whole flock into a kind of 'superindividual' acting as one.

Whether or not there is a signal, or a leader, is still not resolved. Dr Cesar Romero-Sierra, working with Dr Bigu in Ontario on the problem of birds colliding with aeroplanes, has established that the movement in the flock may be involuntary. Shifts in the strength of the electromagnetic field can be detected through a highly complex mechanism in the birds' feathers, which are capable of acting as radiowave and microwave receivers and transmitters. In practice, what happens is that if the field is strong to the right-hand side of the bird, the left-hand side of the bird automatically weakens momentarily. In flight, this is what may cause the apparently patternless dipping and wheeling of the flock – the birds can't help performing in that way, since they are responding unconsciously to an electromagnetic stimulus.

The larger unanswered question is whether man, too, is unconsciously using the microwave range of frequencies for some of his more unusual activities, such as dowsing. Dr Bigu, in a series of experiments designed to distinguish between the theoretically predictable level of radiation, and that actually produced, has shown that all creatures, including humans, naturally emit microwave radiation in significant quantities relative to the background. Although his experiments have not been confirmed, and he himself has not yet detected a non-thermal component experimentally, he is on record as believing that radio waves and microwaves 'play an important role in biocommunication'. Dr Eduardo Balanovski, an Argentinian colleague of Professor John Taylor, told a Parascience Congress in London in 1976 that after many fruitless experiments through the spectrum right up to far infra-red frequencies, there at last seemed to be some promising early results with measurements made at 19 gigahertz. Here, changes of mood – from contentment to anger, for instance – were accompanied by sharp changes in the level of 19-gigahertz radiation. But, as with Dr Bigu, he has not been able to repeat these results consistently.

The electromagnetic dilemma

So it has to be said at the moment that the evidence, from anywhere in the world, is tantalizingly thin. What characterizes such scientists is their persistence in conducting their work within the known framework of science – they believe that the evidence for dowsing and thought transference is too strong to be denied, and they are convinced that it must be fitted into the accepted parameters of knowledge. Dr Bigu, while concentrating on electromagnetic radiation, says that 'a more complete theory should take into account nuclear, electromagnetic, "weak", gravitational, acoustical, and chemical interactions, to name but a few.' Nevertheless, painstakingly complicated though it may be to construct such a model for psi phenomena, he believes it is the only way. 'The alternative, of developing a theory containing unknown forms of energy and unusual properties of matter to suit observed phenomena, seems unjustified at this stage and without much promise.'

Professor Taylor is even more emphatic.

Most people who try to invent new force fields or revolutionary theories of physics simply don't know how satisfying the present state of knowledge really is. Of course, there are dramatic and exciting things happening in science, with important new discoveries being made every year. But they are often discoveries that we have predicted from existing knowledge – we find that a fundamental particle that theoretically ought to exist, really does. We now have a very good and convincing explanation of what happens in all bodies down to 10^{-15} centimetre in size. We have to fill in many areas: for instance, finding out just how sensitive living things are to electromagnetism, and the mechanism which enables them to react. But that's what it is – filling in. Once we have a better picture, there is little reason to suppose that it won't include dowsing, telepathy and the rest.

But still, there are aspects of dowsing which even the most optimistic physical scientist finds it hard to accept, let alone understand and explain. Dr Arthur Bailey, President of the British Society of Dowsers, told a meeting in 1975 that, although a scientist himself, he had been through all the possible scientific explanations and found them unsatisfactory. 'They certainly don't explain the weirdies, like map-dowsing.' When asked to identify which specific laws of physics were contradicted by his dowsing successes, he named two; and if he is right, we can be sure that electromagnetic radiation is at best only a partial answer to how dowsing works.

The first is that dowsing seems, sometimes, to defy the laws of space/time. For instance the length of time it takes to get an answer from a pendulum is unaffected by distance – you can ask a question about life on Mars, and the pendulum will react as quickly as if you were asking about life in the local supermarket. Moreover, there is the phenomenon that the dowsing literature identifies as 'remanence': you may be dowsing for something – hidden treasure, a missing person, a well – and you have a strong pendulum reaction. Yet when you check out the site, you find nothing – but some time ago, even centuries ago, exactly what you are looking for was indeed there.

The second, says Dr Bailey, is the inverse square law – or more broadly, the set of laws that explains how radiated energy steadily decreases with distance. For Arthur Bailey and many other dowsers, the reaction is just as strong over a map as on site; and on site, his reaction fails to get stronger as he approaches the point being sought. Now if he were picking up the very long wavelengths (up to about 100 hertz) of electromagnetic radiation, this would perhaps not be surprising: they circle the earth with scarcely any diminution of power. But as we have seen, they are much too long to convey information about an earth fault/underground stream that may be only six inches wide. Something as small as this would need the precision of a microwave of at least one gigahertz – and here, even a commercial broadcasting station would not expect to send a signal more than about 50 kilometres; and the emission from something as indistinct as an underground stream would perhaps be only a few feet. There may be freak exceptions on the way the inverse square law works (recently, it was found that under certain conditions waves of 70 megahertz could be picked up as a 'second echo' after a complete circuit of the earth, which nobody had thought possible), but in general it would have to be fitted into any electromagnetic explanation of dowsing.

So we have a classic dilemma. The best answer that science is likely to provide already looks inadequate for the facts as reported by dowsers. Faced with the dilemma, the two sets of people tend to take contrary ways of explaining it. The dowser's attitude is generally to say: we know it works, and if science can't find out how it works, no matter. The scientist, on the other hand, would first be sceptical about the dowser's subjective conclusions, and then try to deal with each case one by one to see if there was truly a common phenomenon that defied the known laws.

For if there is, it would be very worrying to science indeed; and of all the candidates, map-dowsing is the most troublesome. During my visit to the Barnothys' home in Evanston, in which we discussed how map-dowsing might work, Jena Barnothy uttered a plea that deserves to be published in full, for it shows just how strongly a good scientist feels when confronted with an impossibly difficult concept:

'If it doesn't have a law, then we are lost. Our lives are dedicated, we keep ourselves alive, to investigate and understand the laws of nature. It would be hard for us to give up and say there is no point in our work because there are things which are completely outside . . . it would mean that all our endeavours, our ambitions, our idealism are in vain because they are meaningless.

'The phenomena of physics, astronomy, chemistry and biology are all being explained by these laws – so why should we be looking for a further force? With so many things explained, why haven't we come across indications of this other force?

'If you tell me that a man can sit on the other side of the Atlantic and look at a map and receive information about something not shown on the map . . . it is impossible. A map can give no clues. It is outside the laws of physics.

'All the four forces of nature decrease with distance – either with the square of distance or the cube of distance. If it is magnetism that a dowser picks up, then it is the cube of the distance from the magnetic dipole. If you start with a magnet of ten gauss in strength, then at one metre distance it is one thousand times less. At ten metres it is one thousand times less again. So in England the anomaly would be a billion billion billion times less – I can't imagine how small it would be. It's just not possible in physics. The most sensitive magnetometer we have couldn't do it, not by orders of many, many billions.'

And then:

'If your dowser can really pin-point something on a map . . . well, it is supernatural.'

Which is, of course, what a dowser like Bill Lewis in Abergavenny does habitually – and what he did for me in an exhaustive research project in 1976.

Part Three: the Psi Connection

No honest scientist can now publish a book on physics without a metaphysical epilogue.
– Arthur Koestler.

7 Inter-continental Experiment

The experiment began with my need to find out about the mega-liths of North America – the strange prehistoric standing stones, burial chambers, rocking stones and so on that are spread throughout New England, and which seem set to become one of the major archaeological controversies of the next decade. Until recently, very little has been written about these sites; indeed, the majority of people in the United States are almost certainly un-aware of their existence. But they are much more than a curiosity. They show such a marked similarity with some of the megalithic sites in Western Europe (which culminated at Stonehenge) that there is now speculation that they were built by the same people. In which case, there would have to have been transatlantic sea crossings by 2000–1500 BC – a date which is unbelievably early, according to orthodox academic thinking.[1]

One difficulty in finding out more about these sites lies in the lack of basic information. Most archaeologists dismiss them as root cellars built by colonial farmers, or as gateposts, and there-fore have not bothered to identify or map them. Although this is not the place to go deeply into the pros and cons of the argument, it should perhaps be noted that this may be yet another example of Occam's Razor being wielded in a way that precludes a full explanation: without doubt, there is much evidence of colonial use of the structures; but anybody looking carefully at the way that many of the 'root cellars' (stone tombs?) were built with huge stones, weighing many tons, and fitted together with subtlety and precision, must be in some doubt as to how a colonial farmer would have found the time and energy to build such a structure, or why he should have bothered. It would seem much more likely that he found them there, built in some earlier time, and gratefully made use of them.

So for a stranger wanting to examine these stones, official

information is somewhat hard to come by. A number of amateur prehistorians in the area have begun the job of cataloguing the sites. But by and large, they keep the detailed locations to themselves, for fear of having them vandalized; landowners are equally reticent, not wanting a horde of tourists. Since I was going to the area in any case, I decided to see if a good dowser could guide me to any of them. At this stage, it wasn't a map-dowsing experiment in a scientific or statistical sense. It was simply a matter of need.

The dowser in question was Bill Lewis, with whom I had been making a film about prehistoric stones near his home in South Wales. He has long been fascinated by the way in which he senses they were sited, instinctively and universally, in certain sacred places where there are special qualities or emanations that can still be felt by sensitive people today. To him, the feeling of power and ancient sanctity at a standing stone or burial mound is as impressive as the nave of a cathedral – perhaps more so, since the sites in Western Europe were chosen when man was emerging for the first time as a settled farmer, before he could read and write, before religion was institutionalized, and when he perhaps had a knowledge of the universe and its rhythms that was lost with the arrival of literacy and the development of intellect.

This general belief is shared by many dowsers, and it is important to the experiment because, in a dowsing sense, Bill Lewis knew what he was looking for. When the time came to search the maps for ancient sacred sites, he had very many years of experience in visiting them, at least in Britain. As a professional map-dowser, he is also highly experienced. Many of the jobs he does are passed on to him by the secretary of the British Society of Dowsers, and they come from many parts of the world. They may involve trying to find the whereabouts of something that has been stolen, or a lost dog; or a request for water on a parched and arid site anywhere in the world; or for information about pipes or cables or historic treasure buried deep beneath the ground.

There are scores of these in Bill Lewis's files, and it is instructive to look at the first far-distant one he attempted. It is recorded on the copy of a 1:1000 map of a farmstead in Australia from which he was asked to find out if there was any good water, and if so where. Geologists in the area had assured the owner that there was nothing but a brackish and undrinkable layer lying some thirty feet below the surface, and a sample bore-hole had shown this to be the case.

When I got the map, the first thing I thought was: how the hell do I go about this job? I didn't have much doubt that if good water was there it should be possible to find it, but all sorts of questions began to clutter up my mind; remember, it was the first time I had tried to find something in Australia. I got worried because it was the other side of the world. Should I have the map upside down? Should I reverse it so that south was north? If it was a radiation I was picking up from all that distance, would there be a two or three second delay? Would the radiation get weaker as it travelled, and give me confused information?

In the end, he made a conscious decision to put all these worries at the back of his mind, and just treat it as a normal map-dowsing job. (This is, of course, a mis-use of the way in which most of us use the word 'normal', but to Bill Lewis and others like him, it is appropriate enough.) When he starts to dowse, he goes through a marked change in his state of consciousness. A detached air of concentration comes over him, rather as if he was trying to pick up a faint signal from a distant loudspeaker, and although he often carries on a fluent commentary to describe what he is finding, he prefers not to have too many questions or comments put back at him until he has finished a particular area of search. Like Bob Ater, he can use a pencil to mark the map with what looks to the outsider like a form of automatic writing; however, he says it is not this – more, he is consciously sensing the position or direction of what he is seeking. On this particular occasion, he drew the direction of two underground streams that, undetected by the geologists, seemed to run beneath the Australian property. Next, by questioning – is it good water? how deep is it? and so on – established the best place to site the well; and then predicted that there would be clear water 37 feet down producing a quantity of 600 gallons a day.

I was just about 100 per cent right. I had a letter saying I was a couple of feet out with the depth, but as I didn't visit the site, I don't know whether they put the drill exactly where I marked it. If they were two or three yards away, it could easily account for the error. In any case, the farmer's still getting his water.

When it came to dowsing for megalithic sites in New England, the first session lasted for about ten minutes, working over an Official Transportation Map of the state of Vermont, sent to me by friends and not seen by Bill Lewis until then; from this he dowsed the supposed position of a stone circle and a burial chamber. In order to achieve more accuracy, so that when I reached the area I would be able to map-read a point sufficiently closely to say whether the megaliths existed or not, we decided to order up one-inch, and where possible two-and-a-half-inch, US Geological Survey maps of the relevant sections.

It was at this point that I realized this could be potentially the most thorough and extended test of map-dowsing yet undertaken; and then and there, decided to make it so. The purpose of the experiment became, fundamentally, to show whether map-dowsing works, and if so how well one particular dowser could do it – whether Bill Lewis was able, using nothing other than a map, to provide information not indicated on the map and not obtainable by chance.

Experimental method
I aimed to collect as much verifiable information as possible from Bill Lewis, and then compare it with similar information obtained by random guesswork. In this way, I would ultimately have two sets of photographs, descriptions and measurements: one of Bill Lewis's predictions of what I would find when I visited the sites he had chosen, and the other of the matching control sites. A comparison between the two would potentially give a significant statistical result (which in the event it did).

To forestall any suggestions that Bill Lewis might be giving me information that he knew already, the maps were ordered by me directly from the US Geological Survey or other US map suppliers, and were not shown to Bill Lewis until the map-dowsing session.

162

All these sessions (a further two, lasting a total of just over three hours) took place in a small office in his home near Abergavenny, and were tape-recorded. As soon as he had identified a site which sounded interesting and relatively accessible, I asked him for additional details – height, orientation, etc. – both to help me identify it, and to provide additional features to fill out the experiment. As the sessions advanced and Bill Lewis began to know better what sort of information I was looking for, he tended to volunteer more sites and more details without being asked. I noted these, together with his answers to my direct questions, and typed them in the form of a record as soon as possible after the session. These were witnessed and dated by a lawyer, and posted to the Society for Psychical Research to be filed for safe keeping. They contain all map references of sites subsequently visited. The three sessions took place on 17 February, 13 and 31 March 1976; my visit to the United States began on 13 April.

Bill Lewis's method of map-dowsing is to fix in his mind what he is looking for – in this case, say, 'an ancient megalithic site', or 'a standing stone', or 'a burial chamber' – and to run an index finger north-south down the left-hand side of the map until it meets what he describes as a slight resistance or stickiness, and then to work left-right across the bottom of the map until the same thing happens. The point where the horizontal and vertical lines from these points meet is now his area of interest, and next, holding a short pendulum made of thread and a wooden bob in his right hand, and a sharp pencil in his left, he works the pencil around and inwards towards this point until he is satisfied he has marked the site as accurately as he is able.

Although there is a somewhat distant air of concentration about Bill Lewis as he works, the tape-recording shows the sessions to have been fairly talkative affairs, punctuated by silences of half a minute or so while he was searching for a response. In general terms, the sessions were controlled by me, in the sense that I would open a map and ask him, for instance: 'Can you find the largest standing stone in this area?', or 'Is there a burial chamber near here that I can comfortably walk to?', at which Bill Lewis would grumble under his breath about my wanting to have everything the easy way.

Once he had pin-pointed a spot that seemed to him promising, information about it emerged from him with the kind of mordant humour that is peculiarly Welsh. 'A burial chamber with spiral markings you want, is it? . . . (pause) . . . What about this, then? They must have put it here for you. Look at it, right in the neck of the river bend . . . (pause) . . . You won't even have to get your feet wet, you lucky devil. It's all silted up.'

'Which way is it oriented, Bill? How big is it?'

'Orientation? . . . (pause) . . . north-west, south-east . . . Mound's visible all right, you can see it above the ground . . . Capstone's all broken and silted up . . . you can see the stones, though, they're sticking above the surface.'

All the time, his pendulum moved, giving him yes/no indications to his unspoken questions.

Finally, we had a list of 22 sites, for each of which were a number of detailed predicted features. These were divided into visual features (size, position, etc). that ought to be capable of immediate verification, and archaeological features (dating, buried objects, etc.), some of which might be proved at a later date if the sites existed, and were properly excavated. Because of the limited time available during the visit, I decided only to look for the visual predictions, and these were collated into a master list containing 63 predictions.

Stage two was to make a random list of predictions similar to those of Bill Lewis, so that should anything that he had map-dowsed turn out to be really where he said it was, I would have a statistical check that he was not getting his result by chance. At a meeting on 2 April, the chairman of the ESP committee of the Society for Psychical Research, John Stiles, took the same maps that Bill Lewis had used, and marked on them – just guessing – where he thought a matching site would be. Thus where Bill Lewis said there was a 10′ 6″ standing stone, John Stiles suggested there was a 5′ 7″ standing stone at another point perhaps half a mile away, and so on. These, with their map references, were similarly filed at the Society for Psychical Research, and were labelled 'Check Sites'.

In the end, I was unable to visit all the sites. In Vermont the snows had just melted, and some of the forested mountains were impenetrable; in South Dakota, some of the sites I had originally hoped to find were too remote for the time available; and in

Arizona, the roads were too bad. But I was able to record my findings at 55 visual features predicted by Bill Lewis, and at 43 matching predictions from the guesswork check list. The features were photographed, and measured with a tape when necessary.

I have compared, or scored them, in two ways. In the first, each prediction is classified as a hit, a query, or a miss. A hit was when there was no possible doubt, or when it was reasonable to say that there was a good match between the prediction and the feature; a query when there were positive but ambiguous indications; and a miss when there was nothing, or such a generalized success that the prediction was meaningless.

This is a somewhat arbitrary division, giving a rough and ready analysis of the results, although it has the virtue that it can be used by people who have not visited the sites concerned. The second way is more subjective, because it depends on personal observation and assessment, but is also more sensitive. I have scored 10 points for what I regard as a faultless prediction. Points are then knocked off for inaccuracy, ambiguity, or the chance of another explanation.

How well did map-dowsing work on this occasion? Whichever way the results are scored, the percentages work out approximately the same. The random check list of predictions comes out around one per cent – exactly what would be expected from chance. Bill Lewis, on the other hand, scores in the 35–40 per cent bracket – a figure that seems at the same time conclusive and astonishing. He had significant success at 5 of the fourteen sites: 35 per cent. I scored 20 hits out of 55 predictions (36.4 per cent); on points, my evaluation is 40.7 per cent.

This is, by any standard, a positive finding. For the record, a full description of what I found on the predicted sites is given below; I have tried to give enough information for people to make their own assessment. The most successful predictions were at Sites one, four, seven, nine and nineteen.

Scoring by hits, queries, misses

SITE ONE

Prediction. Using a 1975 Official Transportation Map of Vermont, with a scale of five miles to one inch, Bill Lewis marked the site of where he thought a burial chamber could be found. He said it would be about 1600 feet above sea level, in fairly open countryside, with two small trees or shrubs growing out of it. It was very much damaged, and not in its original form.

At a later meeting, when a US Geological Survey map on a scale of 1:62,500 was available, it was immediately clear that two of Bill Lewis's predictions were true: the Transportation map had showed neither contours nor vegetation, which the Geological Survey map did; the spot behind the intersection of two country roads which he had marked was precisely at 1600 feet, and was in an open area surrounded by woods. At this meeting he refined his reading to say that some small stones protruded from the earth mound, which at its maximum would be about seven feet above the level of the surrounding ground.

Site description. A large holiday home had been built next to the road junction, and there were signs that this had disturbed the ground considerably. A considerable amount of local stone had been used in its construction, and this stone could also be found, presumably cleared from the fields by colonial farmers, in the dry stone walls that bordered the dust roads. Most of the area was thickly wooded. The exact position of the site marked by Bill Lewis was about fifty yards away from the house, in a field which had once been planted as an orchard, of which a few trees were still scattered here and there.

At first sight, looking from the direction of the house, there seemed to be nothing that might have been a burial mound. The ground appeared almost flat, dropping gently away towards the orchard. But looking back the other way, so that one was standing slightly below the level of the site, the ground was shaped in a way that corresponded more closely with Bill Lewis's description. For a distance of about thirty yards, there was a well-defined rise, at its maximum about seven feet above the general level of the ground; in the middle of it were two small trees, about fifteen feet high; and there were some small boulders where the mound fell away at its north-eastern end.

Evaluation. The elevation of the site, the choice of an open field in an otherwise wooded area, the position of the two small trees, and the height of the mound above ground level, were all remarkably accurate. But was it a burial mound? The 'mound' looked much more like a ridge, or terracing (although it may have been flattened when the house was built); and the prediction of small stones is so generalized, compared with the precise detail which Bill Lewis was able to forecast on other sites, that it is not worthy to be counted as a hit.

Score. Hits: Four.
      Queries: Two.
      Misses: Zero.

CHECK SITE ONE

Prediction. A burial mound would be found in the woods at a point about half a mile away from Site 1. Nearby would be a moss-covered stone wall, and a fallen tree. There would also be two flat stones 'reminiscent of steps'.

Site description. A typical, densely-wooded, Vermont hillside. Nothing to be seen of a mound. There was a stone wall alongside the lane near the site, but not at the site itself. There were many fallen trees, no flat stones as described.

Evaluation. Only the prediction of a fallen tree was accurate, and this (like Bill Lewis's small stones) is so generalized that it ought to be discarded, or at best given a query.

Score. Hits: Zero.
      Queries: One.
      Misses: Three.

SITES TWO AND THREE

Prediction. To the south-west of the small village of Gaysville, Vermont, there would be a standing stone, 5′ 4″ tall, with Indian markings on the face; the lowest markings being 3′, the highest 4′ 6″. A quarter-mile further on would be an ancient burial ground, with a visible mound.

Site description. The narrow road from Gaysville winds

above the White River, with steep, wooded mountains rising to the right, and a sharp fall to the river on the left. No standing stone was found. The site of the burial ground lies beyond the end of the road, where there is now a summer camping area with wooden huts. No mound could be seen, and the clearing in the position marked is so flat and level that it ought to have been readily visible.

Score.   Hits: Zero.
            Queries: Zero.
            Misses: Five.

CHECK SITES TWO AND THREE

Prediction.   At points on hillsides approximately half a mile, and two miles, away from the sites above, there would be a 10′ tall standing stone, without markings, tilted at 45°; and a 'long barrow' (a type of burial mound common to Western Europe *c.* 4000 BC).

Site description.   Both sites were up precipitous mountain-sides, thick with forest and undergrowth. Insofar as it was possible to pin-point the supposed sites accurately, none of the features could be seen In many years of research, I have never, in any case, come upon a standing stone or a long barrow on such steep terrain.

Score.   Hits: Zero.
            Queries: Zero.
            Misses: Five.

SITE FOUR

Prediction.   About half a mile to the south of South Randolph, the Geological Survey map shows a bridge crossing the second branch of the White River. Just there, the river runs approximately east-west, and the road north-south. Bill Lewis marked a spot in the left-hand quadrant, touching the road and nearly touching the river. Here, he said, would be found a burial chamber; the mound visible; stones protruding; covered with silt and much damaged; and oriented NW/SE.

Site description.   The river flows through a flat valley about half a mile wide; on either side the hills rise steeply upwards. Along the valley, glaciation has left behind many rounded humps, most of them 20'–100'. The grass in the valley is used for grazing in the summer; in the winter it is snow-covered; in the past, there has been much flooding.

In precisely the position marked by Bill Lewis, there is a gentle mound rising in the perfectly flat flood plain formed by a bend in the river. It is semi-circular, about thirty yards at its longest, rising about five feet above the plain, and aligned NW/SE; at the NW end stones protrude, including a prominent, 4' tall, standing or marking stone.

Evaluation. He was extremely accurate in the position of the mound and its alignment; the protruding stones, too, may be counted a hit, since the standing stone is an obvious and prominent feature. He was right about the silt, too, and mentioned this feature a number of times when map-dowsing; but a certain knowledge of geography would enable anyone to suggest the same, so as a predictive success it rates no more than a query.

As with Site 1, is it in fact a burial mound? Compared with the rest of the valley, it is probably too small to be a glacial deposit. But it has many of the signs of a silt levée, left behind as the river gradually changed course. An archaeologist with me said he would need more evidence before bothering to excavate.

Score. Hits: Three.
         Queries: Two.
         Misses: None.

CHECK SITE FOUR

Prediction. About half a mile to the south of Site 4, there would be a burial chamber in the shape of a flattened mound, 'with rocky edges, as if hewn from rock'; there would be a visible lintel, cracked and sagging; the mound oriented NE/SW.

Site description. The position is in relatively open countryside on the side of the hill leading up from the valley. There are glacial lumps but none that look remotely like a burial chamber as described above.

Score. Hits: Zero.
         Queries: Zero.
         Misses: Four.

SITE FIVE

Prediction. A quarter-mile to the NW of Site 4 would be an ancient camp site, just inside the woods, where there were still to be found, with difficulty, some minor earthworks.

Site description. On the spot marked, there is a curious terracing that can just be seen outside the woods, and continues inside. It could as easily be formed by erosion as be manmade.

Score. Hits: Zero.
      Queries: One.
      Misses: Zero.

CHECK SITE FIVE

Prediction. There would be a camp site on the hill-side one-quarter mile east of Site 4, with impressive earthworks that could be easily seen.

Site description. Steep and wooded. No earthworks.

Score. Hits: Zero.
      Queries: Zero.
      Misses: One.

SITE SIX

Prediction. A standing stone, 6′ 8″ high, lying on its side near a pathway, would be found about two miles SW of South Woodstock. Three spiral markings were carved on it.

Site description. The area is lightly wooded, with a profusion of boulders, mostly moss-covered and undisturbed for many years. As Bill Lewis had also dowsed the information that the standing stone had been moved down the hill within the past two years, and as it would have been considerably larger and differently shaped from the other stones, one would have expected to have been able to see it, particularly as the 1:25,000 US Geological Survey map made it possible to arrive accurately within about twenty yards of the position marked. However – see Sites 7–9 below and discussion elsewhere in the book – Bill Lewis seems to have been having problems of displacement on this particular map; in light of this, it may be that a search in another area could prove successful.

Score. Hits: Zero.
Queries: Zero.
Misses: Four.

CHECK SITE SIX

Prediction. There would be a 4′ 6″ standing stone, without spirals, inclined at 10° from the vertical, on the other side of the path leading to Site 6.

Site description. The position marked was in a small field. There was no stone.

Score. Hits: Zero.
Queries: Zero.
Misses: Four.

SITE SEVEN

Prediction. Two standing stones, each with two spiral markings, would be found at a spot approximately two miles W of South Woodstock. They would be aligned E/W, with a small burial mound ten feet to the east, and were 6′ 2″ and 5′ 3″ respectively.

Site description. A single stone, 6′ 10″ tall, stood at the entrance to a disused farmyard. It was much eroded, so that it was impossible to be certain of the original shape of the marks that had once been put on the stone. More recent drill-holes showed that it has been used as a gatepost. Ten feet away to the east was a dry stone wall (also running E/W) above a small mound raised above the general level of the ground.

Evaluation. Of all the sites dowsed by Bill Lewis during this exercise, this was the most tantalizing and ambiguous to assess. For instance, I found only one stone, not two, during an hour-long visit to the area. Was there ever another one? The farm has not been inhabited for more than twenty years, so perhaps we shall never know. However, in the judgement of local people, it is very rare to find even one standing stone of this shape and size – nobody I spoke to had heard of any of this height, and of the same slender, needle-like form that characterizes megalithic standing stones in Western Europe, except the ones described in Sites 8 and 9 below.

Again, the precise position of the stone is some forty yards from the spot marked by Bill Lewis. Here we come to something which seems to have affected him while dowsing this map. With this stone, and also to a much larger degree with Sites 8 and 9, goes an error in the predicted position. Mysteriously, at all three sites, they are each displayed some distance away from their true position almost exactly on a NW/SE axis.

Over all, it seems fair to regard Bill Lewis's discovery of the site as a genuine map-dowsing success – to pin-point and describe a very unusual stone (even if he hoped there were two) within forty yards of its position, from some 3000 miles away, ought to satisfy all but the most critical. The E/W alignment of the site is accurate; so is the ten-feet distance of the mound.

As at other sites, only excavation could show if the mound, which is indistinct, contains burials. The existence of spirals among the carvings on the stone is hinted at. However, the estimated height of the stone(s) is outside the margin of error that Bill Lewis would apply.

Score. Hits: Three.
         Queries: Two.
         Misses: One.

CHECK SITE SEVEN

Prediction. Two standing stones would be found in an open space about 200 yards from Site 7, on the other side of the road leading to it. There would be one spiral marking, the heights would be 9′ and 4′ 9″, they would be in approximate N/S alignment, and no burial mound would be visible.

Site description. Position marked was in a field containing a few low shrubs or bushes. Nothing was visible as described. There were some irregularities in the ground, but nothing that would be regarded as a possible burial ground.

Evaluation. For the purposes of comparative scoring, the non-existence of the burial ground is counted as a query. No negative statements by Bill Lewis have been included in his predictions, and he could, of course, have produced a massive tally of hits by saying, e.g., 'there is no chambered tomb to be seen', 'little green men are not visible'. The chances of there *not* being a burial mound in a given place in Vermont must be several thousand (or million) to one.

Score. Hits: Zero.
Queries: One.
Misses: Four.

SITE EIGHT

Prediction. A chambered mound near South Woodstock, of which Bill Lewis was shown a photograph, would be found a few yards to the left of the road about a mile south of the town.

Evaluation. The position was wrong by approximately one mile and 100 yards, displaced to the NW. In general direction from the centre of Woodstock there was an error of 43°. By chance, he would have come as close as this about one time in eight.

Score. Hits: Zero.
Queries: Zero.
Misses: One.

CHECK SITE EIGHT

Prediction. The mound would be found about 200 yards to the north of Site 8, as predicted by Bill Lewis.

Score. Hits: Zero.
Queries: Zero.
Misses: One.

SITE NINE

Prediction. The tallest standing stone on the US Geological Survey 1:25,000 Woodstock South Quadrangle map would be found at a point marked in West Windsor county. It would be 10′ 6″ tall, have Indian markings, the lowest of these being about 4′ and the highest about 4′ 6″.

Site description. The point marked on the map is in a field which has been recently flattened by a farmer, and contains a small artificial lake. If there was ever a standing stone there, it has been removed. However, a stone remarkably similar to the one described by Bill Lewis was found in a field approximately one and a half miles NW of the site marked. It is 10′ 6″ tall, and has ancient markings on it in a band spreading round its four surfaces between approximately 3′ 6″ and 5′ from the ground.

Evaluation. The archaeologist with me, Byron E. Dix, has

probably visited and investigated more of the controversially ancient sites in Vermont than any man alive. He was astonished not to have come across this stone before, and said that in his experience it was not just the tallest standing stone on that particular map quadrangle, but in the whole of Vermont. He thought it extraordinary that a dowser working out of a small room the other side of the Atlantic could have come so close to identifying its position. He was in no doubt that the descriptions given by Bill Lewis were extremely unlikely to apply to any other stone. Some confirmation of this came when I had a letter published in all of Vermont's hometown newspapers asking if readers knew of any similar, or taller stones. Out of twenty or so replies, none mentioned stones that approached this height.

Although the predicted position was a miss, the fact of it being the tallest seems highly probable. Its height was accurate; pre-colonial markings exist (again, later drill-holes for its use as a gatepost can be seen), and they are in a band acceptably close to the predicted height.

Score.   Hits: Four.
         Queries: Zero.
         Misses: One.

CHECK SITE NINE

Prediction.   A standing stone 3′ 6″ tall would be found in an open area near Site 9, bearing a mark like a cross about two feet above the ground.

Site description.   The site marked was in a field surrounded by stone walls and woods. There was a clear view of the terrain, and no upright stone could be seen. (There were many stones 3′ 6″ and more on their sides in the walls.)

Score.   Hits: Zero.
         Queries: Zero.
         Misses: Four.

SITES TEN, ELEVEN, TWELVE

Not visited.

SITE THIRTEEN

Prediction.   Careful searching would find the entrance to a neolithic flint mine, with chippings and bits of flint on the ground outside. The mining area covered several square miles. The mine shaft goes horizontally into the hill-side.

Site description. The hill in question was visited shortly after the snows had melted. The ground was covered with layers of fallen leaves and dead vegetation, which made a proper search very difficult. Mines for other minerals – copper, tin – exist in the area. There were substantial mounds of loose rock chippings beneath the vegetation, which might indicate mine workings in the immediate vicinity. However, none were of chalk or lime-stone that would normally be associated with flint workings.

Evaluation. Without investigating more thoroughly, it is impossible to say whether Bill Lewis's predictions were accurate. The chances are strongly against. However, there is one curiosity that should be marked down on the credit side. Originally, when I asked him to try to find me a neolithic flint mine, all he had to dowse from was the Transportation Map. When the Geological Survey maps arrived, it was clear that he had picked the one area in Vermont which was once rich with mines.

Score. Hits:　Zero.
　　　　　Queries: One.
　　　　　Misses: Two.

CHECK SITE THIRTEEN

Prediction. There would be a flint mine on a hill-side near Site 13, with whole flints visible, and the shaft going vertically down.

Site description. This site was up an even steeper hill-side, making investigation doubly difficult. There was no obvious sign of a mine.

Score. Hits:　Zero.
　　　　　Queries: Zero.
　　　　　Misses: Two.

SITE FOURTEEN

Not visited.

SITE FIFTEEN

Prediction. There would be evidence of an ancient camp site on top of a hill near the flint mine. Worked flints – spearheads, scrapers, etc. – would be visible on the surface.

Site description. Short-cropped grass, with well-spaced trees, covers the top of the hill. I found no flints; maybe, if they were there, they have been collected by people using the log cabins among the trees. The ground is curiously uneven, with many humps, banks and hollows. They did not appear regular enough to be ancient fortifications, but some were steep enough to appear man-made.

Score. Hits: Zero.
        Queries: One.
        Misses: One.

CHECK SITE FIFTEEN
Inaccessible. Not visited.

SITE SIXTEEN
Not visited.

SITE SEVENTEEN
Prediction. There would be a standing stone 6′ 9″ tall on the western edge of the Badlands of South Dakota near Rockyford, with two cup marks on it.

Site description. So far as the site could be traced accurately from an old map, it lay near the dried river bed of a small ravine. No stone was visible. A solitary tree was a feature of the area, with a mound beside it.

Score. Hits: Zero.
        Queries: Zero.
        Misses: Three.

CHECK SITE SEVENTEEN
Prediction. Standing stone on opposite side of road near Site 17, 8′ high, V-shaped mark.

Site description. Similar terrain to Site 17. No stone or other feature visible.

Score. Hits: Zero.
        Queries: Zero.
        Misses: Three.

SITE EIGHTEEN

Prediction. On the Pine Ridge Indian Reservation, one mile south of South Manderson, there would be a 7′ 3″ standing stone.

Site description. Steep, sandstone hills, sometimes eroded into cliffs, sometimes covered with grass from which grow well-spaced conifers, stretch for many miles. The tracks marked on the map, near which the stone should have been found, are indistinct on the ground, and because of the many changing contours and precipitous cliffs, it was difficult to follow the map, and impossible to take a compass bearing and head directly for the site. I can only be sure that I located the general area where the stone should have been, and here there were many fallen boulders from the eroded cliffs above, although none looked to have been placed there by man. Although the area is very sparsely inhabited, there is a farm at the foot of the track leading to the site, and the Indian family there said they knew of no such stone.

Evaluation. On the face of it, this prediction counts as a straightforward miss. However, the Indian family was considerably disturbed to find that we were investigating the site at all, and insisted on accompanying me. While insisting that there was no stone to be found, they refused to let me go to one place where, from the map, I thought the stone might be. They said it was a sacred and very ancient burial ground, of which they were the guardians. I asked my Indian guide to find out if it was unique in any way, and she established that it was 'special', and dated back to a time 'long before our present people'.

Score. Hits: Zero.
       Queries: Zero.
       Misses: Two.

CHECK SITE EIGHTEEN

Prediction. There would be a 4′ tall standing stone near the main road south of Manderson.

Site description. The position marked was on an open grassy plain. It was possible to locate the site precisely. There was no stone as described.

Score. Hits: Zero.
Queries: Zero.
Misses: Two.

SITE NINETEEN

Prediction. Just north of Pine Ridge, there would be a standing stone 7′ 3″ tall, with Indian markings on it, in the sundance
circle. The stone would be off-centre, being placed to the east.
Round the outside of the sundance area would be an irregular
series of stones, ten in all, between 3′ and 4′ tall, put there by
Indians as a modern enclosure to keep out spectators.

Site description. About a quarter of a mile to the north of
Pine Ridge is a piece of deserted wasteland, almost flat, which at
first sight appears featureless except for a few stretches of
abandoned fencing, discarded tyres, and similar debris. The site
is used ceremonially, usually once a year, when a sundance tree
is planted in the position marked by Bill Lewis as where the
standing stone should be. At all other times, this position is
indicated by a metal stake driven into the ground. Above ground,
its height was 7′ 3″.

Only certain Indians may take part in the sundance ceremony.
The rest of them must stay outside an approximately semi-
circular area, roughly defined by ten irregularly-spaced, sturdy
wooden posts 3′ to 4′ in height, set in stone foundations.

Evaluation. This is perhaps the most remarkable of all the
predictions made by Bill Lewis, and may have considerable
implications regarding the processes involved in map-dowsing.
For at the same time as he was wrong about the main object of
his search – the standing stone – he was astonishingly accurate in
finding, first, the most important ceremonial site of the Pine
Ridge Indians, and secondly, the geographical details and
physical features of the site.

His first hit was in finding the site at all. At an early meeting,
when we were plotting my tour of North America, all he had to
work on was the Rand McNally Road Atlas. The mark he made
on this precisely coincided with the site of the sundance circle,
which came to light when a US Geological Survey 1:24,000 map
arrived.

He also scored hits with the height of the marker post, the

position of the post, the number of boundary posts, their height, and their disposition. As they are set in stone, and he qualified his description by saying that they were of later date, and had a different function from the central marker, this deserves a query. He was wrong on the stone and its Indian markings.

Score.   Hits: Six.
            Queries: One.
            Misses: Two.

CHECK SITE NINETEEN

Prediction.   A 4′ standing stone, without markings, would be found about half a mile west of Pine Ridge, in the centre of a circle marked by six stones.

Site description.   The position marked is in an uncultivated field. It was possible to locate it exactly. The field has no local ceremonial significance. There was no standing stone or circle.

Score.   Hits: Zero.
            Queries: Zero.
            Misses: Five.

SITE TWENTY

Prediction.   South of Pinon, on the Hopi Indian Reservation in Arizona, would be a 5′ 7″ standing stone with Indian markings.

Site description.   The area for many miles around is flat, sandy desert, with tufts of scrub grass. Using a compass, it was possible to locate the site precisely, and in any case such a stone would be visible from a considerable distance. There was no stone, nor any other obviously intrusive feature.

Score.   Hits: Zero.
            Queries: Zero.
            Misses: Three.

CHECK SITE TWENTY

Prediction.   There would be a 7′ 6″ standing stone, without markings, at a spot on the other side of the road near Site 20.

Site description.   As Site 20. It was not difficult to locate the position. There was no stone.

Score.   Hits: Zero.
            Queries: Zero.
            Misses: Three.

SUMMARY OF RESULTS (* HIT, ○ QUERY, × MISS)

	Sites chosen by Bill Lewis	Result		*Check Sites*	Result
SITE 1	1. Elevation 1600 feet	*	1. Burial mound	×
	2. Open field	*	2. Stone wall	×
	3. Two small trees	*	3. Fallen tree	○
	4. Height of mound	*	4. Flat stones	×
	5. Shape of mound	○		
	6. Small stones protruding	○		
SITE 2/3	7. Standing stone	×	5. Standing stone	×
	8. 5' 4" tall	×	6. 10' tall	×
	9. Indian markings	×	7. No markings	×
	10. Height of markings	×	8. Tilted at 45°	×
	11. Burial mound	×	9. Long barrow	×
SITE 4	12. Burial mound	○	10. Burial chamber	×
	13. Mound position	*	11. Shape of chamber	×
	14. Mound orientation	*	12. Mound orientation	×
	15. Protruding stone(s)	*	13. Lintel visible	×
	16. Silt			
SITE 5	17. Minor earthworks	○	14. Impressive earthworks	×
SITE 6	18. Standing stone	×	15. Standing stone	×
	19. 6' 8" tall	×	16. 4' 6" tall	×
	20. Lying on side	×	17. Inclined 10°	×
	21. Three spirals	×	18. No spirals	×

		Mark
SITE 7		
22.	Standing stone(s) site	*
23.	Site orientation	*
24.	Mound position	
25.	Burial mound	
26.	Spiral markings	○
27.	Height	○
SITE 8		
28.	Mound position	x
SITE 9		
29.	Tallest stone	*
30.	10' 6" tall	*
31.	Indian markings	*
32.	Height of markings	*
33.	Site of stone	
SITE 13		
34.	Mining area	○
35.	Flint mine	x
36.	Flint chippings	x
SITE 15		
37.	Camp site	○
38.	Flint tools visible	x
SITE 17		
39.	Standing stone	x
40.	6' 9" tall	x
41.	Two cup marks	x
SITE 18		
42.	Standing stone	x
43.	7' 3" tall	x

		Mark
19.	Standing stone site	x
20.	Orientation	x
21.	Height	x
22.	Spiral markings	x
23.	No burial mound	x
24.	Mound position	○
25.	Standing stone	x
26.	3' 6" tall	x
27.	Mark like cross	x
28.	Height of markings	x
29.	Flint mine	x
30.	Flints visible	x
31.	Standing stone	x
32.	8' tall	x
33.	V-shaped mark	x
34.	Standing stone	x
35.	4' tall	x

Site	#	Feature			
SITE 19	44.	Sacred site	*		
	45.	Marker post height	*		
	46.	Position of marker	*		
	47.	No. of boundary posts	*		
	48.	Height of posts	*		
	49.	Position of posts	*		
	50.	Nature of posts		O	
	51.	Standing stone			X
	52.	Indian markings			X
SITE 20	53.	Standing stone			X
	54.	5' 7" tall			X
	55.	Indian markings			X
		TOTALS	20	10	25
		% OF TOTAL	36·4	18·2	45·4

	#	Feature			
	36.	Sacred site			X
	37.	Standing stone			X
	38.	4' tall			X
	39.	Centre of circle			X
	40.	Six-stone circle			X
	41.	Standing stone			X
	42.	7' 6" tall			X
	43.	No markings			X
		TOTALS	0	2	41
		% OF TOTAL	0	4·7	95·3

Prediction	Score	Comment
1. Elevation 1600 feet	10	Very unlikely he would have arrived at this figure by chance.
2. Open field	8	This area is 90 per cent woodland.
3. Two small trees	7	There were also fruit trees in the area.
4. Height of mound	6	Sloping ground made accurate measurement impossible.
5. Shape of mound	3	More like a terrace.
6. Small stones protruding	1	They do in most places in Vermont (although W.L. did not know this).
7. Standing stone	0	
8. 5′ 4″ tall	0	
9. Indian markings	0	
10. Height of markings	0	
11. Burial mound	0	
12. Burial mound	2	A mound, but unlikely to contain burials.
13. Mound position	9	Runs slightly under road, instead of beside.
14. Mound alignment	10	Precise.
15. Protruding stone(s)	7	One prominent stone, not several.
16. Silt	2	Line of river makes this probable.
17. Minor earthworks	3	Ambiguous disturbance of ground.
18. Standing stone	0	
19. 6′ 8″ tall	0	
20. Lying on side	0	
21. Three spirals	0	
22. Standing stone(s) site	7	One stone, not two; 40 yards out of position.
23. Site orientation	10	Precise.

Prediction	Score	Comment
24. Mound position	10	Ten feet from stone.
25. Burial mound	7	Not distinct, but have seen similar in Britain.
26. Spiral markings	4	Eroded and ambiguous.
27. Height	2	Taller than predicted.
28. Mound position	3	Seven chances in eight he would have made worse error.
29. Tallest stone	8	Cannot be certain it was the tallest.
30. 10′ 6″ tall	10	Precise.
31. Indian markings	5	Could be seen, but is a generalized prediction.
32. Height of markings	8	In slightly wider band than predicted.
33. Site of stone	2	$1\frac{1}{2}$ miles from predicted position on map covering $9 \times 6\frac{1}{2}$ miles.
34. Mining area	6	Correct in general.
35. Flint mine	0	
36. Flint chippings	2	Chippings, but not flint.
37. Camp site	4	Ambiguous disturbance of ground.
38. Flint tools visible	0	
39. Standing stone	0	
40. 6′ 9″ tall	0	
41. Two cup marks	0	
42. Standing stone	0	
43. 7′ 3″ tall	0	
44. Ancient sacred site	10	Found sundance circle.
45. Marker post height	10	Precise.
46. Marker post position	10	Precise.
47. Ten boundary posts	10	Correct.
48. Height of posts	10	Correct.
49. Distribution of posts	8	Correct, but more generalized.
50. Nature of posts	10	Correctly predicted to keep out spectators.
51. Standing stone	0	Metal post, not stone.
52. Indian markings	0	

Prediction	Score	Comment
53. Standing stone	0	
54. 5′ 7″ tall	0	
55. Indian markings	0	
TOTAL	**224**	

Out of a maximum possible points of 550, the total of 224 represents a success rate of 40·72 per cent.

On the list of check sites, it is possible to give points for accuracy on only four predictions out of the 43, as follows:

3. Fallen tree	1	Generalized prediction.
4. Stone wall	1	Ditto.
23. No burial mound	1	Negative prediction.
24. Position of burial mound	2	Worse error than equivalent prediction by W.L.
TOTAL	**5**	

Out of a maximum possible points of 430, the random check list thus produced a success rate of 1·16 per cent.

Discussion

John Stiles has called the experiment 'highly imaginative, with interesting results'. On a stringent interpretation of the site-matching, he marked Bill Lewis's score of hits and queries somewhat lower than me – but still significantly higher than the check sites. An independent evaluation, which he also arranged, tallied very closely with my score.

The experiment and the results have now been scrutinized by a variety of people, all of whom have been to varying degrees impressed or baffled. Such reservations as they have had can best be summarized as follows:

The test was not fraud-proof, did not exclude the possibility of collusion. This is true. The nature of the experiment, being basically a practical aid to a personal quest, did not lend itself to

185

a double-blind procedure. However, I took care to catalogue and file the predictions through a third party immediately after they were made, and the tape-recording exists as a record of the way the predictions were made. Bill Lewis has never been outside the United Kingdom, and has no contact with any of the areas visited. In any case, not one of the sites which he dowsed (with the exception of the sundance circle) is recognized locally as an archaeological site, which makes it unlikely in the extreme that anybody would have suggested them to him. The ambiguity of most of his findings also lends credence to this view. There remains the possibility that, with his co-operation, I invented the whole exercise, having first established the sites through my own contacts. All I can say is, I didn't; it would have been one of the most pointless and absurd ways of spending a lot of money that I can imagine.

I did not seek out the check sites with equal diligence. So far as the terrain made it possible, I did. Both Bill Lewis and John Stiles were asked to find accessible sites; Bill Lewis turned out to be rather more successful in doing so. In any case, the lack of an exactly equal comparison only makes the statistics slightly more difficult – it does not destroy the significance of the scores.

Most of the significance comes from only five sites, and at not one of these was there 100 per cent accuracy. The purpose of the experiment was to establish whether Bill Lewis was able to provide information not contained on the map, and not obtainable by chance. As it turned out, he was able to provide some information accurately, but not all. I found the most difficult choice, in the scoring, was whether to include the 10′ 6″ standing stone, because of its considerable distance from the position that was map-dowsed. But even if this is excluded, there are enough other hits to give Bill Lewis an acceptably high above-chance score.

Bill Lewis is used to the contours and other features on a map, and knows from experience where such sites would be. Although familiar with British Ordnance Survey maps, he is not used to any of the four American maps used (and even the best of these do not mark ancient sites as the British ones do, and might therefore be said to give a clue at least as to the general locality of prehistoric remains). It should also be stressed that the two standing stones included in the results are of a size that is very rare. Only one other is known by local archaeologists, at Site Eight, and persistent enquiries that continued after my visit did not uncover any more.

I also have a number of personal impressions of the experiment, in addition to the observations made in the site description. Firstly, the topographical details that Bill Lewis dowsed were often, I suspect, more vivid and accurate than the antiquity which we were both looking for. Of course this cannot be proved except by excavation, but I had this impression at: Site One, where the supposed burial mound with two trees growing out of it looked much more like a ridge; Site Four, where although the mound and its orientation were correctly described, it seemed to have a geological rather than human origin; Site Five, where there was indeed a ground disturbance, but again not obviously man-made; Site Thirteen, where he dowsed the existence of a flint mine (not found) in the middle of an area that turned out to have many disused modern mines; and Site Fifteen, where there were prominent humps and banks reminiscent of an ancient camp site, but again not obviously man-made.

Secondly, in the South Dakota predictions, I felt strongly that Bill Lewis successfully identified some sites that were basically what I was looking for – 'an ancient sacred place'. He unerringly pin-pointed the sundance circle at Pine Ridge, and although for most of the year it looks desolate and abandoned, for generations now it has come to life annually during the sundance ceremony; and I was told it is important that the ceremony takes place just there, and nowhere else. Nor was I in any doubt about the sanctity of the burial ground at Site Eighteen. Several Indians (who incidentally found dowsing interesting but not surprising) confirmed this, and one suggested that Bill Lewis might have picked up the grave of the legendary Sioux warrior Crazy Horse, who rode off wounded into the hills near there but whose body was never found. So you could argue that, in a territory without megaliths, I was guided to the next best thing – although it does not, of course, affect the scoring one way or the other.

Finally, the most successful predictions tended to come at the beginning of a session, or after a short break. Were I to run the experiment again, I should have much shorter sessions – certainly no more than 15 minutes – over more days, with only one map per session to work on. The Arizona map-dowsing, which came at the end of a session, felt like a lost cause even while Bill Lewis was working; he did not like the maps, even though they were newly-revised and distinct, and frequently changed his mind about the sites.

Conclusion

However you adjust the figures to make allowances for the relative inadequacy of the check list, and the ambiguity of some of the site features, there remains an overwhelming balance in favour of Bill Lewis's correct predictions being the result of something other than chance. In this experiment map-dowsing worked, albeit fallibly and inconsistently. Arthur Bailey has written: 'Whilst a statistician would no doubt find all sorts of points to query if he was not prepared to look sensibly at the evidence, nevertheless I find the results conclusive. I would also expect the same conclusion from open-minded persons. It is stretching chance to very large limits to try to explain the results on that basis.'

I agree.

8 The Psychic Spectrum

On the assumption that every event, whether described as paranormal or not, requires a physical transfer of energy from one place to another, John Taylor has conveniently arranged the various categories of 'supernatural' happenings according to the amount of energy that would probably be involved. At the lowest end of the scale come acupuncture, faith healing, dowsing, clairvoyance and telepathy, which he estimates could be achieved with levels of power measured in micro-joules (a joule being a standard unit of energy representing the amount of energy generated by a potential of one volt across a resistance of one ohm – in homely terms, roughly the amount of effort needed to lift a quarter-pound bar of chocolate from ground to waist level). Next come a set of phenomena that include metal-bending, psychokinesis, levitation and poltergeist activity, for which energy of the order of several joules would seem to be necessary. Then, materialization and disappearance, which he estimates would need megajoules of energy. Finally, he collects together an assorted bunch of reported occurrences such as precognition, reincarnation, automatic writings, and 'impossible' coincidences, for which he feels unable to guess at the energy involved; this last group also has in common the fact that some outside agency such as a 'spirit' is often held to be responsible for them, and certainly there are profound difficulties in trying to explain them in terms of the laws of physics.

It is the latest of many attempts to categorize the jumble of happenings that, like dowsing, have always been seen as incompatible with science. Once termed 'supernatural' or 'psychical', they are nowadays most usually called 'parapsychological', 'paranormal', or 'psi effects'. Another way of classifying them has been to say that one class is the result of extra-sensory perception (ESP), and demonstrates itself through strange workings of the mind – telepathy, dowsing, clairvoyance, unexplained knowledge of the future or some far-distant time in the past; the other class, physical in nature, is labelled psychokinetic (PK) – poltergeist activity, an ability to move or deform objects without touching them, or to 'will' the way a dice falls.

Historically, there have been definite fashions in these phenomena. The planchette, a small heart-shaped board on castor wheels that moves freely about a table top and is supposed to trace messages without conscious direction when two or more people rest their fingers lightly on top, was used in ancient China and then emerged again in France towards the end of the nineteenth century. Automatic writing was known in China between AD 1034 and AD 1038, and became the subject of much research and debate in Germany in the 1920s; there have been vogues for séances, stigmata, table-tipping, ouija boards. The appearance of Uri Geller in front of television cameras brought a rash of other spoon-benders and clock-stoppers – but he was not the first of his kind: in 1879, there was an outbreak of poltergeist behaviour in a southern plantation in Georgia, later recounted in the *Nashville Banner*, in which as well as the usual manifestations of smashed furniture, floating objects and so on, dishes and food were reportedly flung about, inflicting painful scalds on the hands of diners, who also found that 'spoons were broken, or suddenly twisted out of shape in their hands'.

In the late nineteenth century, the fashion was for spiritualism: in a new age of science, people desperately wanted evidence of life after death – of the existence of the 'soul' (by which was usually meant the continuance of the personality that had been known on earth). In direct response to this need for proof, the spirits seemingly obliged by materializing in ghostly form, speaking through the mouths of mediums, tapping out messages on tables in darkened séances, and giving accounts of the other world in death-bed visions. It was against this increasingly murky and fraud-ridden background that, in 1882, a group of distinguished scientists and scholars met in London to form the Society for Psychical Research, whose avowed aim was to study these matters 'without prejudice or prepossession of any kind';[1] three years later it was followed in New York by its American counterpart. Ever since, the two bodies have attracted the support of some of the most eminent men and women of their time, and produced millions of words in their meetings, journals, and proceedings. Yet the hoped-for evidence for survival after death is still far from clear, and as we shall see, there are still some extreme sceptics who say that there has never yet been acceptable proof of ESP or PK whatsoever.

Certainly, the research has been dogged with deception and disappointment. Looking back on the early days of investigation into the subject, it is clear that the great minds, though determined to expose fraud wherever they could find it, were still unable to comprehend just how intimately connected the supernatural and the suspicious seem to be. Thus, having looked at the records of one of the best-attested exploits of those times, by the medium Daniel Dunglas Home, who was observed to have floated out of a third-storey window and in at another, the psychologist H. J. Eysenck can now explain it by saying confidently: 'Every stage magician nowadays does more difficult tricks before larger audiences and under conditions of much brighter illumination. It would have been easy for him to have made arrangements beforehand to enable him to appear outside the window of the room containing his friends, either by way of a plank or by swinging from a rope attached to the roof and hanging over the parapet. Investigators who cannot explain every trick performed by stage magicians should consider themselves barred from investigating psi phenomena.'[2]

Certainly, with hindsight, it is possible to explain the way in which many of the inexplicable events in Victorian psychic research *might* have happened; and it is also undoubtedly true that many of the famous mediums of the past, from Eusapia Palladino to Carmine Mirabelli, were caught cheating on occasion. The question is: does this automatically discredit and disprove all the other occasions when they weren't caught cheating, and when there is no easy way of explaining the remarkable effects they were reported to produce? When Home was at the height of his powers, for instance, objects in the room around him erupted into life. With the lights full on, with his legs held or tied, with no attempt at a hushed or suggestive atmosphere, bells would ring, grand pianos float across the room, tables up-end themselves, the floor vibrate, he would speak in strange tongues, objects would materialize; and this happened not once but many times, in front of witnesses who over a period of years must have totalled thousands, in Britain, Europe and America. According to Colin Wilson, who is convinced that most of Home's manifestations were genuine, he was 'one of the few mediums who were never seriously accused of fraud. He passed all "tests" triumphantly.'

Standards of proof

But for a critic such as C. E. M. Hansel, Professor of Psychology in the University of Swansea, South Wales, evidence of this sort is completely inadmissible, because however apparently impressive in sum, each individual observation is subjective, potentially fallible, and therefore unreliable. Indeed, he goes further. For him, the only psi phenomena worth considering are those produced under experimental laboratory conditions, and in his most famous study[3] of these, he chose four series of experiments which are well known and supposedly conclusive evidence of psi. He based his investigation on two premises. The first was that there is an '*a priori* unlikelihood' of ESP, because it is known that rationally and according to all scientific law, such events as telepathy or precognition cannot occur. His second premise was that fraud certainly exists as a well-known human failing, and to have been associated with many alleged examples of ESP. It follows, in his view, that no experiment can be said to be valid unless it has excluded the possibility of fraud.

The experiments he chose all involved telepathy or precognition as shown by above-chance guessing of the symbols on the standard set of so-called Zener cards used throughout the world in such experiments. There are five of them – a star, a square, a circle, a cross, and wavy lines – in a deck of 25 cards. The chances are therefore one in five that, over a period of time, anybody will guess a symbol correctly. Highly sophisticated mathematical techniques have been evolved to establish the probability of guessing significantly more or less than one card in five. In the experiments chosen by Hansel, the subjects had performed in a way to make the odds many millions to one against their results being chance – by any standard, a significant result.

Hansel was able to show, through a study in great depth of the experimental conditions, that fraud *could* have been committed in each case. That, for him, was enough. He gave no direct evidence of fraud, but concluded: 'If the result could have arisen by a trick, the experiment must be considered unsatisfactory proof of ESP, whether or not it is finally decided that such a trick was in fact used.'

Now his is an extreme view, and one it is very hard to argue with in principle. But it is also a narrow and exclusive one. As H. J. Eysenck points out regarding the question of whether psi has been demonstrated satisfactorily: 'Different people require different standards of proof. There is much experimental evidence, collected under sound and well-controlled conditions and properly analysed statistically, which supports the view that ESP certainly, and PK probably, does exist. But if to prove the existence of psi it is necessary to have replicable phenomena that can be demonstrated with certainty and that behave according to certain well-known laws, the answer must be in the negative.'

And on another occasion: 'Unless there is a gigantic conspiracy involving some thirty University departments all over the world, and several hundred highly respected scientists in various fields, many of them originally hostile to the claims of the psychical researchers, the only conclusion the unbiased observer can come to must be that there does exist a small number of people who obtain knowledge existing in either other people's minds, or in the outer world, by means yet unknown to science.'

Majority decision is on Eysenck's side, according to a 1973 survey. The *New Scientist* in London reported that out of nearly 1500 readers, most of them science graduates, who replied to a questionnaire, 67 per cent considered ESP to be an established fact or a likely possibility.

ESP experiments

There is now a vast quantity of parapsychological literature on which this majority opinion is based. For sheer extent, the card-guessing experiments held, from 1930 onwards, under the guidance of Dr J. B. Rhine, Dr Louisa Rhine and Dr J. G. Pratt at Duke University, are probably the most impressive.[4] During a period of more than thirty years, many millions of calls or guesses were made, annotated and analysed, and it is now generally accepted that the probability of achieving by chance the success rate that they did is so small that, according to Eysenck, 'every inhabitant of the earth would have to guess cards continually and unsuccessfully for many centuries in order to render the reported results insignificant'. The successes fall into two categories: a small number of individuals performed very well, enough times for coincidence to be ruled out; and over all, large groups of people have done slightly but significantly better than chance. Rhine's methods have been subjected to many challenges, both on statistical grounds (e.g., ignoring worse-than-average results), and by accusations of fraud. Latterly, however, the statistical side was checked by the American Institute for Mathematical Studies, whose President found that 'If the Rhine investigation is to be fairly attacked it must be on other than mathematical grounds.' So far as the accusations of fraud were concerned, his most persistent critic, G. R. Price, whose article 'Science and the Supernatural' in *Science* in 1955 led to a widespread suspicion of Rhine in orthodox psychological circles, was obliged to retract his views and exonerate Rhine seventeen years later in an apology in the same journal.

A handful of other researchers are usually cited in support of positive evidential proof of psi. Leonard Vasiliev's Russian work showing that telepathically-induced hypnosis can be made to occur over long distances is well thought of.[5] Rhine's successor at Duke University, Dr Helmut Schmidt (formerly a physicist at Boeing Aircraft Industries) has invented equipment which is so completely automated that nobody has been able to question the way in which it produces a random selection of targets for the subject to guess, and is also totally fraud-proof both for experimenter and subject. With this device, his results confirm Rhine's – there are odds of roughly 2,000,000,000 to one that some people are able to guess the future to a small but significant degree.

Dr Milan Ryzl, a chemist with the Institute of Biology of the Czechoslovakian Academy of Science, is the first person to have discovered a subject – a young man named Pavel Stepanek – who can produce evidence of ESP with about the same level of success repeatedly, on demand. Ryzl trained Stepanek, under hypnosis, to be able to say, with approximately 60 per cent reliability, which way up was a hidden playing card, one side coloured green, the other white. This appeared to be Stepanek's only psychic ability – he performed no better than average in many other tests that he tried (and curiously, he was much above average with specific numbered cards).[6] But his consistency, both in America and Czechoslovakia, under widely differing experimental conditions, all of the greatest stringency, has given experimenters, for the first time, a yardstick of psi efficiency; and while 60 per cent accuracy may not superficially seem much, a gambler would certainly welcome much less than that.

All this, evidently, is an attempt to observe and record psi in the analytical/statistical way that has been demanded by scientists of dowsers – and indeed, psi research has undergone exactly the same infuriating difficulties that dowsing tests suffer from, on an infinitely grander scale. In psi, as with dowsing, much the most exciting and superficially convincing examples are on an anecdotal level, which excludes them from the calculations of most scientists. There is also the well-known 'decline effect', in which, rather like a rapidly unwinding watch spring, the target-guessing subject seems to function excellently at the beginning of a test, only to find his powers disappearing as the day goes on. This compares closely with Zaboj Harvalik's 'fatigue effect' in his experiments with dowsers. Both, cumulatively, tend to invalidate the statistical results on which outside scientists are so insistent.

In each area of enquiry, we are back again to the near-irreconcilable standpoints of the sceptical scientist who wishes to have a certain kind of evidence, and the demonstrator who can often offer only another kind. Everybody would agree that one of the characteristics of psi is that it is tantalizingly unpredictable, and that if it functions via a human being, then something odd and strange must be happening to that person's state of consciousness. To expect this mood to persist in laboratory conditions is rather like blindfolding an athlete, to deprive him of his normal sensory reactions, and then expecting him to run a four-minute mile ten times in a row. It is perfectly predictable that the psi faculty is likely to vanish once boredom sets in – or, as many dowsers would express it, when there is an absence of need. The circumstances of card-guessing, according to Dr Charles Tart at the University of California, are identical to the standard psychological techniques, which he has used many times, for deconditioning a human response – 'a technique for extinguishing psychic functions in the laboratory'.

The exclusion of anecdotal evidence has another drawback, too, for there is a sense in which statistical evidence, however good, is arid and self-defeating. Thus, for instance, the sceptical John Sladek in *The New Apocrypha*[7] can in the same breath agree that at least one of Helmut Schmidt's fully automated experiments succeeded in achieving a score with odds against chance of about 10,000 million to one, and at the same time try to diminish this by concluding bleakly that what this really means is that 'some people are capable of seeing into the future at least ·00000025 second, and for at least once every 175 tries' (as if, because the event happened so quickly and so seldom, it somehow didn't matter that it broke all known physical laws); and later that 'the odds against an American's having a social security number whose digits are all the same, e.g., 777–77–777, are 1000 million to 1, yet several Americans must have them' (which is arguable statistically, and in any case who said they must?).

In other words, the search for statistical proof is bound to end controversially. The statistics so far collected would be enough to convince anybody in any branch of orthodox science, were there some framework where psi could be put. Clearly, there are some people who are never going to be persuaded, whatever the statistics say, because it is too much for their imagination or their training to encompass, or because they are unable to work without repeatable experiments.

So there are many researchers who think that the way out of this dilemma is simply to stop bothering about continuing to prove psi *per se* in the old-fashioned way, since enough experiments of that sort have already been carried out that show, according to your choice: (*a*) psi unquestionably exists sometimes, (*b*) there exists a strange set of statistics about unlikely happenings which will one day find an orthodox explanation. So the search is now on for tests which are at the same time more than tests: they may serve a demonstrable need, like mapdowsing; or they may be novel, and therefore interesting on their own account; or they may provide encouragement by means of feed-back devices, like the one Zaboj Harvalik used to programme himself. This new attitude to psi research accepts most of the phenomena as facts, and then tries to analyse how they come about.

Remote viewing

It may be more than a coincidence that the area of psi where the new approach is having the most success, is remarkably similar to dowsing – that is, in the ability of people to 'see' things far beyond what the normal senses can obtain. Whether you accept John Taylor's classification of psi phenomena by energy requirement, or the traditional division between ESP and PK, it is broadly true that there seem to be two separate kinds of paranormal happenings, one passive and the other active. In the first group, what happens is that people are able to perceive things that they ought not, rationally, be able to. In the second group, people make things happen – they cause objects to move or bend or trigger off a spontaneous healing. Now this second group is even more prone to controversy than the first, since much of what happens is a magician's stock-in-trade. In the view of most people, there has never yet been a satisfactory film or video-tape of an object materializing, or of metal bending. The most impressive demonstration that I have seen is Russian film of the Moscow housewife Nina Kulagina, who can be seen to 'will' matches to move across a glass-topped table. It is evident from her concentration and her attitude that she is expending much effort in the exercise. Having seen the film several times, I cannot tell whether the film was faked. Like all Russian research, it remains suspect to most Western scientists because of the vagueness and secrecy surrounding the circumstances of the experiment, and because they have not allowed Nina Kulagina to be tested elsewhere.

Of course, this is not to say that PK doesn't exist; it may just be that it is extraordinarily hard to capture on film in a way that is convincing to a sceptical audience. But mostly, it is a manifestation of psi that lies outside the scope of this book. So far as dowsing is concerned, its relevance lies in the area of spontaneous healing; for it is certainly true that many dowsers have 'healing hands' – they can transmit a physical sensation of warmth or tingling to other people, and sometimes seem to effect cures in this way. However, it is not clear just how 'active' this process is, and how many joules of energy would be involved. As we have seen in the research on magnetic fields, infinitesmal amounts of energy may be enough to trigger major physiological changes.

More light is thrown on the nature of dowsing by current work on psi occurences in the gentler, passive group. These include clairvoyance, telepathy, and out-of-body experiences (sometimes described as travelling clairvoyance or astral projection) – the latter a phenomenon which has been experienced by many dowsers, and may be much more common than is generally recognized. There are subjective differences in the way each of these phenomena feel to the person who is undergoing them, but what they have in common is that they are methods of picking up information not presented to the normal five senses in any known way. Harold Puthoff and Russell Targ, physicists working in the Electronics and Bioengineering Laboratory at Stanford Research Institute in California, have coined the more neutral term 'remote viewing' to cover the way in which, like dowsers, people are able to describe geographical details of far-distant places.[8]

To one who has watched dowsers at work, the most striking aspect of the Puthoff/Targ experiments is the way in which, by different techniques, their subjects come up with the same sort of results as dowsers. Although it is early days yet, their experiments also seem to show that, as with dowsing, remote viewing may be a relatively common but under-used faculty. However, in one respect the work of these two scientists is a striking improvement on anything that has yet happened with investigations into dowsing, and that is in the sophistication with which they have set up their experimental procedure. It is designed to be fraud-proof – 'double-blind', as the jargon has it – and it is also repeatable. Yet at the same time it is intrinsically interesting, which is perhaps why it is achieving such spectacular results. A slight variation has been designed so that any number of people – a club, a study group – can set it up in their own area, using local surroundings. I took part in one such meeting among about fifty people in a part of the University of California at Berkeley, and as others may want to set up a similar experiment, this is how it goes.

The aim of the experiment is to sit a group of people down in a room – 'receivers' – and discover how accurately they can identify and describe a place, whose whereabouts is completely unknown to them, which during the time of the experiment is being visited by some people they know. In other words, the receivers will attempt to pick up the 'thought waves' of the people visiting the site, and describe what they see.

The first essential is to make absolutely certain that nobody in the room, neither receiver nor those running the test, can have the slightest chance of knowing in advance where the target site might be. The Puthoff/Targ method of achieving this is to persuade some independent person, the more distinguished and publicly trustworthy the better, to choose a set of suitable targets, and then stay completely clear of the experiment. This selector should choose at least six target sites, three indoor and three outdoor, as distinctively different as possible, which for reasons of timing should be within half an hour's driving distance from the room where the receivers will be gathered. He should know personally that these places are accessible at the time when the experiment is due to take place, and ideally he should not tell anyone, not even the owner, that he has selected them.

Next, this independent selector must write up a description of each site, in about 100 words, giving its location, and an indication of some of the visual features there – trees, water, road surfaces, walls, buildings, if it is an outdoor site, the contents of the room and the approximate size if it is an indoor site; and he must give directions on how to drive there. He makes two copies of these descriptions and instructions, so that he has three complete sets numbered 1–6. One set he should keep for himself, in conditions of good security, until the experiment is over. The other two sets go into matching numbered envelopes, tightly sealed; these he should also keep to himself until as near the time of the experiment as possible.

When this moment comes, he hands over the two sets of envelopes, unmarked except for a number 1–6 on each, to whoever is running the experiment (a leader plus one or two assistants). The selector then goes and shuts himself away somewhere privately for the duration of the experiment (roughly a couple of hours), and the leader takes over. He explains to his audience briefly the purpose of the experiment – that there are six independently chosen sites described in the envelopes, and that neither he nor anybody else in the room has the slightest idea where or what they are, except that they are within roughly a ten-mile radius.

He has a volunteer from the audience join his assistants, who are given one of the sets of envelopes, and go to their car. Once this team has started driving (for reasons that have emerged through research, it is better that they are actually on the move), they open one of the envelopes at random, and head off towards the target described inside. They have exactly half an hour to get there from the moment they leave the room where the receivers were waiting, and if they arrive early, they should keep driving around the vicinity.

Meanwhile, the leader is dividing the audience into two equal parts – 'receivers' and 'observers'. When the time comes for the team to visit the target site, the receivers will try to pick up what they are seeing, and the observers will record their comments on a sheet of paper. If the audience is new to this sort of thing (which most will be), it is important for the leader to stress that the experiment has succeeded many times, and that, probably, they all have the faculty of remote viewing to a certain extent. Just who becomes a receiver and who an observer, on the day, is by mutual consent – whoever feels receptive, on the day. Everybody should be persuaded to relax by any means that will help: some groups practise meditation for a few minutes before the target is visited; with a new group, it may be a help if the leader quotes some of the more commonly known examples of spontaneous clairvoyance – when people 'know', for instance, that they are going to get a letter or a telephone call, and it duly happens. I think that the state of mind for a successful experiment is not much different than that needed for successful dowsing: stimuli from the immediate surroundings should be mentally shut out, and something akin to a light trance allowed to take place – 'a concentration on nothing', as it were.

At the end of half an hour, the team get out of the car, start observing the target site, and – insofar as it is consciously possible – transmit pictures of what the place looks like. There is a certain amount of evidence that they shouldn't take things too seriously. In Victorian experiments in table-tapping and the like, some of the best effects seemed to have happened in the most uproarious atmosphere of jokes and raucous laughter, and this has been replicated recently by a Canadian group of researchers who, in a well-attested series of episodes, managed to summon up a table-tipping 'ghost', complete with levitation and supernatural noises, once they had created a sufficiently congenial atmosphere. So where appropriate, there is every reason for the team to horse about and enjoy themselves, hug and touch the trees or buildings – anything, in fact, which is a vigorous and positive affirmation that they are where they are. In other words, they shouldn't be overly self-conscious or nervous about what they are doing, since it may be presumed that confidence is as much a necessary factor in transmitting as in receiving.

The transmission should be timed to last for exactly fifteen minutes, during which time, in their experimenters' room, the receivers are busy describing what they are picking up or 'seeing', and the observers writing down these mental images as they are described. It has been found that the first pictures are often the best; afterwards, the details may tend to become confusing or fade away. As in a dream, the pictures are sometimes seen from different viewpoints, and the relationship between them may be illogical. It is important for the observer to note down as much as possible, including all amendments, and also to note the approximate time when the comment was made. To begin with, the Puthoff/Targ transmissions were allowed to last for half an hour, but after a number of them had been evaluated, it was found that virtually all the accurate remote viewing had taken place in the first five or ten minutes – there is, perhaps, a limit to the length of time when the receiver's special kind of concentration can be made to last, just as in the decline effect with card-guessing and the fatigue effect in dowsing. The receivers should also try to draw on paper, however vaguely, what they see – there is often a closer correlation between the shapes perceived in the images, and the shapes of the target site, than there is in the verbal description.

At the end of the quarter-hour, the team gets in the car and heads back. In the room, the leader of the experiment opens up the six envelopes, and writes the names of the sites on a blackboard, reading out the selector's description of each. This is a good theatrical moment, like the half-way elimination in a quiz show; for the first time, people in the audience have an idea how right or wrong they may have been – although they still have no idea which of the six sites was chosen. It is now the job of the observers to match, in order of probability, the remote viewing description by his receiver, against the actual description by the selector, marking them 1 through 6. Thus, if his viewing description were of a bridge above water, and one of the target sites was in fact a bridge above a railway, he might mark it 1, and so on through to the unlikeliest site, which would score 6.

(There are always difficulties in writing down a ranking for the worst matches – at the lower end, where none of the descriptions fit each other, you can usually place 4, 5, and 6 in any order. Nevertheless, it is essential to complete a score, even if it seems pointless to the observer, since only in this way can the viewing description subsequently be included and evaluated statistically in a way consistent with previous experiments.)

As soon as this is done, the papers should be signed by both receiver and observer, dated and timed, and handed in to the leader. Before the team arrives back to reveal which site they in fact visited, the leader should call round the room and total up on the blackboard all the first choices of sites. Thus site 1 might end up with five first choices, site 2 thirteen, site 3 six . . . and so on; it is the climax of the experiment, for usually a clear favourite will emerge, and everybody is waiting for the team to establish whether the remote viewing was successful. In California, I was told that it works every time, with varying degrees of significance.

Certainly, on the occasion of the experiment in which I took part (in the category of an observer), the results showed unambiguously that a degree of remote viewing had been achieved by the audience. There were 48 in the audience (and thus, the same number of first choices in total). The target site was an olive grove by an artificial lake in a park (18 first choices); the other two outdoor sites were a tunnel beneath a freeway bridge (5), and a fishing pier in the bay (15); the three indoor sites were a gymnasium (4), part of a chemistry laboratory (3), and an office (3).

I found several things remarkable about this. Not only did the target site come out top, but the site which was closest to it in terms of atmosphere and surroundings – water, quiet, open-air – scored very nearly as well. At the same time, the choices for outdoor against indoor (38 to 10) was significant. Among the receivers, two people gave astonishingly accurate descriptions. One woman not only named the trees as being olive trees, but had them correctly placed in a circular grove near the pool. On her drawing, there was an indication of a time when a tree seemed to be spinning round – and one of the team then described how she had danced round a tree in a circle, holding on to it with one hand.

The other oddity was that the receiver whose remarks I was noting, whom I had not met before, gave an equally accurate description, complete with drawing, of the freeway tunnel which the team had never visited. So – was he picking up information by clairvoyance from inside one of the envelopes? Or was it just coincidence, that should therefore be used statistically to cancel out the accurate description of the olive grove?

The original Puthoff/Targ experiments were different from this in that they used individuals rather than groups to perform remote viewing; their control procedure was rather more sophisticated, since the target was chosen by a random-number generator from 100 independently selected locations, and their judging was handled independently of the subject or the researchers. In principle, the experiments were designed to answer the same question: can someone describe the details of a randomly chosen site, at a given moment, where he is locked away in a laboratory with no knowledge of where the site may be?

As with the group experiments, success does not seem to depend on whether people believe themselves experienced or gifted at psi. Two US Government scientists, a man and a woman, who visited the Stanford Research Institute to check on how stringently the double-blind procedure was being observed, were persuaded to take part in a series of experiments. The woman, during her three tests, steadily improved with practice, and by the time she came to the third target, a merry-go-round in Palo Alto, she drew a circle with hoops on it, and a central axis, that was unmistakably the right shape. The man, in his first experiment, describing some of the details around his target (a windmill in Portola Valley five miles away) achieved, according to Puthoff and Targ, remarkable results: 'He began his narrative, "There is a red A-frame building and next to it a large yellow thing" – a house and a tree – "further left there is another A-shape. It looks like a swing-set, but it is pushed down a gully so I can't see the swings" – all absolutely correct. He then went on to describe a lock on the front door that he correctly said "looks like it's made of laminated steel, so it must be a master lock".'

Out-of-body experiences

But just as there are dowsers whose abilities transcend the normal run of dowsing ability, so Puthoff and Targ have found that there are a number of psi professionals, men and women who consistently exceed, in the quality of their remote viewing, the isolated successes of unskilled subjects. 'The principal difference between experienced subjects and inexperienced volunteers is *not* that the latter never exhibit the faculty, but rather that their results are simply less reliable, more sporadic.'

Two of these psi professionals seem to me especially interesting because of the way that their experiences and their achievements overlap and illuminate some aspects of dowsing. The first is Pat Price, a renowned California resident, sometime police commissioner in Burbank and city councilman, who died in 1976. By all accounts he was a tough, abrasive man, at least until middle age, whose psychic powers came upon him quite suddenly at the age of fifty. The other is a quite different personality, the friendly, well-dressed, successful New York artist Ingo Swann, whose paintings often portray elements of psychic vision such as auras and energy fields.

Both men, Puthoff and Targ have found, have demonstrated the same ability 'to describe correctly details of buildings, roads, bridges and the like'. In the case of Pat Price, this detail often extended to 'structural materials, colour, ambience and activity'. When Ingo Swann met the two scientists, they asked him if he felt he could alter the magnetic field in a 'squid-type' magnetometer (the superconductive quantum interferometric device used, among other things, for measuring brainwaves) buried in the basement of the Stanford Research Institute. The magneto-meter is shielded by an aluminium container, copper sheets, and most importantly, a superconducting canister. In rigorous tests, this shielding had withstood the effects of a field of several thousand gauss applied from the outside by a powerful electro-magnet; the level of field on the inside showed up as a steadily pulsing sine wave on a recording chart in an office above.

Hal Puthoff reported: 'Swann was shown the set-up and told that if he were to affect the magnetic field in the magnetometer it would show up as a change in the output recording. He then placed his attention on the interior of the magnetometer (his description) at which point the frequency of the wave was doubled for a couple of cycles, or roughly ten seconds. We were amazed. We commented that it would really be something if Swann could stop the sine wave altogether. He proceeded to do just that for a period of roughly ten seconds. He then "let go", at which point the output returned to normal.'

The implication for dowsing of this remarkable PK effect is that Ingo Swann feels that he achieved this change by inducing in himself an out-of-body experience (OOBE), in which he mentally left his body behind and 'visited' the magnetometer in its under-ground well. In this way he was able as well as affecting the field, to give an accurate description as a dowser might, of various features of the magnetometer which, because of its individual design, could not conceivably have been known to him in ad-vance.

This ability to achieve an OOBE at will, which the Sussex dowser Robert Leftwich is able to manage for short times during a period of about a week in a six-week cycle, was also enjoyed consistently by Pat Price during the later years of his life, in-cluding the period when he was involved in experiments at Stanford. For those of us who have never felt what it is like, it is not an easy concept. Yet to those who have undergone such an experience, voluntarily or not, it is unmistakable (and from accounts in the literature, relatively common). It is variously described as 'floating away from oneself', or 'being detached and somewhere else'. Sometimes people can observe their own body sleeping or sitting wherever they have left it behind, sometimes not; in occult and spiritualist literature there are frequent references to a golden or silver cord attaching the physical body to the ethereal one – a kind of escape route, or guide-line with which to return home. But this is by no means always the case. In a survey conducted for the Institute for Psychophysical Research in London, more than 80 per cent of the respondents said they had never seen such a cord, and for Pat Price, down-to-earth and practical as he was in every other respect, it was as straightforward an experience as flying. He described vividly what happened after Hal Puthoff had given him a map reference, and asked him if he could find out, by means of an OOBE, what the countryside there looked like:

After I got home, my natural tendency was to get a map and look up where the hell those co-ordinates intersected; then I decided that wouldn't be necessary – I'd just locate them on my own.

All of a sudden, it was like boom! Those particular co-ordinates happened to intersect on the East Coast of the United States, in mountainous country. There I was, looking down on the scene, when I spotted a mountain about 5000 feet in altitude. I was at 15,000 feet at the time and decided to dip down and take a look round.

The first thing I found was a stream, and I wondered if there were any trout in it. So I felt it – no, I thought, it's too warm for trout. I did observe some other fish, though. Then I elevated.

I found myself looking clear down at the Gulf of Mexico to the south and up into Canada to the north. There was this big storm pattern developing, so I charted it, noting the time. I located some freeways and drew out maps, even though I hadn't been requested to do so. As it turned out later, they proved accurate.

Just so someone wouldn't think I was generalizing, I decided to dip down in a Civil War battlefield where there was a monument with an inscription. I read it, wrote it down, then noted its location in precise terms of degrees, minutes, and seconds. Later, after I'd reported my findings, Hal Puthoff had the monument located and checked. It was exactly where I'd said it was, and I'd written the inscription correctly.[9]

The OOBEs of Ingo Swann and Pat Price are important because they join the growing list of cases which prove that the experience is not just a subjective phenomenon – a fantasy or hallucination no more significant than a private dream – which is what the bulk of the literature on the subject consists of: personal descriptions of what it feels like, and of speculations about how it has given the person a new insight into the existence of life after death. But increasingly, the anecdotes on a level that can be checked, such as Robert Leftwich's out-of-body visit to his bank manager's safe, or another occasion which he described to me, when he had some friends to dinner:

They wanted proof that when I said I left my body, I really did so, and they suggested I go to their home in Brighton and describe what the front room there was like. So I drifted off, and when I got there I had a look round the room, and noticed that their baby-sitter, an aunt, was reading a book. I noted its title, and the number of the page she was reading. Then I came back into my body, pulled myself together, and told them what I'd seen.

They were astonished. I told them about their furniture, its colours, and where it was placed. You should understand that although it seemed extraordinary to them, for me it was perfectly straightforward. I knew what I'd seen, and that was that. Then I told them about the book, and straight away they telephoned to check. They asked their aunt the page number, and it was one or two further on than I'd said – during the time I'd been talking, she had read a couple more pages.

Experimentally, Charles Tart has established that a typical OOBE lasts between half a minute and half an hour, and that there are often different physiological symptoms compared with dreaming – a lack of the rapid eye movements that accompany dreams, for instance. He also set up a test which is remarkably similar to Robert Leftwich's viewing of the bank safe combination number. A young woman had reported frequent occasions at night when she had the sensation of floating near the ceiling of her bedroom and looking down on her body. So Tart invited her to sleep in his psychophysiology laboratory for four nights; each night he wrote a five-digit number, taken from a random number table, and placed it on a shelf seven feet above her bed.

For the first three nights, in spite of having felt several times that she had floated away from herself, she did not get into a position to see the paper. On the fourth night, however, she correctly identified the number as 25132 – which if guesswork had been involved, has odds of 100,000 to one against. Throughout the time she was sleeping in the laboratory, she was wired to an electroencephalograph, so that she could not have left the bed without disturbing the machine. The only thing wrong with the experimental procedure was that she was not constantly observed, and the somewhat unlikely suggestion has been made that she could have managed to glimpse the numbers without getting out of bed or leaving an EEG trace by putting a small mirror on the end of a telescope stick (though neither a stick nor a mirror were ever found).[10]

It may be that out-of-body experiences are much more common in dowsing than is usually thought. Bill Lewis, for one, believes so. John Shelley, formerly president of the American Society of Dowsers, became so sensitive that he was able to discard his pendulum and pick up information directly from the site; he got to the point where he could answer telephone requests for help in finding water by visualizing the place to be dowsed, and then giving a detailed description to the caller as to where the well should be sunk. Bob Ater's account in chapter 1 has obvious similarities with this.

The mysterious business of tracing missing bodies, may also occasionally owe something to this gift of instant, direct viewing. Gerard Croiset, the Dutch clairvoyant, arrived during 1976 in Tokyo to be greeted by the Press, and the distraught mother of a missing child. Having used a map and pendulum to discover the approximate area where he thought the child would be, he then described features of the site – reeds, water, paths – and their relationship to one another in such a way that the place could be unmistakably identified. By next morning, the child's body had been discovered exactly where he said, and the police chief in charge of the case, whose men had been searching a completely different area, could be seen on the television news shaking his head in disbelief.

There was a similar case in Austria shortly after the Second World War, when an elderly dowser named Franz Hertz, working in Vienna, was asked to help find a young girl who had disappeared from her home some weeks previously. A friend watched how he went about it:

> Franz held a pendulum over a map of the district and after nearly fifteen minutes' concentration he said: 'I want to go to a place about six miles from here.' There was a car at the door and I drove him and the parents to a lonely spot on the outskirts of the city.
>
> We left the car and followed Franz along a narrow lane which opened on to a clearing at the edge of a wood. There, a large pool of stagnant water attracted his attention, and again he held the pendulum and remained a long time staring into the water. 'We must go further,' he said quietly.
>
> We drove about two miles further on, very slowly as he instructed. Next time we left the car, Franz walked directly to a ditch half full of stagnant water, and in it he found the body of the girl, who had apparently been murdered.
>
> Much later, when I spoke to Franz about the case, he said he had 'seen' the girl lying under stagnant water when he was staring at the map, and that the pendulum had in some way helped to set in action his unconscious mind.[11]

The obvious link between dowsing and the various other types of remote viewing has not yet been the subject of experimental enquiry, and perhaps it is now time for this. The two activities seem to complement each other, like two sides of the same coin. Whereas with map-dowsing the object is to discover the location of something or somebody, remote viewing involves describing what the location looks like. Where dowsing usually relies on a painstaking and somewhat restricting question-and-answer procedure, viewing occurs as a series of fleeting, dream-like and not always accurate mental images. It is possible that a combination of the two techniques would be irresistible.

Some idea of a way forward has been indicated by Ingo Swann's most recent activities. Like a dowser he has been applying his viewing faculty to real discovery, and was immediately successful in finding a gas field for the Red Feather Gas and Oil Company. At the same time, in his experiments with Hal Puthoff and Russell Targ, he has been dictating two lists for them to record – one list of objects which he 'sees' but does not think are at the location, and the other list those things which he is fairly sure are there. In physics, this would be known as improving the ratio of signal to noise, and it is also very closely akin to the way in which a dowser sorts out the features of what he is seeking by getting yes/no answers to his questions.

But perhaps the most hopeful aspect of the common thread that joins dowsing and the experimental successes of other psi effects is the growing body of proof that the gift of seeing hidden things may not be as exclusive as was once thought. In the words of Puthoff and Targ after more than fifty experiments: 'Remote viewing may be a latent and widely distributed perceptual ability.'

In other words, there's something of the psychic in every one of us – and always has been.

9 Dawn of Understanding

'Today's interest in the occult is born of a revulsion from science,' Dr John Beloff, Professor of Psychology at Glasgow University, Scotland, said in his 1976 inaugural lecture as President of the Society for Psychical Research. Maybe the word revulsion puts the matter too strongly. What seems to be happening is that a new generation of both students and teachers is demanding that science should encompass the study of phenomena that for a long while have been held outside the scope of legitimate enquiry. Such things as miracles, apparitions, pre-destination, astrology, magic, altered states of consciousness, telepathy – in short, the ancient 'mysteries' – are once again instinctively felt to be part of the grand pattern, and as such must be included in any attempt by science to explain how the universe works.

Increasingly, some scientists are making the difficult attempt to come to terms with the reality of psi, and it is nowadays over-simplistic to go on portraying 'psi' and 'science' as if they were at war, or were necessarily on opposite sides of the fence. A more accurate metaphor might be the confrontation of two strangers, both slighly suspicious of the other's background, who find it very difficult to speak one another's language. For each, words alone are inadequate. The psychic finds it impossible to verbalize his personally felt experience and instinct; the scientist, searching to explain the symmetries of natural law, can only do so through mathematical theorems and formulae. Seeking to prove his point, the psychic might say, 'I feel it, therefore it is'; the scientist, 'it can't be measured, therefore it isn't'. From the psychic point of view, there are some experiences, certain states of consciousness, that are simply indescribable. To which the scientist would have to reply that such things cannot, being indefinable, lie within his sphere of competence.

But the attitude between the two, while still wary, is becoming somewhat less strained. Partly this is because quantum physics, which embraces the unpredictable, is speculatively providing a number of methods of reconciliation. But in many other disciplines also – anthropology, zoology, neurology, psychology – there is a growing number of people who feel that only by accepting the existence of a psychic component in the area they are studying, can they fully understand it. Sophisticated laboratory work in France, for instance, has shown that mice are able to foretell the future. A number of them were placed in a cage that was separated into two halves by a low barrier. From time to time, the floor on one side of the cage or another was electrified, giving the mice there a mildly unpleasant electric shock. The timing and choice of side to be electrified were made by a random number generator, so that neither the experimenters nor the mice could, in theory, know when or on which side it was going to happen. Yet after a short while, the mice learned to avoid the shock by anticipating what the generator would choose, and leaping the barrier before the floor became live.[1] (The author of this experiment, an eminent French biologist, decided to publish the results under a pseudonym, for fear of ridicule by his orthodox colleagues.)

An explanation via ESP is also increasingly being put forward for some of the classic puzzles of animal behaviour. In spite of years of work that has established some of the clues which migrating birds use – the stars, the earth's magnetic field – it is still not enough, according to the latest research study, 'to fully explain how an individual bird finds its way between its breeding territory and its wintering grounds'. Nor has anyone satisfactorily explained how it is that cats and dogs have found their way home, or to their mates, across entire continents (this ability seems to function less well if their whiskers are cut off – as if their aerials had been removed); nor how some animals, such as elephants, are able to detect underground water when there are no visible surface indications.

What these aspects of animal behaviour have in common is that they are responses to basic, primal urges – for water, for reproduction, for communication, for safety from danger – and dowsers say with one voice that these instinctive abilities were once shared by man. As prehistorical evidence of this, they quote their belief that ancient megaliths – including those in New England observed during Bill Lewis's map-dowsing experiment – were always placed over the crossing of underground streams. I have watched experienced dowsers, who are seldom wrong in water-finding, tracing the paths of these streams beneath megaliths often enough to be convinced that this is true; if so, it is an indication that the dowsing faculty, at least in the form of water-divining, may be as old as man himself.[2]

But dowsers also sense that these ancient sites, which are spread throughout the world, were once capable of a wider use, for psychic healing and telepathic communication; and that psi effects today are simply a faint echo of this distant knowledge. So far as the stones are concerned, there is some support for this in legend and folk-lore, and as recently as the nineteenth century there are contemporary accounts of attempts to use ancient sites in a miraculous or paranormal way. In Europe, when the supposed healing powers were being invoked, there were ceremonies that called for them to be touched or walked round in certain ways, often on important days in the calendar. Of course, there is no reliable evidence as to whether the cures worked, but it is nevertheless of some significance that the sites were believed to have this vestigial power, particularly as it is confirmed by similar reports in North America and Australia. Here, one can assume a continuous use of the sites since early times, uninterrupted as in Europe by several centuries of Christian teaching, and in both continents the sites seem to have been thought to have powers of re-vitalization and re-generation.

In Australia, there were numerous stones which aboriginal trackers stopped by for an hour or so, gaining, they said, the equivalent of a night's rest. In America, there was a strikingly well-observed example, reported to the US Bureau of Ethnology in the 1880s, of Apache Indian medicine men rubbing their spines against a sacred stone in order to re-vitalize their powers of telepathy and healing.

Psi and anthropology

Dowsers claim a natural kinship with such people, who even today may represent a long line of psychic tradition stretching back unbroken to prehistoric times. General Scott Elliot told me once: 'I went on a visit to South Africa and was introduced to one of their witch doctors – a nice chap. The strange thing was the way we were able to communicate without really understanding one another's language. He sat there throwing his bones, and I sat there with my pendulum, and in our own ways we were getting just the same answers.'

Certainly, some anthropological reports on primitive tribes quote instances that seem indistinguishable from interviews with modern psychics in paranormal studies. Thus Ronald Rose, writing of Australian aboriginals in *Living Magic*, tried to find out how they saw messages in smoke.

'Is the message in the smoke?'

'No . . . it makes me think, but I do not think. There is a great feeling rises up in me . . . it is like wind from the head.'

'How would you send a message?'

'I would make a good fire with green boughs that makes a good smoke. When he sees it he knows it is not a camp fire and gets to thinking. And I am thinking too so he thinks my thoughts.'[3]

Norma Lee Browning, another researcher, regards Australian aboriginals as 'undoubtedly the most hypersensitive race of people in the world, the most highly suggestible, the most non-talkative, and the most psychic in the truest literal sense of the word, that is: *sensitive to non-physical forces*'. She tells the story of an aboriginal woman called Queenie who walked into her office at Maningrida early one morning and said: 'My brother bin properly-dead-finish.' The brother was in Cape York, 200 miles away, and almost immediately a wireless message came through confirming that the brother had died at 5 a.m. When Queenie was asked how she could have known this, she replied simply: 'I just knew.'[4]

This kind of incident is so common among aboriginals that most people take it for granted. Few statistical studies exist, mostly because people who use psi as a matter of course in their day-to-day life regard card-guessing as even more pointless than a Western psychic or dowser who is personally assured of his powers. However, Ronald Rose was able to persuade fifty

Australian aboriginals to co-operate in an experiment, and then a number of New Zealand Maoris, and obtained 'highly significant above-chance deviation' in both cases. But, Samoan natives failed to do better than average, and so did a group of native teachers in another experiment in New Guinea.

Such conclusions as can be drawn from this, as well as from the vast body of anecdotal evidence, suggest that however widespread the belief in psi may be, and however widely practised, each society has just a relatively small number of exceptionally gifted people. For the Australian aboriginal, these were termed 'clever men'. The Chippewa Indians, near Lake Winnipeg, had *shamans* who put their gifts to the practical uses of foretelling the approach of the enemy, finding lost objects, locating wild game, and warding off invisible cannibal monsters who threatened the security of the tribe. To achieve this, they went into a 'shaking tent', a séance in which spirits were invoked to answer questions, and spirit-voices emerged to give clairvoyant advice. As late as the 1930s, about ten per cent of the tribe were capable of this faculty, and it was said that earlier, before the white man came, about double that number could manage it.

In recent times, much the most remarkable studies of native psi have come from Africa. Robert and Linda Sussman, from the department of Anthropology in Washington University, St Louis, Missouri, studied the Sakalava of Madagascar, where divination is used in cases of sickness, in discovering the identity of thieves or in finding lost objects, in finding a wife, for advice about crops and livestock, and in predicting the future – with the possible exception of the last, a range of events extremely close to those covered by dowsing. They found that although most people in the tribe knew something of the techniques and used them to solve minor everyday problems, it was the doctor, or *ombiasa*, who was called in for more serious matters; he divined by a complex procedure that involved the use of about 140 acacia seeds and their formation into rows and patterns.

The Sussmans were convinced of the ombiasa's powers on two occasions. The first time, he told them with complete certainty that a lost cigarette lighter was in their car. After searching it, they thought he must be wrong, but several weeks later found it there in an almost inaccessible place. On the second, he knew exactly the day they would arrive back from a trip, even though they hadn't told him – 'He had arranged for our host to be in his house to greet us, instead of in the rice fields where he should have been planting.'[5]

Another scientist to have discovered talents among the witch doctors more or less identical to those of dowsers was the noted South African psychiatrist Dr B. J. F. Laubscher. He chose to make a lengthy investigation of the South Eastern Cape Bantu, especially the Tembu tribe, where he knew that their few most senior diviners, the *isanuses*, were generally believed by local Europeans to be able to find stolen animals and lost property. He tested one of these, Solomon Daba, by burying a purse in Queenstown, sixty miles from Daba's home, and then driving at an average speed of thirty-five miles an hour (to defeat the possibility that runners were bringing distant information) to meet Daba. To make the test more difficult, he had wrapped the purse in brown paper, buried it in the ground, and then placed on top a flat brown stone covered with a grey stone. Solomon Daba, during the séance-dance which he used as his method of divining information, described all these things correctly in minute detail.[6]

All of which goes to show that, however different the methods (tent-shaking, dancing, 'knowing'), the divining ability is widely distributed. But lately, there has been one truly exceptional case that as well as describing the reality of psi, throws genuine insight on its nature when it is practised at the very highest level.

Adrian Boshier is a British archaeologist in his thirties, somewhat reserved and academic by nature, who has undergone the extraordinary experience of being fully initiated as a witch doctor with a tribe of Zulus. In this part of the world, a witch doctor means the priest, prophet, physician, herbalist, psychiatrist, healer, diviner, and historian of the tribe, more commonly a woman than a man, who is known as a sangoma.

Many of the tasks which sangomas are expected to undertake are common to healers, diviners and shamans in other countries. One thing that is notable (although it also happens in other societies) is the way in which the process of becoming a sangoma starts involuntarily and becomes irresistible. Adrian Boshier told a conference on parapsychology and anthropology in

London in the summer of 1973 how a very senior witch doctor, who had herself trained thirty others, foresaw and told him how he would be 'going on a different journey (from the ones he normally took); you're going over the big water, and the place you're going to, people are going to know about us, us sangomas, and you must tell them . . . that we sangomas have no choice. We might have been converted to any of the Western religions. When the spirit takes us over, we have no choice but to be trained.'

The woman's father was in fact an ordained Methodist minister, whose fellow churchgoers did all they could to dissuade her. But the signs were unmistakable. When somebody is genuinely about to become a sangoma, an illness known as *moya* takes hold of them, which may make him or her bedridden up to three years (in the case of Boshier himself, six months), whose symptoms of fits and foaming are something like those of epilepsy.

After this comes an extended period of training – again, up to about three years – in which the initiate learns daily through songs, special dancing, drumming, bodily purification, and continual instruction, how to strengthen and use the 'spirit' which is possessing them, and which speaks through them in a special voice (male or female) and often in different tongues. Adrian Boshier explained how the initiate 'is called day or night to find things that the *Baba* (teacher) has hidden in the village. At first the teacher will tell the *bwasa* (recruit) that something is hidden for her, but as the training progresses the Baba will no longer inform the initiate verbally, but will call her employing telepathic methods.'

At the coming-out ceremony the initiate has to find a goat which has been hidden somewhere in the village, and is then, when it has been slaughtered, required to drink some of its blood. Adrian Boshier comments on his own initiation: 'My Baba informed me that we had to call up the spirits and only this blood-taking ritual could ensure such communication. And so I found myself enacting a custom which in numerous writings I have claimed to be one of man's earliest religious rites.'

Thereafter, a sangoma may go through another twelve stages of training, always guided by the spirit, which may come at any time, unbidden. The way in which a sangoma diagnoses illness echoes strikingly the way in which a dowser will announce spontaneously that a part of someone's anatomy is not functioning properly. 'An African suffering from any misfortune, physiological, psychological or otherwise, will go to the home of a sangoma and simply demand that the sangoma tell him what he has come for. "I want to know" (*sia cou lega*), will be his only statement. With no further prompting whatsoever the sangoma must tell the patient exactly why he has come, and how to cure or remedy his troubles.'

One final extract from Adrian Boshier's narrative sounds a sympathetic chord with the belief of most dowsers that there is a commonalty, or universality, in the existence of psi: 'During one of my initiation ceremonies, I asked an old woman who was presiding whether she had any regrets, fears, or doubts that she was initiating me into a tribally orientated ceremony, as I was not only European, but actually came from England. I had not been born here, and none of my ancestors had been in South Africa.

'She replied that it made no difference whatsoever, she had seen my ancestors in her dreams, and my ancestors and her ancestors spoke to one another – all spirits were the same, when we die we all go to the same place. She said, "today you and I are different, we live differently, our culture is different, but long long ago we all came back from a common source and when we die we go back to the old people – back to the old days, to our ancestors, and on that side there is no difference, we are all the same." She went on, "I can only accept you as a witch doctor because my ancestors and your ancestors have agreed that this should be so, and that is why I invited you here".'[7]

Brainwave patterns
Another area of new-found interest to scientists for which dowsers have an instinctive sympathy is what might broadly be termed the Eastern way of life. Mostly – since this is the way Western science goes about its business – this research takes the form of measuring physiologically what happens during acupuncture, or observing the pattern of brainwaves during altered states of consciousness, or trying to discover if the seven chakras of the body described in Indian teachings as vortices of energy, have any existence in reality. For dowsers, the appeal is more in what

is seen, subjectively, as a close parallel between the state of mind needed for their work, and that which a yogi strives for. As with native divination, there are differences in technique; also, the intentions are somewhat different. But there is still a marked affinity between the way that many dowsers describe the way they are able to pick up information, and, for instance, Norma Lee Browning's description of the states of yoga training:

1. Pratyhara, or sense withdrawal. The yogi learns to restrain the flow of external sense impressions on his mind.

2. Dharana, or concentration. This is not the same as 'concentration' in the Western sense. Its final phase is characterized by the highest state of complete *thoughtlessness*, or a totally blank mind.

3. Dhyana, or contemplation. In dhyana, the yogi begins to perceive new and subtle aspects of his contemplation.

4. Samadhi, or trance. The desire of all yogis is to reach this stage. Many fail. There are five stages of this trance, according to the manuals. In the final stages of samadhi, the yogi is supposed to achieve an ecstasy of the highest form attainable, sometimes characterized by 'super-conscious' or 'super-normal' perception, transcending space and time.

It is this last, comments Norma Lee Browning, that has given rise to the widespread but mistaken belief in the yogi's powers of extra-sensory perception. A true yogi, she says, is not interested in occultism, magic, supernaturalism, or any aspects of psychic phenomena.[8]

Nevertheless, the first two stages of yoga training that she describes could equally well have been taken from any dowsing manual, and it is illuminating to find that many of the physiological and neurological measurements that have been taken during these stages have a marked similarity to those observed in dowsers. The consistent appearance during meditation of a slowed heart rate, reduced oxygen requirement, and reduced body temperature, for instance, is precisely the same as that found by a team of doctors at Guy's Hospital in London when they examined Robert Leftwich during one of his out-of-body experiences.

219

There also seems to be a link between the characteristic brain-wave patterns in yoga training, psi manifestations generally, and at least one dowsing experiment. All of us produce these brain-waves, since our brains are complex, weak electrical instruments. The invention of the electroencephalograph (EEG) in 1929 by the German scientist Hans Berger allowed people for the first time to identify how much current the brain produces and at what frequencies; a number of electrodes – usually eight – are placed on the scalp, and the electrical impulses from the brain are recorded in familiar traces on a moving strip of paper. It has been found that the frequency range stretches from about thirty cycles per second to half a cycle per second or possibly lower; most of the time, waking, the adult brain operates at the top end, from 30 down to 14 *cps*, and anything below this is known as an altered state of consciousness – for instance sleep, dreaming, meditation, hypnosis. All these states have familiar signatures which, after some years of study, can be recognized and identified by experienced observers. The frequency range has been some-what arbitrarily divided (see *Diagram 5*) into beta, alpha, theta and delta waves.

Edward P. Jastram, a scientist from Rehoboth, Massachusetts, told a meeting in 1975 what happens in a typical EEG recording when you drop off to sleep: 'You would find that at the moment when you drift into a period of floating or peacefulness just before sleep, alpha rhythms would emerge. Then sleep takes you through alpha and theta to delta, then gradually back again to alpha, where you spend some time dreaming. This trip to delta and back takes about ninety minutes. Then you go to theta again, varying back and forth between alpha and theta in approximately ninety minute periods for the rest of the night.'[9]

Some of the general characteristics of states of mind associated with the various frequencies have been classified:

Beta: Especially prominent when there is nervous tension and anxiety. Most heavy smokers stay at high beta most of the time.

Alpha: Besides dreaming, a feeling of well-being and relaxa-tion, and also of the increased awareness that comes from meditation. The average person usually has a burst of alpha waves several times a minute, and it seems to be established that

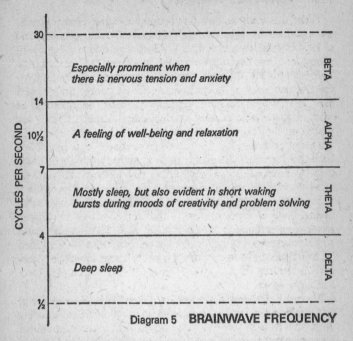

CYCLES PER SECOND

30 — Especially prominent when
there is nervous tension and anxiety — BETA

14 — A feeling of well-being and relaxation — ALPHA
10½

7 — Mostly sleep, but also evident in short waking
bursts during moods of creativity and problem solving — THETA

4 — Deep sleep — DELTA
½

Diagram 5 **BRAINWAVE FREQUENCY**

the more this happens, and the lower in the spectrum normal, waking beta waves are, the more contented and efficient a person will be.

Theta: Mostly sleep, but also becomes evident in short waking bursts during moods of creativity and problem-solving.

Delta: Deep sleep.

You might therefore predict that alpha waves are the important ones for dowsing, and you would almost certainly be right. Edward Jastram described an experiment with the Cape Cod dowser William Broadley, who uses a small forked rod held in the tips of his fingers. Seeking answers to questions by dowsing methods (i.e. a question followed four or five seconds later by a dip of the rod), it is quite clear from his EEG recording (*Diagram 6*) that about one second after the question, there is a marked period of alpha activity.

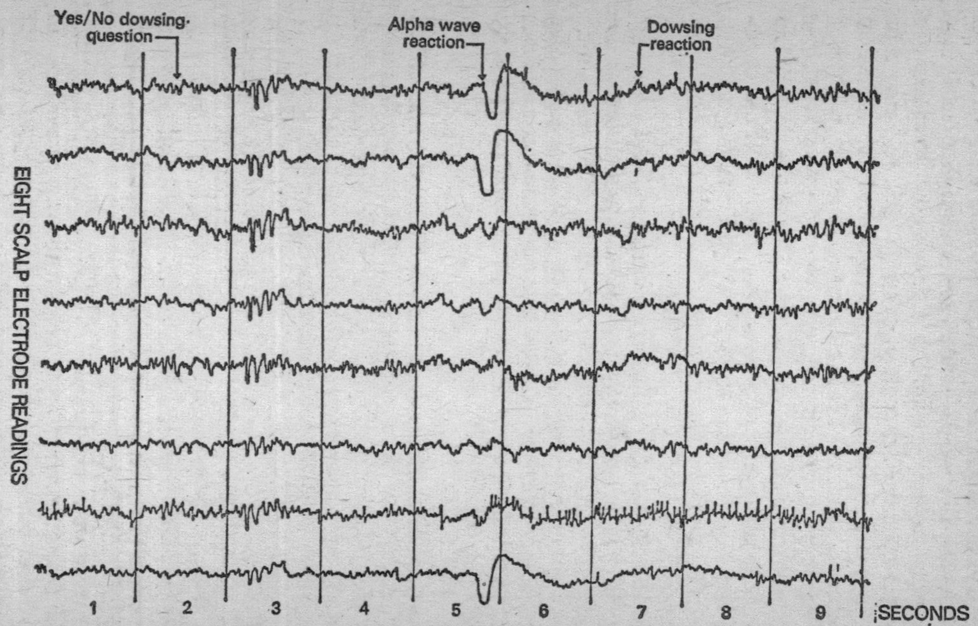

Yes/No dowsing question
Alpha wave reaction
Dowsing reaction
EIGHT SCALP ELECTRODE READINGS
1
2
3
4
5
6
7
8
9
SECONDS

Diagram 6 **EEG READINGS ON WILLIAM BROADLEY**

In scientific examination of yoga, the most renowned experiment involved forty-eight Zen Buddhist monks aged from twenty-four to seventy-two who undertook a closely-monitored series of meditations in the University of Tokyo in 1960. As a control, a similar group of untrained volunteers imitated the method of meditation, which was to sit cross-legged, hands clasped, gazing for about thirty minutes with open eyes at a position on the floor about three feet in front of them. The results showed that where the control group's beta rhythms remained active throughout the half-hour, the monks quickly slipped into alpha, and then gradually down the spectrum into theta, still with their eyes wide open.

Edward Jastram thinks there may be another link between the dowsing faculty and alpha rhythms. In the growth of a child, the brainwave pattern is almost exclusively delta in the womb, and is predominantly so until about eighteen months. At about one year, theta begins to appear, and strong theta shows from about eighteen months to three or four years. Thereafter, until puberty, alpha takes over:

So the child from three to twelve years is largely in theta and alpha, and this is the time when it is most creative, sensitive, and learns at the most rapid rate. During this period the child will have considerable psychic ability, particularly if its parents are willing to recognize it and not suppress it.

The American Society of Dowsers has tested children in the five to twelve year group, and finds that probably 90 per cent of them can dowse quite well with little instruction. The baby operating in delta is very sensitive and aware, but non-verbal. He has good communication at the non-verbal level, mostly in terms of feeling: a mother and child achieve excellent rapport without any words.

When we as adults enter into these altered states of consciousness deliberately, as we can do with certain mental exercises and training, and seem to do in dowsing, all sorts of awareness and modes of communication become open to us. With practice, we can even get all the way down to delta while remaining consciously aware of our surroundings, and the effect of doing so in the presence of a baby is something to see;

the baby thinks/feels that it's just great – here's someone he can 'talk' to.

It appears to be the case that in beta we are all strangers to one another, while in alpha, theta and delta we are all subconsciously communicating with each other all the time.

Inner and outer minds

Neurologists have also recently found the probable way in which the brain operates the change from one state of consciousness to another. In the brain stem at the base of the skull is a crucial network of nerve cells known as the reticular system, which acts as a complex filter and switch mechanism for the barrage of sights, sounds and other sensations that constantly overwhelm us. The way it works has been throwing new light on what happens during hypnosis – and at the same time, offering an equally good explanation of what may happen in the brain during the unconscious process of dowsing.

Hypnosis is itself an altered state of consciousness in which, like dowsing, alpha rhythms predominate; the mystery has long been how a hypnotic subject is able to ignore most of the information presented by his normal five senses (like a dowser or a Zen Buddhist), and remember only the message given by the hypnotist. The latest research findings, contradicting orthodox theory, suggest that all our nerve impulses – the information carriers between the sensory organs and the brain – go along parallel trackways. One track leads directly to all parts of the cerebral cortex (the myriad grey cells that make up the brain), but the impulses lie there unactivated and unheeded for the time being; the other trackway goes via the reticular system, which sorts out whether a particular impulse is immediately important or unimportant and instructs the cerebral cortex accordingly. The system either activates the first set of impulses to allow perception and appropriate action, or inhibits those first impulses so that perception does not occur.

Dr Gordon Flint, a member of the British Society of Medical and Dental Hypnosis, explained to a meeting in 1975 how this seems to account for the way hypnotic suggestion works:

Immediately before hypnosis, the subject is using his five

senses normally, and the reticular system is activating those bits of information that he needs to tell him where to sit down, what to say, and so on; you might call this the outer mind – that part with which we interpret the world around us with our five basic senses and which has reasoning ability, a critical faculty.

There is also an inner mind – that much larger part, perhaps ninety per cent, which is a memory store of all our experiences and which caters for what one might call general housekeeping – temperature control, pulse rate, blood pressure, breathing, glandular secretions and other aspects of general maintenance and repair. This inner mind has no or only minimal reasoning capacity.

In hypnosis, what may happen is that when the hypnotist starts a session, the subject is using his outer mind to attend to what is being said. As he goes into a hypnotic state, he switches over, by using the reticular system, and allows his inner mind to accept the suggestions of the hypnotist. At the same time, most of his conscious sensations are inhibited or modified, so that the only nerve impulses that become activated are auditory – the ones that relay the messages coming from the hypnotist's mouth.[10]

Dr Flint suggests that something very similar happens in dowsing. A dowsing signal comes in, which the reticular system recognizes and activates, causing a neuro-muscular response that is felt and seen in the rod or pendulum movement; simultaneously, the dowser's reticular system inhibits the unrequired senses, producing the state of receptive concentration needed.

The mystery signal

All of which goes to show that, in various ways, a considerable body of scientific attention is being directed towards dowsing and related phenomena, certainly to an extent that would have been unthinkable even ten years ago. However, this kind of observation and analysis still leaves the most fundamental questions unanswered. For however illuminating it may be to discover a similarity between dowsing and primitive psi, or the importance of alpha waves, or the mechanism in the brain that may enable us to distinguish a signal from background noise, the deepest challenge still remains: just what is the nature of the signal? where does the information come from? how is it carried over great chasms of space and time into our inner minds?

The plain answer must be that, as yet, nobody knows; and by the same token, there may not be a single solution for all psi phenomena. John Taylor and Eduardo Balanovski, concentrating on the electromagnetic frequency band from 500 megahertz to three gigahertz, have had isolated results which seemed to indicate an excess of energy here radiating from the hands of a number of healers. This is promising, for if confirmed, it might provide the basis of a physical explanation for many so-called 'miracle' cures; as we have seen, the newly-discovered facts about the human body's sensitivity to minute levels of radiation, and its capacity to react and adapt under the influence of tiny environmental changes, make it entirely feasible that a measurable energy passing from one person to another would be enough to trigger off a healing. In the same way, it might become possible to understand the well-observed sensation of tingling which some dowsers – Bill Lewis and Henry Gross among them – are able to transmit to another person, by violently revolving the pendulum as if it were a dynamo.

Similarly, we could build a hypothetical model of how the ancient megaliths may have been used.[11] We know that the passage of water through the earth, as in underground streams above which they were built, creates a small electrical current, which appears on the surface as a magnetic anomaly. This, in turn, may somehow be amplified by the mass of the megalith (two recent magnetometer surveys suggest this), and the changed magnetic field could theoretically – as in the Presman/Barnothy experiments – affect the human body. In this way, an explanation would be available for all the legends of healing and re-vitalization; and also for today's accounts, told to me and observed on many occasions, of how the stones sometimes feel as if they are rocking, or giving off an emanation that can be felt as a tingling through the fingertips.

Our newly proved sensitivity to low levels of radiation also forms a framework of belief for all the dowsing stories about the harmful effects of underground 'black streams'. Even within dowsing circles, this is probably the most contentious of all current issues, and outside, perhaps the most difficult for a sceptic to accept. But basically, what is being said is very simple. Many dowsers – perhaps nearly all dowsers who have studied the subject – believe that certain underground streams can cause arthritis, cancer, and have other harmful effects if a person is exposed to them regularly and too long, such as by sleeping in a bed or working at a desk over one; and that the effect of these streams can be modified by various methods such as by driving stakes into the ground at a certain point directly above them.

Stated as baldly as that, it is a very hard proposition for an outsider to take. A geologist wouldn't even agree that such streams exist, a physicist wouldn't have equipment sufficiently sensitive to distinguish and measure their supposed emanations, a physiologist would say that there is no evidence that illness can be caused in this way, and a psychologist would ask for a survey of claimed cures with proper controls to prove to him that the whole idea is not fictitious nonsense. The emotional link between the driving of stakes and medieval witchcraft and vampirism doesn't help; nor does the fact that dowsers themselves are hopelessly divided about the nature of the streams (even whether they are streams at all), how they can best be diverted, and whether this can be done permanently.

And yet . . . there still remains something mysterious that needs to be explained. With one possible exception, each of the excellent dowsers whose activities have so far been described believes that the theory is in some degree true, and has his own examples to offer. Much of modern dowsing literature is absorbed with how to investigate it further. Jack Livingston showed me a map of a small village in California which he knows well, with houses running up each side of the main street. For some years now he has kept a record of deaths in the village, for he once dowsed the existence of a harmful stream that runs under the houses on one side – and sure enough, there has been an exceptionally high rate of cancer deaths in them, whereas the other side has been completely clear.

Now this is in no way scientific proof, but it goes a long way to explain dowsers' preoccupation with the subject. Jack

Livingston explains the dilemma with utter conviction: 'What the heck am I supposed to do about it? I can't go and worry a lot of nice folk by telling them individually that unless they move house they will probably die. Altering that stream would be a big job, and one that I would probably have to keep going back to. And anyway, there's hardly a chance that any of them would believe me if I told them.'

Enid Smithett has many similar stories to tell. Bill Lewis says: 'Just because we can't fully understand the streams doesn't mean that they don't exist. We disagree about them because their nature is very complicated and difficult.' Herbert Douglas, a family doctor living in Arlington, Vermont, has kept records of fifty-five consecutive cases of arthritis which he examined in a period of two years. 'Every single one was sleeping over underground veins of water that crossed right beneath the part of the body hurting most. Over a period of time, twenty-five of these people agreed to move their bed to a part of the house free of these underground irritations, and in each case the pain was substantially lessened or completely eliminated.'[12]

Herbert Douglas describes the state of our knowledge in such matters as comparable to our knowledge of TV in the year 1900, and this may well be the fairest way of looking at the whole disputed area. The Russian radiation research reported by Alexandr Presman could be crucial.[13] If it can truly be established that extremely low levels of certain types of radiation have a greater effect on the human body than relatively high ones, and if interrupted doses of exposure are cumulatively more effective than continuous exposure – both of which he claims to be proved – then at least there is a basis from which to start a serious investigation of black streams, and to discover what type of emanation may be involved. Zaboj Harvalik speculates that it may be some form of the harmful gamma rays, high in frequency in the electromagnetic spectrum, which are normally shielded from us by the ionosphere, and in one of his experiments with Wilhelm de Boer, he has sought to prove that minutely low levels can be detected by the human body. A phial of Cobalt-60, giving off gamma rays at a rate of 3 milliroentgen/hour, was shielded by 23 cm thickness of lead, which he says attenuated the radiation 'to almost cosmic rays background'. Even so, he says that Wilhelm de Boer was able to distinguish the radiation at a distance of five feet.

So research into electromagnetism as an explanation for at least some psi phenomena is showing promising advances. But even its most enthusiastic advocates find grave difficulty in applying it to all reported cases of dowsing and telepathy. Remote viewing experiments with Ingo Swann and Pat Price were sometimes carried out when they were enclosed in a double-walled copper-screen Faraday cage, which gave 120-dB attenuation in the spectrum range from 15 kilohertz to one gigahertz. At the upper end, this is precisely the frequency band which John Taylor suggests as being theoretically most suitable to carry information, and 120-dB attenuation means that virtually none of it was able to penetrate the Faraday cage. Yet neither Ingo Swann nor Pat Price found any subjective difference in their ability to perceive distant sites, and their statistical successes in remote viewing were not significantly different from the times when they operated outside the Faraday cage.

Harold Puthoff's and Russell Targ's own suggested explanation is that, since extremely low frequency waves (up to about 10 hertz) are able to penetrate the cage with little attenuation, the search for the information carrier, if electromagnetic, must be looked for here. Their answer to the overwhelming objection to this – that the wavelengths are too long to carry detailed information – is that the imagination may be 'filling in the blanks'.

So neither frequency band is at the moment satisfactory as a complete answer, and as we have seen, electromagnetism simply does not square with the dowsers' own feelings and observations. Even Zaboj Harvalik, who as a physicist yearns for an answer within his scientific understanding, has been forced to conclude that 'something else' is operating. He visited Australia a few years ago, and was challenged by a member of the Sydney Water Board to locate the main reservoir serving the city, and to tell him how far away and how deep it was. Now although Zaboj Harvalik does not regard himself as a great dowser, he knew well enough that under the right circumstances, this was the kind of information that ought to be obtainable by dowsing methods, so he agreed to try. First he spun his body round the horizon until his rod dipped – the direction of the reservoir, he said: correct. Then he counted the distance – twelve and a half miles: correct.

Finally the depth – 68 feet: wrong, said the Water Board member – the true depth was 75 feet. As it happened, their itinerary that afternoon took them to the reservoir . . . and the current drought had lowered the level to 68 feet. 'Try as I have, I can't work that out through electromagnetism,' he says. 'The direction and the distance, possibly they're some kind of remote viewing. But not the depth – it was too exact. In any case, I didn't "see" the location. I just let the rod do the work.'

But if the information carrier isn't electromagnetism, what can it be? John Taylor incisively summarized the various theories, and the objections to them, at the 1976 Parascience Conference in London, and proved at least that there is no shortage of ideas, and no theoretical reason to suppose that there is a single explanation for all phenomena. Most of the proposals hover on the outermost fringes of what is known about the fundamental particles that make up the universe, and are incomprehensible except in terms of mathematics. However, he thinks they are all in their own way unsatisfactory. Here are some of the easier ones, with a simplified version of some of his criticisms.

(1) Beams of the other three known forces – nuclear, radio-active and gravitational – or of cosmic rays as information carriers. 'Improbable because of the amount of energy needed to activate them; and because the way they act is well understood.'

(2) Other dimensions – the idea that other worlds exist in space and time alongside us, and that occasionally there is an interaction between our world and this other existence. 'This causes severe divergence difficulties in quantum field theory.'

(3) Tachyons – faster-than-light particles which, if they exist, could overcome the difficulties of penetrating into the past or the future. 'There is no experimental evidence for them; indeed, in the whole of physics, there has never yet been an observation of a causal effect. And the amount of energy needed theoretically to activate them is colossal.'

(4) Various theories based on quantum physics – the 'Copenhagen interpretation', the 'branching universe', and so on. 'Not

only do these change the existing rules, but each does so in a different and arguable way; and it is difficult to see how the theoretical behaviour of minute particles, which is what quantum mechanics is all about, can be applied to something as massive as a human body.'

(5) The idea that the sum total of the energy put out by all human brains, added together, produces a random noise which can be used both as a source and a carrier of information. 'Even though this has supposedly been "proved" in theory, it depends on two arbitrarily chosen mathematical constants.'

Direct knowledge

Yet in spite of the objections, there remains the notion that there is a fifth force as yet unknown to science which is used during ESP, or that there is a vast and all-embracing concept known as Mind, or cosmic consciousness, from which we obtain our paranormal information. To this, John Taylor would retort that there is no experimental evidence of a fifth force whatsoever, and by now there should be – 'to say that some event is the result of ESP is just another way of saying that you don't understand it'.

He is right, of course, and perhaps the most important thing is that we don't understand, yet. But this belief in the existence of a consciousness outside what can be measured has proved remarkably resilient, persisting through the scientific revolution that occurred when the laws of Einstein succeeded those of Newton, and now, according to some scientists, finding common ground with the newly discovered paradoxes of sub-atomic particles.

Undoubtedly there is still a very great deal that science does not know. Ray Willey, in his lectures, sometimes lists around fifty mysteries which he feels that scientists regard as proven, but are in fact just assertions. In physics, he says that the nature and source of the force of gravity is not properly understood; nor is the nature of electricity; nor is it known what carries the waves of the electromagnetic spectrum. In biology, he says that nobody knows the thermostat that maintains body temperature; nor the method of controlling the chemical composition of the blood;

nor the action of aspirin when taken in the body; and he says that there are some 700 contemporary medicines in use that have been selected on a trial-and-error basis, with no understanding of the chemical/biological reactions. 'The above are obvious – we actually know little about internal human mechanics, its chemistry and physics, and above all, its controls.'

Moreover, this list does not include what is perhaps the biggest mystery of all – the nature of thought itself. The brain, whether it is looked at by a neurologist or a biologist or a psychologist, is one of those systems described as holistic – that is, the total effect is larger than the sum of the effects from individual components. It can be compared with the workings of a computer – but it is more than that. There are analogies with the workings of the brain of higher animals such as primates – but it is infinitely greater, in its ability to muse and to draw conclusions from apparently unrelated events. And yet, for reasons that nobody knows, at least 75 per cent of our brain cells already remain unused.

There seems to be no Darwinian purpose for this huge inactivity; all that can be guessed is that within this pulsating mass of electrical impulses and connections lies what Gordon Flint has called the inner mind, the vast repository of all the information that we have ever received through our senses; and it is in the unconscious workings of this mind that many great scientists have come to believe, often at the end of their careers, that there is some unifying force in the universe that is beyond measurement, yet indisputably real. Sir Arthur Eddington summed up the paradox: 'All through the physical world runs that unknown content which must be the stuff of consciousness. Here is a hint of aspects deep within the world of physics and yet unattainable by the methods of physics.'

One way to advance towards this ultimate mystery, and at the same time throw light on the fundamental question of how a dowser can have instantaneous knowledge of a distant subject, is by looking at some of the marvellously strange faculties of this mind. For instance, it is now recognized that it almost certainly contains information and has abilities beyond what could have been obtained by means of the five senses. An innate capacity to measure time is one example: there are many cases of people being hypnotized and told to carry out an action a certain number of days, hours and minutes after being awakened – and they are able to do so to an accuracy of one or two minutes. The inner mind can even translate such a command when given in seconds: in one celebrated experiment, an action was carried out precisely 616,500 seconds (a little more than a full week) afterwards, as instructed. It may be by the same internal process that some people are gifted with the ability of instant calculation – they often explain their talent with a phrase such as 'the answer just appears' – or are born to become musical prodigies, since it has been shown that music, harmony, and rhythm are closely linked with a sense of time and numbers.[14]

The important thing is that such inborn talents may have their roots not just in the comparatively recent development of *homo sapiens sapiens* (say, 40,000 years ago), nor even in the development of earliest man 2,000,000 years earlier, but in the emergence of the first reptiles and lower animals aeons ago in the earth's history. Dr Ruth Borchard, a British psychologist, has done much to publicize the work of the American physiologist and anatomist George Ellet Coghill, who spent forty years of his life studying the embryonic and larval stages of the development of the nervous system in *Amblystoma*, a primitive amphibian salamander. 'Only towards the end of his life did he reach the conclusion that the primitive and largely independent early nervous system observed by him possesses mentation and the innate faculties of time, space, and orientation, independent of the senses,' she has written. Moreover, Coghill's work proved that this inborn capacity 'was developed long before the sensory apparatus evolved which eventually culminated in the brain of animal and man and finally in consciousness.'[15]

Mentation is defined as mental action, or a state of mind; so in other words, deep in our inner minds – for Coghill specifically says there is nothing in his work that prevents the same concept of development being applied to man – there is a primeval and vestigial memory of movement through space and time that has nothing to do with the five senses, but which is common to all living things. It is through this basic and universal harmony,

Ruth Borchard believes, that dowsers are able to gain their information.

It is biological evidence, perhaps, for Carl Jung's collective unconscious, through which he believed we were all able to communicate;[16,17] and there is also a striking echo of what Adrian Boshier's sangoma told him in South Africa: 'Today you and I are different, we live differently, our culture is different, but long long ago we all came back from a common source, and when we die we go back to the old people . . .' But it is possible to go even further than that, for you can demonstrate philosophically that beyond this common understanding of the movement and rhythms of the universe, there are matters which exist outside the concepts of space and time.

The simplest way of imagining them is to think of an idea.

Ideas, by their very nature, are immeasurable. There is no doubt that they exist – sometimes powerfully enough to change the course of history. But how big is an idea? What does it weigh? Does it make your brain any heavier or any larger?

These are rhetorical questions, for there is evidently no way of quantifying the size of an idea. The nearest that science could come to pinning it down would be to describe the paper on which this paragraph is written in terms of atoms and molecules, or in equations of electrons, protons, and so on existing in space/time, in a way that would apply equally well to another piece of paper with the same words on it. The equations would be worked out according to rules that have been proved by their repeatability. Science could then go on to explain, within a framework of radiation and wavelengths, how you visually perceive the words, and say that you subsequently, by a mechanism not properly understood, decode them in your brain.

But there is no way in which science could measure the quality of the idea behind the words, nor the private sensation that you have when you read them. Science is able only to describe the structure and behaviour of nature in physical and mathematical terms – not the thought itself which has enabled a scientific structure to be erected.

The world of mind and ideas is not subject to measurement, or, as it has been put, 'ideas in themselves, and the minds which conceive them, betray none of the properties of either space or time. They subsist in a world where space and time are not appropriate descriptions of the mode of being. Here, space is replaced by co-presence and time by eternity. Eternity is not endless time but complete contemporaneity. We sometimes catch glimpses of the quality of eternity when we experience a sense of timelessness in the contemplation of beauty. The religious mystics undoubtedly have similar and more sustained experiences which they try – in vain – to express in words belonging to the world of space and time.'[18]

Now this is a liberating concept, for if ideas can exist outside space and time, then logically so can knowledge, which begins with ideas. There is thus no point in trying to find a wavelength through which Queenie on the Australian bush station discovered that her aboriginal brother had 'bin properly dead-finish'. For a brief flash her mind had realized its eternal co-presence with her brother's. Maurice Maeterlinck wrote: 'The more one thinks about it the more it appears impossible that we should be only what we seem to be: only ourselves, complete in ourselves, separated, isolated, circumscribed by our body, our mind, our conscience, our birth and our death. We only become possible and real when we transcend all of these and prolong ourselves in space and time.' And if you reach a position where you feel personally that psi does not need a scientific explanation – or that, when a scientific explanation emerges, science itself will have much expanded the criteria on which it bases its conclusions – then it is philosophically possible to accept direct knowledge as part of all life.

It may be, then, that the difference between the outer and inner minds is not just of function, but of their essential nature. The outer mind, using the five senses, conscious, ratiocinative, deals with material reality, the inner mind with qualitative sensations that transcend objective observation and measurement. Traditionally, science is concerned with the first, religion and philosophy with the second, and psi phenomena can be seen as contemporary examples of faith and miracles that have been part of our consciousness since the emergence of man.

There are now several hundred documented cases of out-of-body experiences to show that this consciousness operates independently of our physical body or brain. Many of these are accounts by people who, after an accident or a sudden illness, were pronounced dead but subsequently revived. During the period of 'death', when all signs of life were missing for periods up to twenty minutes, they commonly reported the experience of floating above themselves, watching with serene detachment the activity going on in the 'real' world around their physical body. Later, when they had returned to life (and their body), they were able to describe in accurate detail what they had seen.[19]

Not that this would have seemed surprising to the Hawaiian islanders who, up to the first part of this century, practised the philosophy of Huna. This views people as being composed of three selves: the subconscious, the conscious and the super-conscious. Man's purpose for existence is to unite the three selves, which is accomplished by continually communicating with the other levels of consciousness until all are united in continuous communion, at which point man exists in harmony with his environment. They perceived the link between the levels of consciousness as being by means of *aka*, threads of a shadowy, sticky substance just like those reported by many of the people who have briefly left their bodies; and the *aka* did not merely provide each person with his own internal communicating link, but also joined him to every person he had ever met, and every place he had ever visited – he was part of an endlessly branching and interconnecting web of experience.

Nor would Eastern mystics find it hard to understand this notion of a consciousness that unites the universe; what is perhaps more surprising is the way that quantum physics is heading relentlessly towards the same conclusion. Several writers have noted the extraordinary similarity between the deep riddles of Eastern religions and the paradoxes of the new physics, where particles can be seen simultaneously as solid matter and as a wave, destructible and at the same time indestructible, here and yet not here.[20] According to the physicist Fritjof Capra: 'All particles can be transmitted from other particles; they can be created from energy and can vanish into energy. In this world, classical concepts like "elementary particle", "material substance" or "isolated object" have lost their meaning; the whole universe appears as a dynamic web of inseparable energy patterns.'[21]

Since the beginning of recorded history, every society has

produced its own explanation of the psychic (a word which comes from *psyche*, meaning soul or mind), recognizing a form of energy that is at the basis of life, and which is part of us while at the same time part of the cosmos. For the ancient Chinese, in Confucian and Taoist teachings, it was *ch'i* (in Japanese, *ki*), the vital force without which nothing could exist. For the yogi of India and Tibet it was *prana*. The author John White has written: 'The same concept can be found in practically every culture. The Polynesians and Hawaiian kahunas call it *mana*. In Christianity it is the *Holy Spirit*. To the Sufis it is *baraka*. It is *yesod* in the Jewish cabbalistic tradition. The Iroquois call it *orenda*; the Iture pygmies, *megbe*. These and other traditions claim to recognize and, in some cases, control a vital cosmic energy underlying paranormal phenomena.'[22]

Within this continuing esoteric tradition, it may be that dowsing today holds a special place because of the way it is uniquely able to provide a practical and personal proof of the existence of the paranormal. Maybe we should not even call it paranormal – rather a precious, half-forgotten, and under-used faculty which deserves to be re-discovered and better understood.

Most handbooks and introductions to dowsing encourage beginners to practise it because of its mundane day-to-day use – in finding lost objects, tracing references in a library, pinpointing an available plumber in the telephone directory, checking the age of an antique, finding the fault in an automobile, detecting a fake, deciding whether a certain food suits you – and certainly it can do those things, at least with a degree of reliability. But potentially it can achieve much more, in the way that it can open one's mind to another world, and in the unsuspected insights that it offers.

It is no longer surprising, for instance, that many North American Indians, or primitive tribes in South America and Africa, are reluctant to have their photographs taken, for they may know instinctively that in the hands of a sensitive person a photograph can reveal very much more information than the image which it shows. Nor is it odd that some buildings feel haunted, and others welcoming; knowing what dowsers say about the traces which all of us leave behind, it is entirely possible that the fabric of walls and ceilings retain something of

237

the human emotions to which they have been cumulatively exposed over the years, and which can be sensed by people who are aware enough.

Dowsing may also be important in helping to overcome the widespread nervous scepticism about the occult. For a new generation of scientists, it is a relatively respectable and well-attested activity which, unlike some psi effects, can be observed and to some extent analysed. I think it highly likely that good dowsers, while using the non-physical world of direct knowledge for most of their relevant information, are also exceptionally sensitive to normal radiations, and that this is the explanation for the inaccuracies that often occur when they try to find underground substances in a clay soil, or when they are in the presence of strong fields created by power lines or radio transmitters. This same sensitivity should make them excellent subjects/advisers for experimental work in the potentially dramatic development of low-level electric and magnetic fields in relation to healing and prevention of disease.

For the rest of us, dowsing is above all a gentle and homely way of fulfilling what has doubtless always been a universal desire to know about events beyond the range of the normal senses – but a desire which for centuries most of us in the Western world have been taught to avoid. A caution should perhaps be said about this. Ruth Borchard has pointed out that man shares these powers with animals – but only he is in a position to mis-use them. He should therefore take note of the three ancient esoteric rules of the *Zohar* that were laid down to limit their use:

They must not be used for the accumulation of money or status or power, material or spiritual;
They must not be used to read the future;
They must not be used for demonstration or experiment – there must be a genuine need and quest.

Within these guide-lines, dowsing can achieve many things. An atmosphere compounded of mistrust and fear surrounds most of the manifestations of the paranormal: ouija boards, materialized spirits, crystal balls, table-tapping, ghosts, levitation – all these are tainted generally with stories of fraud and tragedy.

Dowsing, perhaps because of its common association with the countryside and with water, the most basic of man's needs, has remained largely free from suspicion. Yet in its own way it is no less dramatic a method of gaining access to another world, and a new understanding of the mysteries of consciousness.

The world of psi, you might say, at your fingertips.

Sources and Select Bibliography

Abbreviations: *AD*   *American Dowser* (quarterly journal of American Society of Dowsers)
JBSD *Journal of British Society of Dowsers*

Chapter 1

1. For what a squid can achieve, see two articles on magneto-encephalography (MCG) by D. Cohen in *Science*, 161 (1968) and 175 (1972).

2. Harvalik's experiment is briefly reported in 'A Biophysical Magnetometer/Gradiometer' in *Virginia Journal of Science*, vol. 21, no. 2 (1970). The account does not make it clear why he supposes the dowser was picking up magnetic brainwaves; the emanation, if it was one, might equally well have been an electromagnetic radiation, as in the Taylor/Balanovski experiments mentioned on page 133.

3. The American Society of Dowsers, Inc., Danville, Vt 05828. The British Society of Dowsers, 19 High Street, Eydon, Daventry, Northants NN11 6PP.

4. J. C. Maby and T. B. Franklin, *Physics of the Divining Rod*, London 1939, is a classic but ultimately inconclusive scientific investigation that includes physiological measurements. Berthold E. Schwarz, *Parapsychology* IV (2), reports on physiological tests of the noted Maine dowser Henry Gross (see note 13 to chapter 4), and summarizes the literature.

5. Whitaker's report is contained in Sir William Barrett and Theodore Besterman, *The Divining Rod*, originally published in 1926, currently through University Books Inc., New York 1968.

6. E. M. Penrose, *Adventure Unlimited*, London 1958.

7. *Saturday Evening Post*, May/June 1976.

8. T. E. Allibone *et al.* (ed.), *The Impact of the Natural Sciences on Archaeology*, O.U.P. 1970.

9. An excellent study of Leftwich is in Colin Wilson, *Strange Powers*, Sphere, London 1975. Leftwich has written his own short book, *Dowsing: the ancient art of rhabdomancy*, Aquarian Press 1976.

10. J. Scott Elliot, *Dowsing: One Man's Way*, Neville Spearman, London 1977.

11. Clarke's work is summarized in *JBSD*, 127 (March 1965); for Trench see *JBSD*, 135 (March 1967) and *JBSD*, 138 (December 1967).

12. Burgoyne, *JBSD*, 107 (March 1960).

Chapter 2

GENERAL READING

The standard historical works are Barrett and Besterman, *op. cit.*, mentioned above, note 5 to chapter 1, and Arthur J. Ellis, *The Divining Rod: A History of Water Witching*, United States Geological Survey 1917.

1. J. Mullins, *The Divining Rod*, was privately published in 1893, but a later edition is available on loan from the library of the British Society of Dowsers (which sends a full catalogue of all its books to each new member).

2. Hans Möring, *JBSD*, 110 (December 1960) contains useful additional historical material.

3. R. Raymond, 'The Divining Rod', in *Transactions of American Institute of Mining Engineers*, vol. 11, 1883.

4. This translation of the *Cabbala* quoted in Howard V. Chambers, *Dowsing, Water Witches and Divining Rods for the Millions*, Sherbourne Press, Los Angeles 1969.

5. Pogson's work was recorded in a series of papers published by the Government of Bombay, 1925–7, entitled *Report on the Work of the Water Diviner to the Government of Bombay*.

6. Penrose, *op. cit.*, note 6 to chapter 1.

7. Abbé Mermet, *Principles and Practice of Radiesthesie*, Stuart and Watkins, London 1967.

8. Henri Mager, *Water Diviners and their Methods*, London 1931, is a work in English that encapsulates his thinking.

Chapter 3

GENERAL READING

The most recent how-to-dowse books on either side of the Atlantic are Raymond C. Willey, *Modern Dowsing*, Esoteric Publications, Arizona 1976, which is comprehensive on the various techniques, and contains the hope that it will standardize the terminology; and Tom Graves, *Dowsing: its Techniques and Applications*, Turnstone Press, London 1976, which is well illustrated and takes readers on a step-by-step progression. It is highly recommended by Arthur Bailey, although newcomers to the British Society of Dowsers are given F. A. Archdale's *Elementary Radiesthesia* as an introduction. Many dowsers of the traditional school have come to the subject via W. H. Trinder's *Dowsing*, London 1939.

1. Books by T. C. Lethbridge are a delight. Although, to current thinking, his technique became complicated with pendulum lengths and 'rates', his enthusiasm for unorthodox archaeology, dowsing, ghosts, folk-lore and many other subjects comes out idiosyncratically in *A Step in the Dark* and *The Monkey's Tail*, Routledge and Kegan Paul, London 1967 and 1969, and *E.S.P. – Beyond Time and Distance*, Sidgwick and Jackson, London 1974.

2. Harvalik's statistics mentioned on page 116.

Chapter 4

1. If read cautiously, Ostrander and Schroeder's *PSI: Psychic Discoveries behind the Iron Curtain*, Sphere Books, London 1973, remains the best general account. But most of the references are virtually unobtainable.

2. Martin Ebon (ed.), *Psychic Discoveries by the Russians*, Signet Books, New York 1971, is a collection of translated papers invaluable for understanding the background to psychic research in that country.

3. L. Vasiliev, *Experiments in Mental Suggestion*, Gally Hill Press, Hampshire 1962.

4. Bird's lecture in *AD*, August 1972.

5. John Sladek, *The New Apocrypha*, Hart-Davis MacGibbon, London 1973.

6. R. A. Foulkes, 'Dowsing Experiments', *Nature*, 229 (1971).

7. A. C. Williamson, *JBSD*, 118 (December 1962).

8. Leftwich's test was for Granada TV's *Margins of the Mind*, May 1968.

9. Maby and Franklin, *op. cit.*, note 4, chapter 1.

10. D. H. Rawcliffe, *Occult and Supernatural Phenomena*, Dover Publications, New York 1959, is a sceptical and comprehensive account, and together with Sladek, *op. cit.*, mentioned above, note 5 to chapter 4, and Christopher Evans, *Cults of Unreason*, Panther Books, London 1974, an excellent antidote to credulity.

11. D. M. Lewis, *JBSD*, 164 (June 1964).

12. E. S. Vogt and R. Hyman, *Water Witching, U.S.A.*, New York 1959. Although somewhat partial in dealing with individual cases, the book also contains two thorough larger-scale surveys in which dowsers as a whole fared no better than average.

13. Kenneth Roberts, *Henry Gross and His Dowsing Rod*, *The Seventh Sense*, and *Water Unlimited*, Doubleday, New York 1952, 1953 and 1957; as well as being highly readable, the three books give a vividly realistic picture of how dowsing is often spontaneous and unexpected, and therefore inexplicable even to the dowser himself.

Chapter 5

1. Maby and Franklin, *op. cit.*, note 4, chapter 1.

2. S. W. Tromp, *Psychical Physics*, Cleaver-Hulme, New York 1949. More of his research and summary in 'Review of the Possible Physiological Causes of Dowsing', *International Journal of Parapsychology*, X, 4 (1968).

3. Yves Rocard, *Le Signal du sourcier*, Dunod, Paris 1963. Not yet translated into English, but summary in M. F. Barnothy (see note 7 to chapter 6).

4. J. G. Llaurado *et al.* (ed.), *Biological and Clinical Effects of Low-Frequency Magnetic and Electric Fields* (report of a 1973 Colorado symposium), Charles Thomas, Illinois 1974. Detailed

material from this important symposium is mostly included in chapter 6, but the introductory lecture by James B. Beal, with its references, has been drawn on here.

5. Harvalik's work has appeared almost without interruption in successive issues of *AD* from vol. 10, no. 4 (1970) to the present time. Mostly its presentation does not fulfil the requirements of the *Nature* reviewer (see page 103), but the intentions are imaginative and determined.

6. Charles C. Conley, *Review of the Biological Effects of Very Low Magnetic Fields*, NASA TN–D–5902 A–3415. Originally part of research into the effects of such fields on astronauts, it contains an excellent list of references, including those concerning the effect of magnetic reversals on genetic development.

7. The thermal/non-thermal arguments were summarized by Paul E. Tyler in an introductory paper in *Annals of the New York Academy of Sciences*, February 1975.

8. Gymnarchus niloticus . . . M. F. and J. M. Barnothy (see note 7 to chapter 6).

9. Bird migration . . . W. T. Keeton, *Scientific American*, December 1974.

10. A. S. Presman, *Electromagnetic Fields and Life*, Plenum Press, New York 1970.

Chapter 6

GENERAL READING

N. Balfour Slonim (ed.), *Environmental Physiology*, C. V. Mosby Company, St Louis 1974, is the key modern text-book on the previously unsuspected effects of small changes in our surroundings, natural or artificial, and contains more than 1000 references, as well as suggestions for further reading. Much of it is hard going for a non-scientist, or even a non-specialist in the particular discipline. Some of the earlier research findings were popularized by Lyall Watson in *Supernature*, Hodder and Stoughton, London 1973.

1. Frank A. Brown Jr has written a definitive article in *Environmental Physiology* (mentioned in General Reading above). Otherwise see 'Living Clocks', *Science*, 130 (1959).

2. R. Wever, 'Effect of Electric Fields on Circadian Rhythms in

Men', *Life Sciences and Space Research VIII*, North-Holland 1970.

3. Rat desynchronization . . . J. R. Lott and H. B. McCain, 'Some Effects of Continuous and Pulsating Electric Fields on Brain Wave Activity in Rats', *Int. Journal. Biometeor*. XVII, 3 (1973).

4. For Becker's summary of his work, see M. F. Barnothy, note 7 below. Psychiatric admissions and behaviour dealt with in Friedman, Becker and Blackman's papers in *Nature*, 200 (16 November 1963) and 205 (13 March 1965). Limb regeneration in Becker's 'Electromagnetic Forces and the Life Process,' *Technology Review*, vol. 75, no. 2 (December 1972).

5. Bone healing . . . L. S. Lavine and I. Lustrin, 'Electric Enhancement of Bone Healing', *Science*, 175, p. 1118 (1971).

6. Project Sanguine . . . J. G. Llaurado, *op. cit.*, note 4 to chapter 5.

7. M. F. Barnothy (ed.), *Biological Effects of Magnetic Fields*, vols. 1 and 2, Plenum Press, New York 1964 and 1969. Papers by Rocard (vol. 1) and Becker (vol. 2) are especially relevant. More recently, M. F. and J. M. Barnothy's 'Magnetobiology' in *Environmental Physiology* (mentioned in General Reading above) summarizes the whole field, giving 100 references. Interviewed, they have particularly recommended the work of D. E. Beischer with squirrel monkeys at Pensacola, Florida.

8. J. G. Llaurado, *op. cit.*, contains Bigu's summary of his work.

9. Harold S. Burr, *The Fields of Life*, Ballantine, New York 1972, according to Colin Wilson, 'could be just as important as the Origin of Species'.

10. M. A. Persinger, 'ELF Waves and ESP', *New Horizons*, vol. 1, no. 5 (January 1975).

11. Cole and Graf in J. G. Llaurado, *op. cit.*, note 4, chapter 5.

12. Bird flock synchrony . . . F. H. Heppner and J. D. Haffner in J. G. Llaurado, *op. cit.*

Chapter 7

1. Barry Fell, *America B.C.*, New York Times/Quadrangle Books, New York 1976, proposes an Iberian Celtic colonization *c.* 900 BC. My own account of North American megaliths and

their relationship to the rest of the world is in *Earth Magic*, Cassell and Co., London 1976, William Morrow, New York 1977; it deals especially with their mysterious emanations as felt by Bill Lewis and others.

Chapter 8

GENERAL READING

As a massive introduction, Colin Wilson's *The Occult*, Hodder and Stoughton, London 1971, is an all-embracing look at the subject from prehistoric times; Geoffrey Mishlove's *The Roots of Consciousness*, Random House/Bookworks 1975, covers the same ground and is particularly strong on recent research. Guy Lyon Playfair, *The Indefinite Boundary*, Souvenir Press, London 1976, and Stuart Holroyd, *Psi & the Consciousness Explosion*, The Bodley Head, London 1977, are excellent contemporary surveys. Rosalind Heywood, *The Sixth Sense*, Pan Books, London 1966, and G. N. M. Tyrell, *The Personality of Man*, Pelican Books, London 1948, were landmarks of insight and common sense from an earlier generation of researchers.

1. Alan Gauld, *Founders of Psychical Research*, Routledge and Kegan Paul, London 1968.

2. H. J. Eysenck wrote the *Encyclopaedia Britannica* article on theories of parapsychological phenomena, and also covered the subject in *Sense and Nonsense in Psychology*, Penguin Books, London 1957.

3. C. E. M. Hansel, *ESP: A Scientific Evaluation*, MacGibbon and Kee, London 1966.

4. J. G. Pratt, J. B. Rhine, B. M. Smith, C. E. Stuart and J. A. Greenwood, *Extrasensory Perception After Sixty Years*, Henry Holt, New York 1940, is the definitive summary of this period. Louisa Rhine's *Mind Over Matter*, MacMillan, New York 1970, up-dates it.

5. L. Vasiliev, *op. cit.*, note 3 to chapter 4.

6. John Beloff (ed), *New Directions in Parapsychology*, Elek Science, London 1974, contains Schmidt, Ryzl and others.

7. J. Sladek, *op. cit.*, note 5 to chapter 4.

8. The work of H. E. Puthoff and R. Targ was published in *Nature*, vol. 252 (18 October 1974). A longer report, together with

an excellent list of 81 references covering the history of modern psi research, is in *Proceedings of the Institute of Electrical and Electronic Engineers* (IEEE), vol. 64, no. 3 (March 1976).
9. Price quoted in David Hammond, *The Search for Psychic Power*, Bantam Books, New York 1975.
10. Tart's work in J. Mishlove *op. cit.*, General Reading above.
11. Hertz in *JBSD*, 110 (December 1960).

Chapter 9

1. Mice precognition in *Biological Aspects of Psi*, John Beloff, *op. cit.*, note 6 to chapter 8.
2. For the power in ancient sacred places, F. Hitching, *op. cit.*, mentioned above, note 1 to chapter 7; also John Michell, *The View Over Atlantis*, Garnstone Press, London 1969; Lyall Watson, *Gifts of Unknown Things*, Hodder and Stoughton, London 1976.
3. Ronald Rose, *Living Magic*, London 1957.
4. Norma Lee Browning, *The World of Peter Hurkos*, Doubleday, New York 1970.
5. Sussman's work in Allan Angoff and Diana Barth (ed.), *Parapsychology and Anthropology* (Proceedings of an international conference in London 1973), Parapsychology Foundation, New York 1974.
6. B. J. F. Laubscher, *Sex, Custom and Psychopathology*, London 1937; also see 'Psychical Phenomena Among Primitive Peoples'; G. E. W. Wolstenholme and E. C. P. Millar (ed.), *Ciba Foundation Symposium on Extrasensory Perception*, London 1956.
7. Adrian Boshier's account in Angoff and Barth, *op. cit.*, note 5.
8. Norma Lee Browning, *op. cit.*, note 4.
9. Jastram in *AD*, August 1976.
10. Research on reticular system in Professor Barry Wyke's paper 'Neurophysiology of Attention and Inattention' given to the Scottish branch of the British Society of Medical and Dental Hypnosis, 1974.
11. Megalith magnetometer surveys in TV documentary based on F. Hitching, *op. cit.*, note 1, chapter 7.

12. Douglas in *AD*, November 1971, November 1973 and February 1977; the first two reprinted in *JBSD*, 157 (September 1972) and 164 (June 1974).

13. Presman, *op. cit.*, note 10 to chapter 5.

14. Hypnotic memory in Rawcliffe, *op. cit.*, note 10 to chapter 4.

15. Ruth Borchard's work in *JBSD*, 123 (March 1964), *JBSD*, 131 (March 1966) and *AD*, February 1975.

16. C. G. Jung, *Synchronicity*, Routledge and Kegan Paul, London 1972.

17. Arthur Koestler, *Roots of Coincidence*, Hutchinson, London 1972.

18. This concept of ideas by Walter Shepherd in *JBSD*, 118 (December 1962).

19. Raymond A. Moody Jr, *Life After Life*, Mockingbird Books, 1975.

20. Lawrence le Shan, *The Medium, the Mystic and the Physicist*, Turnstone Press, London 1974.

21. Fritjof Capra, *The Tao of Physics*, Wildwood House, London 1975; Fontana Paperbacks, London 1976.

22. Survey of X-energy in Stanley Krippner and John White (ed.), *Future Science*, Doubleday/Anchor 1976; and by Martin J. Parkinson in *JBSD*, 128 (June 1965).

Index

Dowsing Pack Offer

Make dowsing easy for yourself with a dowsing pack specially produced by Thomas Salter Ltd for readers of this book.

The pack contains a pendulum, angle rods with swivel handles, a forked rod and full instructions, which will help you become a successful dowser.

To take advantage of this special offer, complete the form at the bottom of the page, enclose a cheque or postal order for £1.75p and send to:

> Thomas Salter Ltd,
> (Dowsing Department),
> Woodside Road,
> Glenrothes,
> Fife, KY7 4AG.

This offer is available to U.K. readers only

Please send me . . . . dowsing pack(s).

I enclose cheque/postal order No. . . . .

Name . . . .

Address . . . .

. . . .